THE THEOLOGY OF THE EPISTLES

STUDIES IN THEOLOGY

THE THEOLOGY OF THE EPISTLES

BY

H. A. A. KENNEDY, D.D., D.Sc.

PROFESSOR OF NEW TESTAMENT EXEGESIS AND THEOLOGY
NEW COLLEGE, EDINBURGH

DESORMAIS

LONDON: DUCKWORTH & CO.

3 HENRIETTA ST., COVENT GARDEN

1919

IN

AFFECTIONATE REMEMBRANCE

OF

DR. JAMES DENNEY

PREFACE

THIS volume scarcely requires a preface, as the method which has been followed in discussing the subject is fully described in the Introduction. One matter alone calls for remark. I have deliberately refrained from dealing with the thought of the Johannine Epistles, because that could not be adequately treated apart from the Fourth Gospel. All students of theology are aware that any such discussion must extend far beyond the limits of a handbook like the present.

I have tried to limit the references to literature. But I trust I have not missed any contribution of first-class importance.

It is once more a pleasure to acknowledge the large debt I owe to my friend and colleague, Professor H. R. Mackintosh, D.D., D.Phil., who, besides helping me to correct the proofs, has, by his fine sensitiveness of ear and mind, enabled me to improve both the thought and its expression.

H. A. A. KENNEDY.

NEW COLLEGE,
EDINBURGH, *May* 24, 1919.

CONTENTS

INTRODUCTION

PART I

PAULINISM

CHAPTER I

CHAPTER II

CHAPTER III

CHAPTER IV

CHAPTER V

CHAPTER VI

PART II

Phases of Early Christian Thought in the Main Independent of Paulinism

CHAPTER I

CHAPTER II

PART III

The Theology of the Developing Church

M. or (M.) denotes Professor Moffatt's *Translation of the New Testament*.

THE THEOLOGY OF THE EPISTLES

INTRODUCTION

(a) Method

THERE can be little question that the ideal method of reaching the significance of the Theology of the Epistles is to deal with it as an integral section of the history of early Christianity. The fundamental matter in that history is the religion of the first disciples of Jesus, and of those who were won for His allegiance by their missionary labours. The vital thought of the Epistles is the precipitate of the religious faith inspired by Jesus, and deriving its support from Him. But the task of relating this thought to the complex play of events and influences which gave it shape in the apostolic age is one of extraordinary difficulty. The data at our disposal are meagre. Most of them are supplied by the Epistles themselves. The brief outline of history in Acts supplements them here and there, but its view of the circumstances often creates new problems. A connected survey of the apostolic age is impossible of achievement. We have only to compare Paul's passing references in Gal. i. to the events which followed his conversion, with the vague account of the situation given in Acts ix., to realise the many gaps which confront our investigation. Delicate questions such as the precise relation of Jewish-Christian thought in the Diaspora to that of Palestine and the mother Church, and the influence of each of these factors on Paul's early Christian career, elude our instruments of investigation.

A

Nor can we with any certainty determine the various forms assumed by Christianity on heathen soil.[1]

Further, for a complete estimate of primitive Christian thought, it would be necessary to trace the affinities which it presents with those faiths from which it gained the majority of its adherents, notably Judaism and Hellenism, as well as the syncretistic influences which surrounded it in an age when the civilised peoples of the Roman Empire were rapidly becoming unified. Here, it may be admitted, the materials for arriving at a judgment are accumulating in bewildering variety. Hasty conclusions are attractive, and usually erroneous. In no field of inquiry is it more needful to resist large generalisations, until the evidence has been adequately sifted, and its bearings carefully weighed.

(b) Scope

A final problem is concerned with the scope of the investigation. In the opening centuries of our era, the Church was led to construct a Canon or authoritative selection of sacred writings. Certain documents received universal recognition within the Christian community at a very early date. But as late as the beginning of the third century several of the Catholic Epistles, e.g., were regarded with hesitation, if not rejected, by some sections of the Christian Church.[2] On the other hand, in the same period, the writings of the so-called Apostolic Fathers were occasionally cited as Scripture. Thus Irenæus assigns Scriptural authority to a quotation from the ' Shepherd ' of Hermas, which he groups with passages from Genesis, Matthew, and Ephesians. The facts remind us that the boundary between ' canonical ' and secondary Christian writings was still fluctuating. But this condition of things is reflected in the contents as well as the history of various documents. It is practically impossible to draw a sharp distinction between the apostolic and the sub-apostolic age. Hence, such writings as 1 Clement and the Epistles of

[1] See Wrede, *Aufgabe u. Methode*, p. 69.
[2] *E.g.* the Syrian Church.

Ignatius have, in many respects, as good a claim to a place in the history of early Christian religion as, say, 2 Peter and Jude. And recent writers on New Testament Theology have extended their survey to the sub-apostolic period.

Apart, however, from the inherent difficulty of approximating to the ideal treatment of our subject which has been sketched above, the limits prescribed for a handbook like the present make it impossible to attempt a systematic association of the religious thought of the Epistles with the history of the Christian Church out of which it has arisen. To essay the task would mean the covering of a bare skeleton of facts with a thin tissue of ideas. Our aim is wholly different. Our starting-point is the clear recognition that the Theology of the Epistles is not an exercise in system-building, but the transcript of a living Christian experience. If we make the experience the regulative factor in the interpretation of the thought, we shall to that extent guard against the danger of placing the ideas in a false proportion. We shall be able to distinguish those that are normative from those which emerge incidentally in a given situation. Ultimately, the interpretation of the ideas will prove the surest clue to the essential history of early Christian faith. For they will themselves, in large measure, supply their own context. The inner processes of thought and feeling will give life to the meagre historical outline which we are able provisionally to reconstruct from our various sources. In any case, we shall be compelled at every step to fill in as much of the background as is needful to explain the origin and character of those phases of Christian experience which the writers of the Epistles set in the forefront. Thus we shall at least avoid dealing with the material for our study as a *hortus siccus*, in which lifeless specimens are arranged in artificial order. There is, no doubt, a place for the history of New Testament conceptions in the various stages of their development. But that must be supplementary to New Testament Theology in the strict sense, and not its main content.

(c) Paul's ' Letters '

The formulation of Christian thought in the Epistles
must be estimated in the light of the nature and genesis of
the documents in which it is embodied. Much recent discussion has turned on the distinction between the *Epistle*
and the *Letter*.[1] And for our inquiry there is point in
recognising that the Epistle constitutes a definite type of
literature, intended for publication, while the Letter is a
private interchange of thoughts and sentiments, the expression of a well-marked mood. Obviously the writings
of *St. Paul*—even so elaborate a production as the Epistle
to the Romans—must be classified as genuine Letters.
Yet their unliterary character must not be exaggerated.[2]
The truth is that Paul cannot be placed under any of the
ordinary categories. ' This style of letter,' says one of the
most eminent living authorities on Greek Literature, ' is
Paul, nobody but Paul. It is not a private letter and yet
not literature, something between which cannot be
imitated.' [3] And he declares that Paul's uniquely individual Greek, depending on no school or model, but
welling up from a heart full of joyous vitality, makes
him ' a classic of Hellenism.' That is justly said. These
documents contain an animated monologue abounding in
personal feeling, reflecting the subtlest shades of the
speaker's mood. Yet it is not ordinary conversation. For
the apostolic note is there, a tone of authority not anxiously
claimed, but assumed as by the ambassador of Christ.
So we reach a criterion for estimating Paul's conceptions.
He addresses himself in his Letters to certain definite
situations, and these determine the emphasis laid on
particular ideas. But he never hesitates to apply eternal
principles to the passing circumstances of his correspondents,
and he arrives at his principles not by reference to any
external authority, but as he has discovered their operation

---

[1] See especially Deissmann, *Bibelstudien*, pp. 189-252.
[2] As by Deissmann, *e.g. Licht vom Osten*, p. 167 f.
[3] Von Wilamowitz-Moellendorff, *Die griechische Literatur d. Altertums*
(in *Die Kultur d. Gegenwart*[3]), p. 232.

in his own experience, an operation of the very life and energy of God Himself. Hence we have to keep in view, on the one hand, the artless and occasional character of Paul's Letters, and, on the other, their claim, born of a personal assurance of contact with the Divine, to be the medium of a Gospel, a redeeming message, which has a right to challenge attention and obedience. If we give each of these aspects its due place, we shall be able to avoid two easy misconceptions : we shall not demand a rigid logic in the apostle's pastoral counsels and instruction, nor painfully labour to harmonise apparent inconsistencies in order to reach completely rounded ideas ; and we shall remember that he does not write as a contributor to the sum of human knowledge, even the knowledge of God, but as a man redeemed by Christ, who is convinced that he holds the Divine secret of peace of conscience and life eternal for all the burdened children of men.

(d) Catholic ' Epistles '

The *Catholic Epistles* [1] reveal numerous affinities with those of Paul. Their authors share with him the stock of ideas which are the common property of the Church. Hence, in attempting to interpret their thought, we must guard against hasty conclusions as to their dependence upon Paulinism, although that, of course, is an element which has to be reckoned with. A notable characteristic of these Epistles is their impersonality. The reader of James or Jude, or even of 1 Peter, receives no clear-cut impression of their authors. ' It is not so much an important man who speaks, as an important subject.' [2] They might therefore be properly classified as ' Epistles ' in the strict sense. And yet a point must be stretched if we are to regard them as primarily literary compositions. They are certainly intended to reach a widespread

---

[1] The Johannine Epistles do not fall within our survey, as explained in the Preface.

[2] Deissmann, *Bibelstudien*, p. 246.

audience. But they are more than general treatises.
They presuppose special situations in the communities
which they address. These situations, which seem to be
common to many localities, are sufficiently important to
call for definite treatment. This treatment is invariably
practical. And the religious ideas emphasised in the
documents serve mainly to provide motive power for urging
home their exhortations. Accordingly the argument from
silence is in this case peculiarly hazardous. We are often
compelled to form a judgment of the standpoints of the
writers rather from the general atmosphere of their thought
than from any detailed doctrines.

(e) Scheme of Treatment

The real background of the Theology of the Epistles
is the faith of the primitive Christian community, having
its direct basis in the impression created by the historical
Jesus, and confirmed by the conviction that He had conquered sin and death. But, as has already been indicated,
our direct evidence for the earliest type of Christianity
is scanty in the extreme. ' We are restricted to some
information in Acts and the Pauline Epistles, to inferences
from the Gospels and Paul, and to that which may be
gathered from the nature of the historical situation.' [1]
We must attempt to fill in this dim background as the
opportunity offers. Meanwhile, we are confronted with a
mass of unchallengeable and illuminating data when we
approach the Letters of St. Paul.

1. *Paul.* No figure in early Christianity stands out
before us in such glowing clearness as its greatest missionary.
The frankness of his self-revelation, the overmastering
sway of his personality, the sheer force and sweep of his
Christian faith, the enthusiasm of his devotion to Christ,
all combine to focus our interest on this master-builder of
the early Church. Consider the range of his influence.
It was Paul who liberated Christianity from the trammels of

[1] Wrede, *op. cit.*, p. 65.

Judaism, and thus opened up for it a world-wide mission.
There were tendencies, no doubt, in the Christian consciousness of Jewish believers throughout the Diaspora,
which helped to prepare the way for his achievement.
Jewish Christians, e.g., had inaugurated a mission to Greeks
at Antioch.[1] But a penetrating insight into the mind of
Christ and a dauntless energy of purpose were needful
in order to carry through a movement which to many
devout souls must have appeared treachery to the revealed
will of God. But not only was Paul responsible for the
real creation of heathen-Christianity. Although we have
no immediate evidence, the subsequent history of the Church
is sufficient proof that his influence reacted on the Jewish-
Christian section of the community. He may have remained more or less suspect in the eyes of Palestinian
believers,[2] but for Christian Jews throughout the Empire
his positions must have acquired, at least up to a certain
epoch, an increasing validity. It was only in some heretical
Jewish-Christian sects that the tradition of hatred towards
Paul remained influential.

The secret of his constructive power lies primarily in
his own Christian experience. For that experience, from
its very nature, led him beyond the realm of his personal
interests. It made him first of all an ardent missionary.
But his mission-work involved the interpretation not
merely of that epoch-making contact with Christ which
gave him his Gospel, but also of the facts and processes
which lay behind it. He was compelled to formulate a
Christian apologetic, wide in scope and admitting of varied
applications. For the very sum and substance of his
message was ' to Jews a stumbling-block, to Greeks folly '
(1 Cor. i. 23). Hence, a vital element in his missionary
enterprise was the elaboration of Christian ideas on the
basis of actual experience, and the relating of these, on the
one side, to minds steeped in the religion of the Old Testament, on the other, to a mixed multitude of cultivated and
ignorant Greeks and Orientals. But his task did not end

[1] Acts xi. 20.   [2] Acts xxi. 21.

with the presentation and defence of Christianity. The training of converts would be almost as pressing an obligation. So to Paul fell the duty of disclosing the ethical bearing of the central Christian truths, and the process shed back new light on the fundamental conceptions of the faith. But the man who showed such concern as to the life and conduct of those whom he had won for Christ must have been careful to give directions for the regulation of their existence as communities. It is certain that during his lifetime there was much elasticity in the matter of organisation, for we can gather from various passages that the guidance of the Church was associated with special ' gifts ' rather than fixed offices.[1] Still we may infer from the answers given to the questions referred to Paul by the Christians in Corinth, that his practical wisdom largely determined the lines along which a definite organisation gradually took shape.

We are justified, then, in making the religious thought of St. Paul the starting-point of our investigation. The considerations already emphasised determine the method to be followed. When Paul became a Christian, he was an ardent Pharisee, who had made full use of his training in the Rabbinic schools of Jerusalem. But by birth he was a Jew of the Diaspora, and most of his Christian career was spent in a Hellenistic *milieu*. We must therefore attempt to estimate the significance of his education and environment for his work as an interpreter of Christianity. But no influence in his history can compare with his conversion. To form any intelligible idea of this crisis, we must examine his experience in Judaism, laying special stress upon those elements to which he himself makes constant reference in describing human helplessness and need. Thus we shall be able to judge what his conversion meant, more especially as a summons to new life and service. In the light of his new vocation as a missionary of Christ, we shall try to discover the normative influence of his conversion for his religious thought. But it is

[1] *E.g.* Rom. xii. 3-8 ; 1 Cor. xii.

necessary to recognise that when Paul entered the Christian Church, he found there the beginnings of a theology. Those elements in it which were predominantly Jewish were familiar to him already. The new thing was the tradition of the life and teaching of Jesus, and the Church's endeavour to reach an adequate interpretation of it. This situation must have affected at various points the conclusions at which he had arrived as the result of his conversion. In these conclusions, as to some extent modified by the current Christian tradition, we shall look for the fundamental positions of Paulinism.[1]

2. *Post-Pauline Christianity.* The Christian experience of Paul must not be regarded as normal in early Christianity. His was a unique individuality. And he had to pass through a singular crisis. Hence we need not be surprised to find that, while his influence in the Church of the first century was epoch-making, some of his profounder conceptions were not grasped by average Christian thought. Moreover, as time went on, reactionary influences asserted themselves. Even in Paul's day many of the converts from heathenism had been prepared for the step they took by their connection with the worship and doctrine of Jewish synagogues. Jews in large numbers had entered the Christian community. Thus, when the burning controversy as to the necessity of the Law for salvation had died away, the fundamental ideas of Jewish monotheism were bound to exercise their sway. The second generation of Christians would be specially concerned with problems of conduct in a heathen environment. Now much of the best Hellenistic thought was at this

[1] The Epistles to the Thessalonians, Galatians, Romans, Corinthians, Colossians, Ephesians, and Philippians will be used as sources in this investigation. These, with the exception of Ephesians, are accepted by most modern scholars as Pauline. Space does not admit of a detailed argument in favour of the present writer's firm conviction that Ephesians is a typically Pauline document. Readers may consult Professor Peake's careful discussion in his *Critical Introduction to the N. T.*, pp. 53-57. There they will also find a well-balanced statement of the reasons which prevent us from citing the Pastoral Epistles as evidence for Paul's religious thought (pp. 60-71).

period occupied with similar questions. So the demand for
definite guidance in the details of practical life brought in a
new legalism, whose influence was to grow with the development of the Catholic Church. Besides, as the first enthusiasm of the early days began to fade, a formal Christian
tradition would gradually take shape, which, because of its
lower level of conviction, would be less exclusive of influences from outside. This attitude is reflected in varying
degrees in the literature which may be described as embody-
ing the Theology of the Developing Church. But before we
discuss that phase of early Christian thought, we must
examine the religious ideas of two documents, one of
which seems to reflect the best type of Christianity current
in the Church contemporary with Paul, while the other
represents a markedly individual outlook, revealing points
of affinity with Paulinism, but still more the Alexandrian
interpretation of Judaism, baptized into Christianity.

a. First Peter. The *First Epistle of Peter* consists largely
of exhortations to various communities of heathen-
Christians in Asia Minor, who were exposed to persecutions
of a private and perhaps also of a public character. The
religious convictions of the author are introduced, not for
their own sake as instruction in Christian truth, but as
the driving power behind his exhortations. To a marked
degree, therefore, the ideas emphasised are determined by
the situation of the readers. But they give an interesting
glimpse of the ground taken by an authoritative Church-
leader, who has learned something from Paul's view of
Christianity, and yet is far from being a mere echo of the
great apostle.

The Letter bears the name of Peter, and, if we follow
so eminent a scholar as Mommsen in believing that the
persecutions which constitute the one clear datum of the
Epistle may reasonably be placed as early as the reign of
Nero, there is no need to doubt a claim which has un-
usually good external evidence.[1] There is little force in

[1] For the details, see the admirable discussion in Moffatt's *Introduction*,
pp. 319-342.

the objection that the Epistle ignores the life and teaching of Jesus, which Peter knew at first hand, and concentrates attention on His sufferings, death, and resurrection.[1]

The selection of material is determined by the purpose in hand, and, in any case, these crucial events must have held a commanding place in the hearts and minds of all the early disciples. Nor is there any real difficulty in the affinities with Paul. That which the two apostles had in common, as belonging to the authoritative Christian tradition, must have far surpassed their differences. Moreover, it is not unlikely that an impressionable nature such as Peter's would at various points reveal the influence of the dominating intellect of his brother-missionary. But even if the Petrine authorship be disallowed, the Epistle presents an impressive picture of the solicitude of an earnest pastor who has at his command a rich store of weighty Christian arguments resting on convictions which were central for the Christian community of his time.

β. *Hebrews.* So much of the Pauline spirit was felt to pervade the *Epistle to the Hebrews* that for a long period it was included by many sections of the Church among the writings of Paul. More careful research has shown that the book is unique in New Testament literature. Its affinities with crucial conceptions of Paulinism are obvious. But it especially represents the blending of a distinct type of culture with Christian belief, and serves to remind us of the varieties of thought which found a home in the Christian society. The comparison of the Old Covenant with the New, which forms the kernel of the Epistle, is elaborated with all the skill of Alexandrian theological equipment. Yet here, too, the end in view is chiefly the practical one of sustaining a faith which falters under trials.

γ. *The Theology of the Developing Church.* The *Pastoral Epistles*, while incorporating genuine Pauline fragments and traditions, we are unable to regard in their present form as compositions of the apostle Paul. Therefore we group

---

[1] Heinrici notes the comparatively frequent points of contact in 1 Peter with the Sermon on the Mount.

them with Jude, James, and 2 Peter as monuments of the
general religious thought of the developing Church. They
are characteristic products of that post-Pauline evolution
which has been sketched in the introductory paragraph of
this section. They are ' Catholic ' Epistles in the strict
sense, having in view a wide circle of Christian communities
and dealing principally with the perils which beset Christian
life and doctrine between, say, 90 and 150 A.D. We have
no space for the treatment of detailed questions as to
authorship, readers, etc. For these reference must be
made to such works as Professor Peake's *Critical Introduction* (cited above) and Professor Moffatt's *Introduction
to the Literature of the New Testament*, with whose
fundamental positions regarding the Epistles in question
the present writer is in agreement. We shall attempt to
show that these documents reveal the same general religious
atmosphere, that they presuppose the same type of problems, and that, while each writer maintains his own
individuality, he is exposed to the pressure of similar
influences, Hellenistic and Jewish, which mark a definite
stage in the development of early Christianity. This
development appears in such sub-apostolic writings as
1 Clement, the Epistle of Barnabas, and the ' Shepherd '
of Hermas.

PART I

PAULINISM

CHAPTER I

IT is a common modern fallacy to suppose that a phenomenon may be adequately explained, if only its origin can
be accounted for. The risk of error is most serious when
we are dealing with individualities. The man is larger than
his heredity and more potent than his environment. And
his superiority to training and circumstances increases in
the ratio of his creative power. The apostle Paul is, of all
men, the least likely to satisfy mechanical tests. His was
one of those spontaneous, ardent, conquering natures,
whose vitality and daring were subject only to the mind and
will of Christ. Yet we should fail to understand the real
significance of his religious experience and the forms
in which it finds expression, did we not attempt a brief
review of the influences amid which he grew to maturity,
and the spiritual forces which were bound to leave their
mark upon him.

(a) Judaism

There is a ring of natural pride in Paul's enumeration
of his ancestral and acquired privileges : ' If any one pre-
sumes to have confidence in outward prerogatives, I more :
circumcised the eighth day ' (as contrasted with proselytes),
' of the race of Israel, of the tribe of Benjamin ' (which had
remained loyal to the Davidic house), ' a Hebrew born of

Hebrew parents, as regards the Law a Pharisee, according
to the legal standard of righteousness blameless.' [1] And
his bewilderment at the refusal of his nation to recognise
the fulfilment of the Divine purpose for them in Christ is
intensified, as he recognises the gifts bestowed upon them
in the providence of God : ' To whom belong the sonship and the manifestation of the Divine glory, and the
covenants, and the Divine legislation and the worship and
the promises, from whom, as regards natural descent, the
Messiah has sprung.' [2] Although as a Christian missionary,
describing his methods, he can take up so detached a
position as to say : ' I became to the Jews as a Jew, that
I might win Jews,' [3] he had never lost his absorbing
interest in the race which gave him birth. No more convincing evidence could be found than the argument by
which, in face of invincible difficulties, he wrestles to
explain the rejection of the Christian revelation by the elect
nation as a temporary aberration which is being overruled
for good.[4]

No hasty conclusions must be drawn from the fact that
Paul was born in Tarsus, a city of Cilicia, which formed
part of one of the provinces of the Roman Empire. It is
true that a more liberal attitude to non-Jewish society
prevailed among Jews of the Diaspora.[5] But a treatise like
the 'Aboda Zara, intended to regulate the relations between Jews and the heathen peoples among whom they
sojourned, puts us on our guard against the impression that
anything like laxity was permitted. [6] No doubt there
were Jews who proved disloyal to their obligations.[7] But
Paul's description of himself as having surpassed his contemporaries in his burning devotion to the ancestral
traditions of Judaism [8] is sufficient evidence that he came

---

[1] Phil. iii. 4-6.   [2] Rom. ix. 4, 5.
[3] 1 Cor. ix. 20.   [4] Rom. ix.-xi.
[5] See Bertholet, *Die Stellung d. Israeliten u. d. Juden zu den Fremden*,
p. 317 f., for requirements for converts from heathenism. Philo's attitude,
as disclosed in his works, is peculiarly instructive.
[6] See, *e.g.*, '*Aboda Zara* (ed. Elmslie), I. i. p. 4.
[7] An inscription of Miletus apparently marks the place allotted to Jews
in the city theatre ; see Deissmann, *Licht vom Osten*, p. 326 f.
[8] Gal. i. 14.

of a family which kept to orthodox paths. Jerome hands down an interesting report that Paul's parents had come to Tarsus from Gischala, a town in Galilee. The story need not be an invention. Many Jews were taken captive in Roman expeditions, and removed to various parts of the Empire, and some at least of these received the privilege of Roman citizenship.[1]

The youth was trained at Jerusalem in the school of one of the most celebrated rabbis in all Jewish history, Gamaliel I., of whom it was said : ' Since Rabban Gamaliel the elder died, there has been no more reverence for the Law.' [2] The chief element in his education would be the art of interpreting the Old Testament according to the approved Rabbinic methods. These methods were pre-eminently allegorical or typological. Good examples in Paul's letters are Gal. iv. 21-31, where he uses the Genesis-story of the quarrel between Sarah and Hagar as an allegory of the struggle between the servile religion of legalism and the freedom which belongs to the religion of Christ ; and 1 Cor. x. 6-11, where the temptations which overcame the Israelites in the wilderness are regarded as a direct warning written down for the sake of Christian readers in after ages. Occasionally he follows the Rabbinic custom of taking an Old Testament passage entirely out of its connection, when he can make apt use of it as an argument ; so, e.g., 1 Cor. xiv. 21, where he introduces a sentence from Isa. xxviii. 11, ' by men of alien tongues and by the lips of aliens shall I speak to this people,' into a discussion on ' speaking with tongues ' in the primitive-Christian sense. He also has a predilection like the Rabbis for constructing centos of quotations from various parts of the Old Testament to support some thesis : e.g. Rom. iii. 10-18, in which is demonstrated the universality of sin. No better instance of deftness in constructing an argument in the very language of Scripture could be cited than Gal. iii. 7-18, which seeks to establish the position that the

[1] See Zahn, *Einl. in d. N. T.*, i. p. 48 f., note 16.
[2] *Sota*, ix. 15, quoted by Schürer, *H. J. P.* (E. tr.), ii. i. p. 364.

true heirs of the promises made to Abraham are the members of the Christian community.

But this scholastic technique, important as it was reckoned, by no means furnished the most vital part of Paul's education. That lay in his acquaintance with the sacred book itself. The Law came first : then the Prophets and the ' Writings,' more especially the Psalms. No doubt for an ardent Pharisee like Paul the Law stood supreme. But righteousness at this period included more than ceremonial. The Law abounded in moral demands, and from beginning to end of the Epistles we are conscious of the moral discipline which formed the background of his religious life. He was also completely at home in the Prophets and Psalms. It is true that these held a secondary place in Jewish estimation as compared with the Law.[1] But they were read in the public services of the synagogue, and the use which Paul makes of them as a Christian missionary is sufficient evidence of the impression they must have left upon his mind at an early period. Yet there can be little question that he rediscovered their significance in the light of his Christian experience. A superficial glance may see in Paul's debt to the religious heritage of his nation little more than frequent survivals of that later Judaism in which he was reared. But those who look deeper will find that he has grasped the religious content of the Old Testament in its fundamental aspects. Only, it has been so closely woven into the very texture of his ideas that these must be analysed in order to disclose their basis. It goes without saying that this applies to the Messianic bearing of many sections of the Old Testament. By an amazing spiritual intuition Paul catches sight of the organic unity of the Divine self-manifestation. Often in such instances he makes no quotations. Yet one cannot study, *e.g.*, his view of the value and significance of the Death of Christ without perceiving that the Suffering Servant of Deutero-Isaiah stands in the background. So also his great conceptions of the ' knowledge ' of God,

[1] Cf. Holtzmann, *N. T. Theologie* [2], i. p. 51.

the ' Spirit ' of God, the ' righteousness ' of God, and many
more presuppose the positions taken by prophets and
psalmists.   But just as the teaching of Jesus has been so
fully assimilated by him that direct references are only
necessary when detailed problems arise, so we may expect
to find the foundation-truths of the prophetic religion as
implicit rather than explicit factors in his theological
construction.   It is always, at least, wise to exhaust the
possibilities in this direction, before we venture to postulate
the influence of Hellenistic ideas.   At no point does Paul
stand more directly in the lineage of Jesus than in his
maintenance of the prophetic tradition.

The recognition of these facts ought not, however, to
blind us to the influence upon Paul of the Jewish Theology
which had developed in the Rabbinic schools.   When we
use the term ' theology ' in this connection, we must not
think of any elaborate system.   That was alien to the
mind of pre-Christian Judaism.   But a vast number of
elucidations and applications of the sacred text had
accumulated which were at a later date to be codified in
the Mischna.   These were due to the wisdom of many
teachers, of whom the most famous were the so-called
Tannaites.[1]   This exegetical tradition of the schools had
attained a virtual equality of authority with the Law
itself.   It is exceedingly difficult to determine the chronology of the various strata in the material.   Hence it must
be used with caution in any attempt to reconstruct the
Judaistic background of Paul.

We are on surer ground in the endeavour to determine
those religious ideas of Judaism with which Paul must have
been familiar, when we turn to the apocalyptic literature
which was so influential in the first century before and the
first century after Christ.   This literature was, in the main,
a product of Pharisaism, but, while it may be going too far
to say that it was a deliberate reaction against the more
formal piety of Scribism,[2] it certainly seems to represent a

---

[1] See Bacher's invaluable compilation, *Die Agada der Tannaiten.*
[2] So, in effect, Baldensperger, *Die Messianisch-Apokalyptischen Hoff-
nungen d. Judentums* [3], *e.g.* p. 83 f.

wider outlook and a deeper religious need. At many points
its ruling conceptions can scarcely be distinguished from
those to be found in the later prophets, as, *e.g.*, Joel. Like
these, apocalyptic literature looks forward to a cata-
strophic intervention of God in history, an intervention
in which His chosen people shall be vindicated, a new
order of salvation established, and the enemies of the Most
High, who are also the enemies of the elect nation, visited
with merited punishment. The content of the apocalypses is therefore largely eschatological, and the events
of the end are closely associated with those Messianic expectations which had for centuries agitated their minds.

Certain features in the apocalyptic picture were of
special importance. The entire course of things was
divided into two ' ages.' The present was evil, an age of
sin and suffering under the sway of malicious powers.
But the coming age was to be the inauguration of perfect
felicity under the rule of God Himself. The conceptions
of this blissful future show much divergence. In some
apocalypses it is delineated as life on a transfigured earth.
In others it belongs to a transcendental order, akin to our
own conception of ' Heaven,' in which material well-
being is exchanged for spiritual. In any case, it means
the final establishment of the dominion of God and the
vanquishing of all those forces which oppose Him. This
new epoch was frequently, although by no means invariably,
associated with the figure of the Messiah, who was regarded
as the vicegerent of God. Here, again, there are noteworthy
variations in the picture. Some writers describe the
Messiah as a monarch of the house of David, supernaturally
equipped for his unique functions. For others he is a
dim transcendental figure, perhaps of angelic rank, who
is revealed from heaven for purposes of judgment and the
wielding of Divine authority. It would be precarious to
determine what precise conception of a personal Messiah
prevailed in the environment to which Paul belonged.
And it must not be forgotten that often all Messianic
offices were ascribed to God alone. Whichever of these

views might be dominant, the new epoch was introduced
by resurrection and judgment. The pictures are often
inconsistent, and cannot be harmonised. The resurrection,
in the view of some apocalyptic writers, only embraces the
righteous. For others, it is universal. The judgment
includes all within its sweep, although the representations
of it are confusing. Retribution has come to take a fundamental place in Jewish piety, and now, owing to the growth
of individualism in religion, men are not judged in the
mass, as in earlier Hebrew thought, but each separate
person receives his verdict from God. In the one case that
will be deliverance from His wrath, salvation, eternal life.
In the other it is death, or destruction. At a later stage
we shall see how definitely the apocalyptic forecast, briefly
sketched above, has left its mark on the thought of Paul.
Meanwhile, let us review certain aspects of Jewish theology,
attested both by apocalyptic and rabbinic literature, which
must have formed integral elements in the apostle's early
religious position.

Paul brought with him into the Christian Church his
convinced monotheism. And even his high Christology
never detracted from that. But his idea of God assumed
a new colour in the light of the revelation of Christ, and so
it will be serviceable to have before us a brief sketch of the
view of God which dominated that Judaism in which he
was brought up. It is needless to observe that for a
Pharisee the supreme revelation of God was to be found in
the written Law, which was regarded as His revealed will.
Now the larger part of the ritual which the written Law
codified was concerned with the regulation of the approach
of impure men to an all-holy Deity. The conception of
God's holiness, therefore, partly physical, partly possessing
a real moral grandeur, dwarfed for the average worshipper
the other qualities which men yearn for in God. Hence
it was inevitable that a great chasm should be felt to lie
between the all-holy One and His frail, sin-burdened
votaries. We do not wish for a moment to minimise the
thought of God's grace and loving-kindness which is

certainly visible.[1]   But it is overshadowed by the fear of
transgressing wittingly or unwittingly the code of precepts
which represents God's mind for His people.   And so the
priest comes in, to begin with, as man's representative
before God ; and later, the rabbi or scribe as the interpreter of the sacred documents, whose judgment may be
followed in situations which are difficult of decision.   But
even ' the very conception that God had spoken once for
all in the Law removed Him further off from the ordinary worshipper, and in combination with other influences
yielded the post-exilic idea of the transcendent God, who
deals with His world only through the agency of innumerable intermediate beings.' [2]

This necessity for mediating powers between God and
the world accounts, no doubt, for the remarkable development in angelology which appears in Judaism after the
Exile.   Traces of it are to be found in Daniel, where the
archangel Michael is the champion of Israel.[3]   But in some
apocalypses, as, e.g., 1 and 2 Enoch, it takes the form of
vast hierarchies of angelic beings subordinate to God, often
identified with the forces of nature, and sometimes, as in
the Book of Jubilees, associated with the giving of the Law.
Many scholars connect these orders of angels with Persian
(and ultimately, Babylonian) influence.   Whether this be
their origin or no, it is probable that they occupied an even
more prominent place in popular belief than they did in
theology.[4]   It is sometimes difficult to distinguish between
forces of evil and forces of good in these ' powers and
authorities,' as Paul calls them,[5] but Judaism certainly
conceived of a spiritual realm of wickedness, whose head
was Satan or Belial.   Probably in the lower strata of
popular ideas the belief in evil spirits had always been
present, but in the Old Testament they have no important
rôle.   In Paul they cannot be said to take a prominent

---

[1] See, e.g., the Psalms, passim.
[2] H. W. Robinson, Religious Ideas of Old Testament, p. 126.
[3] Dan. x. 13 ; xii. 1.
[4] See Bousset, Religion d. Judentums [2], p. 379.
[5] E.g. Col. ii. 15.

CH. I.]ST. PAUL'S ENVIRONMENT21

place, although obviously he reckons them among the
deadliest foes of the Christian life.[1]

In the famous product of Hellenistic Judaism known as
the *Wisdom of Solomon*, which Paul appears to have read,[2]
it is said that ' God created man for immortality and
made him in the likeness of his own proper being, but by
the envy of the devil, death entered into the world '
(ii. 23, 24). As death is for Judaism the wages of sin, this
statement would connect sin's origin with the devil. But
other explanations are more common. In some Jewish
documents sin is attributed to the ' evil impulse ' (Yetzer
hārā) in the heart of man.[3] The Fall of Adam is also a
frequent subject of speculation. It is constantly described
as having brought misery upon his descendants,[4] and yet
there is no clear doctrine of inherited sin. Death has come
upon his posterity through Adam's transgression, but
apparently each individual is regarded as responsible for
his own sin.[5] The bearing of this idea upon Paul's speculations must be noted immediately.

It is plain that Jewish thought took a dark view of
human frailty and imperfection, although it is an exaggeration to call it ' ethical pessimism.' [6] Over against this
vitiated human nature stood the claims of the Divine
Law. Before religious individualism had asserted itself,
it was not so difficult to conceive a right relation between
the community and their God. But 4 Ezra feels as
poignantly as Paul the burden for the individual of facing
the Law's requirements. Yet the way of obedience is
the only path on which righteousness can be won. For
righteousness before God, acquittal in the day of reckoning,
is the reward of service. The righteous man is declared to
be righteous, *i.e.* is ' justified.' The unrighteous is condemned. So inadequate was the obedience of the average
man that the need was felt of supplementing it, and there

---

[1] *E.g.* Eph. vi. 11, 12.
[2] See Grafe, in *Abhandlungen C. v. Weizsäcker gewidmet*, pp. 253-286.
[3] *E.g.* Sirach, xxi. 11 ; Kidduschin, 30*b* ; Pirke Aboth, iv. 2.
[4] *E.g.* 4 Ezra vii. 11 f.   [5] See esp. Apoc. Baruch liv. 19.
[6] So Bousset, *op. cit.*, p. 462.

are traces of the idea that the surplus merit of notably
pious individuals might be reckoned to those who could
feel no confidence about their own. Holtzmann lays
stress on the conception that the suffering of another as
well as his special merit could atone for transgression.[1]
Unquestionably the idea finds remarkable expression in
the fifty-third chapter of Isaiah. But it would be precarious to argue from this unique passage to any general
Jewish doctrine, and the bulk of the evidence, as Holtzmann
himself admits, is decidedly late. The general outlook,
however, serves to remind us of the positions from which
Paul started as a Pharisee.

(b) Hellenism

It is probable that there was far less fundamental difference between Hellenistic and Palestinian Judaism than is
usually assumed. Wendland has most instructively shown,
e.g., the intimate contact between Palestinian and Hellenistic exegesis.[2] And this relationship no doubt held good
over a large area. So that we dare not start with the
notion that because Paul was a Jew of the Diaspora he
must have stood in a wholly different relation to Hellenism
from that of the average Jew of Palestine. And yet we
must no less clearly recognise the full significance of the
fact that Paul grew to maturity in a typically Hellenistic
city, and that his most memorable work was carried on
among a Hellenistic population.

Attempts have been recently made to show that Paul
had the advantage of a training in a rhetorical school, which
formed a regular element in a good average education,[3]
a training which might be received under Jewish auspices.
The evidence for this is found in his acquaintance with
certain terms current in popular Stoicism, the use of
rhetorical art in the construction of paragraphs, the play

---

[1] Op. cit., i. pp. 79-82.
[2] Die hellenistisch-römische Kultur [2], p. 201.
[3] E.g. J. Weiss, Das Urchristentum, pp. 133, 134 ; Böhlig, Die Geistes-
kultur von Tarsos, p. 154.

upon words, the elaboration of antitheses, and especially
the points of contact which appear between his style and
that of the Cynic-Stoic Diatribe, that form of popular discourse which was a chief instrument in philosophical
propaganda. There can be no question that he used words
belonging to the vocabulary of Stoic moral teaching, and
Bultmann has carefully traced various links of connection
between Paul and the Diatribe. But he admits that Paul
puts a stamp of his own on these popular types of expression, and refuses to venture on a conjecture as to how he
became master of them.[1] Much irrelevant theorising has
been expended on the rhetorical technique of Paul's composition. A few traces of current practice may be discernible.[2] But it is noteworthy that in the masterpieces of
his spiritual genius, such as 1 Cor. xiii. and Rom. viii. 31 ff.,
he approaches far closer to the forms of Hebrew poetry
than to the approved ' figures ' of Hellenistic art.

In attempting a brief survey of Paul's relationship to
his Hellenistic environment, it is of vital importance first
of all to remember that his Bible was the LXX. But the
LXX, with all its literalness of rendering, was, like every
translation, to some extent an interpretation. Of course
Paul was well acquainted with Hebrew. But his religious
thought is expressed in terms of the LXX, and language
necessarily affects ideas. Now it is no doubt true that
this translation, in a sense, simplified the conceptions of
the original and so far adapted them to their new Hellenistic *milieu*. The fact, for example, that the Hebrew
Jahweh was rendered by κύριος, ' lord,' a term already
laden with religious significance for the Oriental and
Hellenistic world, suggests how the thought of the apostle
might be almost unconsciously adapted to the audiences
whom he had to address.[3] This criterion might be applied
to words like πνεῦμα, ' spirit,' ψυχή, ' soul,' σάρξ, ' flesh,'

---

[1] *Der Stil d. paulinischen Predigt*, p. 108.
[2] See Wendland's very careful estimate, *Die urchristlichen Literatur-
formen*, pp. 354, 355.
[3] See Deissmann, *Die Hellenisierung d. semitischen Monotheismus*,
pp. 13-15.

σῶμα, 'body,' and others, which are, of course, direct renderings of Old Testament terms, and yet may carry with them a Hellenistic shade of meaning. But it is surely an exaggeration to say that 'the historic pre-supposition of Paul's piety is the religious content of the Old Testament in Greek.'[1] This is to postulate an influence of terminology on thought which is inconceivable in the case of one who must have been an expert in the Hebrew original.

There are good grounds, if not absolutely conclusive, for believing that Paul was acquainted with the Alexandrian *Wisdom of Solomon*. This work reveals the influence of Greek ideas throughout. The 'formless matter' of Plato, the 'world-soul' of the Stoics, the conception of immortality and of the body as the prison of the spirit, all find a place.[2] Such notions may have determined the emphasis at various points in the apostle's thinking, but we have only to compare him with a contemporary Jew of the Diaspora, Philo, to recognise the vast difference which has to be allowed for between temperaments exposed to the same general atmosphere, but shaped to diverging issues in virtue of their individual experiences.[3]

At the same time we must not ignore Paul's deliberate statement that to 'those outside the Law' he had become as 'one outside the Law,' in order to win them for Christ.[4] How much does this mean? Recent investigation has shown that in the Hellenistic area in which Paul laboured, genuine religious aspirations sought satisfaction, roughly speaking, in two chief directions: in a supernatural redemption from the uncertainties and calamities of life through some sort of communion with the Divine, or in a patient self-discipline, based on the idea of a rational world-order, whose outcome must be a moral life. The one tendency found a home in the numerous religious

---

[1] Deissmann, *Paulus*, p. 70.
[2] *E.g.* xi. 17; viii. 1; ix. 15, etc. For Paul's relation to *Wisdom*, cf. Wisd. xiii. with Rom. i. 18-32.
[3] See an admirable paragraph in Wernle, *Einführung* (ed. I.), p. 185.
[4] 1 Cor. ix. 21.

associations which were grouped round Mystery-cults.
The other followed the guidance of that quickened Stoicism
which sought to rouse men to self-knowledge, and offered
rules for ethical practice.   There were movements also in
which both these tendencies had a place.[1]   It is impossible
to say whether Paul was, in any definite sense, alive to
these movements as a youth at Tarsus.[2]   In any case, as an
active Christian missionary who was bound to seek for
common ground with his Hellenistic audiences, he must
have become acquainted, to some extent, with the currents
of thought and feeling which were moving in the minds of
men.   Like the Mystery-religions, he proclaimed a great
' redemption.'   Like them he could speak of possession by
the Divine.   Like them he could point to a ' knowledge '
of God which meant not intellectual apprehension but
practical fellowship.   Like them he could think of a transformation into the Divine likeness which was the very
goal of being.   This parallelism would be all to his advantage as a preacher, and an educator of those whom his
preaching had won.   But his presuppositions were different.
Redemption from sin was primary with him, not redemption from fate.   The Spirit in whose might he could do
all things was the Holy Spirit which cleansed the heart.
The ' knowledge ' of God, in his view of it, was not reached
through any esoteric ritual but by faith in Jesus Christ,
whose self-sacrificing death was the supreme revelation of
the Divine love to sinful men.   Thus there is complete
justification for Wendland's wise caution : ' Even when
separate statements and doctrines look alike, the ultimate
motives and fundamental positions which have prompted
them may be quite different.' [3]

It may be admitted without discussion that Paul adopted
a variety of terms and ideas from popular Stoicism.   Thus

[1] Perhaps we may so describe the influence of Posidonius, when looked
at in its broader aspects.

[2] Böhlig finds some interesting parallels between Paul and Athenodorus,
the famous Stoic of Tarsus, as also between Paul and the popular philosophical teacher, Dion of Prusa, well known in Tarsus.   But the evidence
is very slight : see *op. cit.*, pp. 107-128.

[3] *Op. cit.*, p. 228.

he speaks of 'conscience,' 'nature,' and 'the unfitting.'[1]
In demonstrating that all men alike, both Jews and
heathen, are without excuse for their sins, he attributes
to the heathen the possession of an unwritten moral law
implanted by nature in their hearts,[2] a fundamental tenet
of Stoic ethics.[3]   In his terrible indictment of heathenism
he makes use of the argument that a knowledge of God
may be gained from His created works, and this we know
was a regular Stoic position.[4]   Possibly he was impressed
by the idea from its presentation in the *Wisdom of Solomon*,
ch. xiii.   And the fact suggests that he came into contact
with current conceptions of the popular philosophy through
what may be called the Jewish apologetic literature of the
Diaspora.   In any case, no mistake must be made as to his
normal attitude towards the 'wisdom' which is 'of this
world.'   That, he declares, 'is folly in the sight of God.'
For him, the true wisdom is embodied in Christ, and it
consists of 'righteousness and sanctification and redemption.'[5]   These things are not the attainment of unaided
human effort.   The Stoic doctrine of self-sufficiency counted
for little with Paul.   He certainly puts a high value on
every virtue which may be manifested in human character.[6]
But his exhortation to his converts to work out their own
salvation, which from the very nature of the case involves
a life of moral effort,[7] is based on the conviction of the living
presence with them of the living God Himself.[8]

Yet Paul was no bigot.   The common life of the great
cities which had claimed his labours is reflected in the
illustrations he employs and the metaphors which give
vividness to his utterances.   Nay, we may go further and

---

[1] *E.g.* 1 Cor. viii. 7 ; xi. 14 ; Rom. i. 28.   The idea of conscience, however, is much more prominent in Philo than in Stoicism.

[2] Rom. ii. 14 f.

[3] Cf. Cic., *de Legibus*, i. 6, 18 : *lex est ratio summa, insita in natura,
quae jubet ea quae facienda sunt prohibetque contraria.*

[4] See the valuable evidence in Lietzmann's note on Rom. i. 20, and
J. Weiss, *op. cit.*, p. 179, note 2.   For a further important example of his
contact with Hellenistic ideas, see chap. vi. (*f*), *infra*.

[5] 1 Cor. iii. 19 ; i. 30.

[6] *E.g.* Phil. iv. 8.

[7] Note the sequence of thought in Rom. xii.

[8] Phil. ii. 12, 13.

say that the political organisation of the Roman dominion made its mark on his whole programme of service ; and his lofty conception of the unity of men in Christ Jesus, essentially spiritual as it was, must have gained in directness and power from his consciousness of citizenship in an Empire which had unified the known world.

CHAPTER II

(a) *Presuppositions*

THE experience which is born of the reaction of the individual nature upon its environment is a far more potent
force in shaping a man's view of the world than the influence
of the environment in itself.   Hence, while Paul's Jewish
nurture and his contact with Hellenistic civilisation must
have counted for much in the evolution of his spiritual
life and thought, his inward religious history remained the
decisive factor.   We know from his own testimony that
the epoch-making event of that history was his conversion.
But if we are to form a true estimate of the significance
of an event which gives the clue to his theology, we must
endeavour to understand something of the spiritual processes which culminated in that extraordinary experience.

The only available evidence is contained in Paul's own
Letters, although it can be supplemented here and there
from brief notices in Acts.   Now some authorities consider
that it is futile to attempt to reconstruct any part of
Paul's pre-Christian religious experience from the extant
data.   They hold that his conversion wrought so complete
a revolution in his life that his subsequent descriptions of
his spiritual past can in no sense be taken as accurate.   To
the man who has come forth into a marvellous light, the
twilight in which he has lived before appears total darkness.
Such a view is only partially true.   There is, no doubt,
always the tendency to heighten the contrast between the
past in which the soul was tempest-tossed and the present
in which it has reached the haven of peace.   But surely the

scars of such a struggle are ineffaceable. And throughout
the ages minds less sensitive than Paul's have been able to
record the phases of unrest through which they journeyed
before reaching the goal of their striving. Yet one or two
cautions are quite relevant. We have to recognise first of
all that Paul invariably interprets his spiritual past in the
light of his *Christian* consciousness. How could it be
otherwise ? The growth of religious life cannot be divided
up into completely isolated sections, like those which
compose a machine. Commenting on the most famous of
all Paul's autobiographical delineations, Rom. vii. 7-25,
Dr. Denney aptly says : ' No one could have written the
passage but a Christian : it is the experience of the un-
regenerate, we may say, but seen through regenerate eyes,
interpreted in a regenerate mind. It is the apostle's
spiritual history, but universalised : a history in which
one stage is not extinguished by the next, but which is
present as a whole to his consciousness, each stage all the
time determining and determined by the rest.' [1]   Further,
although Paul often seems to universalise his own experience, we must remember that on many sides it was unique.
It was the expression of a nature which had no room for
half-hearted, compromising attitudes in the life of the soul.
Most men live by easy compromises with their ideal. They
are content with the second-best. Paul's passionate thirst
for God chafed at the commonplace. There must have
been many even of the devout Jews of his time who were
at least provisionally satisfied with the possession of a legal
standard of righteousness, and the attempt to conform to
it, however inadequate. What we know of Paul's pre-
Christian days suggests that even then his principle was
that of his later years : ' This *one* thing . `. . I press
towards the goal.' [2]

(b) *Sense of Failure*

In Paul's enumeration of his Jewish prerogatives he
describes himself as ' blameless according to the legal

[1] *Expos. G. T.*, ii. p. 639.   [2] Phil. iii. 13, 14.

standard of righteousness.' [1]   Probably this is not to be
taken as a studied confession of his Pharisaic attainments,
but rather as a large general statement such as he is fond
of making, intended to emphasise the contrast between
past and present.   Yet so far from clashing with such self-
revelations as those of Romans vii., as some scholars
assert, it brings them into clearer light.   It reveals the
difference between Paul's own ideal and that current
among many of his contemporaries in Judaism.

The risk which attends every legalistic scheme of religion
is the exaltation of the trivial at the expense of the weightier
obligations.   It is easier to fast twice in the week, or to
pay tithes on mint, anise, and cummin, than to do justice
and to love mercy.   The nature which finds satisfaction
in this view of man's relation to God, whether in ancient
or modern days, is that which delights in the possession of
rules, authoritatively laid down, which cover an immense
variety of possible situations.   To believe that one is
pleasing God by offering a definite number of prescribed
sacrifices, or repeating a special group of petitions at
certain fixed hours by day or night, relieves the conscience
of much of the dissatisfaction due to failure in more serious
moral responsibilities.   Unquestionably a large expendi-
ture of time and energy is necessary to attain a high level
even in this type of obedience.   But once the habit is
formed, such obedience can be rendered almost mechani-
cally.   And there are temperaments which feel a glow of
satisfaction in following a routine.   Now the Jewish Law,
as formulated in the Pentateuch, embodied a vast number
of ritual prescriptions.   The regulations regarding physical
purity form a noteworthy instance.   The tendency to
emphasise external minutiæ had increased under the
influence of the Pharisees, more especially in connection
with the Sabbath law.[2]   But the authoritative code of
Judaism had a much wider scope.   The contents of
Deuteronomy reflect at many points the moral ideal of the
great prophets.   The so-called Book of the Covenant

[1] Phil. iii. 6.   [2] See Schürer, *H. J. P.*, II. ii. p. 96 f.

(Ex. xx. 22, xxiii. 19), which is probably earlier than Deuteronomy,[1] and the 'Ten Commandments,' bear witness to the high place occupied by ethical demands.

Here we touch the *crux* of Paul's problem. His fulfilment of the required observances reached, no doubt, a very high level. He had in this respect left his contemporaries in the shade.[2] But obedience of such a character left his spiritual nature starved. It brought no inward freedom, no sense of harmony with God. What of the ethical claims of the Law ? Must not real satisfaction be reached in this direction ? At this point the apostle lets us see into the depth of his experience. 'I should not have known what sin was except by the law : that is to say, I should not have experienced evil desire unless the law had said : Thou shalt not covet. Thus sin, finding its starting-point in the commandment, produced in me all manner of evil desire.' [3] The words reveal one fundamental element in the situation, the constant conflict between self-will and the claim of a higher order identified by Paul with the will of God, which succeeded the period of childish innocence. To that higher order his better nature assented, but the power of sin was ever present, thwarting his aspirations.[4] Plainly the incessant struggle in his effort to reach his ideal had haunted his soul like a nightmare. And his case was not exceptional. The failure of his fellow-countrymen was equally conspicuous. Nothing could be more instructive than his deliberate indictment of Jews who boast of their privileges as possessing in the Law 'the embodiment of knowledge and truth,' and yet lamentably fail to fulfil its requirements.[5] This reminds us of the wide significance of the situation for Paul. He was too earnest a Pharisee not to feel that the impossibility of keeping the Law had far more than a personal bearing. It was indissolubly bound up with the dearest hopes of the nation. For it had become a fixed dogma of Judaism that the Divine inauguration of the new Messianic epoch

[1] See Robinson, *op. cit.*, p. 66.   [2] Gal. i. 14.
[3] Rom. vii. 7, 8.   [4] Rom. vii. 22, 23.   [5] Rom. ii. 17-25.

depended on the faithfulness of the people to their obligations. So that failure in obedience involved the gravest
consequences. The purpose of God was being hindered.
How could the nation enjoy His favour? To so
penetrating a mind the case must have seemed almost
hopeless. For Paul was fully alive to the principles of
legalism. This comes out again and again. Quoting
from Deut. xxvii. 26 he declares: ' It stands written,
cursed is every one who does not abide by all that is
written in the book of the law, to do it ' ; [1] and, later in the
same Epistle, ' I testify again to every man who submits
to circumcision that he places himself under obligation to
perform the whole law.' [2] That this is no mere personal
dictum is evident from such passages as James ii. 10, and
parallel Rabbinic sayings.[3] Here is revealed the serious-
ness of the position. As we have seen, multitudes could be
satisfied with compromises. But Paul and others like-
minded refused to be contented with anything short of
complete conformity. The words of Leviticus xviii. 5
had sounded like a knell of doom in his ears : ' The man
who performs it ' (i.e. the righteousness demanded by the
Law) ' shall live by it.' [4] No less exacting criterion would
be applied to the sum-total of his conduct by a holy and
righteous God, who was entitled to demand flawless
obedience. And the penalty for disobeying was death.

In the light of these considerations it is easy to understand Paul's persecuting zeal when some of Jesus' more
outspoken followers, like Stephen, began to reveal their
detachment from legal obligations,[5] and to proclaim their
Master as the promised Messiah. The situation was true
to human nature. The earnest Pharisee, with his settled
belief in the high destiny of his nation, was tortured by
doubts which were sapping his religious position. These
doubts he was striving with all the force of reason and feeling to overcome. And now, although he would refuse to

---

[1] Gal. iii. 10.   [2] Gal. v. 3.   [3] See Mayor on James ii. 10.
[4] Rom. x. 5. Cf. the lament in 4 Ezra over man's powerlessness in
presence of the requirements of God, esp. vii. 45-74.
[5] Acts vi. 11-14.

acknowledge the truth to himself, they were reinforced by this movement whose centre was a crucified impostor. In sheer self-defence he was compelled to lead the assault on the Nazarenes, scarcely realising that in thus coming to close quarters with them he was in truth being led with growing insight to discern the instability of his own religious attitude.

(c) Power of Sin in the Flesh

Before we attempt to estimate the impression made upon Paul's mind by the disciples of Jesus, we must pause to examine his own explanation of the failure of legal religion, as that is fundamental for his entire religious out-look. Now, although it may be impossible to bring all his utterances on the Law into a consistent scheme, we receive a quite definite answer to the question : Why has the religion of the Law failed to bring men into a completely satisfying relation to God ? Because of the power of sin in the 'flesh.' Paul speaks of 'the powerlessness of the law, that wherein it had no might through the flesh.' [1] And again, taking his own case obviously as representative of universal experience, he declares, 'Left to myself, with my mind I serve the law of God, but with my flesh the law of sin.' [2] What does he mean by this law of sin in the 'flesh' ? It is important to note that Paul usually speaks of sin not as individual transgression nor as abstract tendency to wrong-doing, but as a quasi-personal power which takes possession of human nature and leads it astray. We emphasise the fact in order to make it clear that he holds no theory of the inherent evil of matter. Man as created was not evil, but now, as a truth of experience, his nature has proved to be tainted with sin. Paul uses the term 'the flesh' to describe this evil nature. The term has its roots in the Old Testament. There 'flesh' is often used to designate human nature in its weakness and in-

[1] Rom. viii. 3.   [2] Rom. vii. 25.

adequacy, as contrasted with God, who is ' Spirit.' [1] There is a closely allied use of the very term (σάρξ), which Paul employs in Plato and the later Platonic schools with reference to the body as the lower element in man in contrast to the soul.[2] But the Hellenic idea rests on a different basis. Matter is evil as phenomenal, as belonging to the realm of Becoming and not of Being. Paul, like the Old Testament, is not concerned with metaphysical distinctions.[3] He does not speculate on the lines of a cosmic dualism. What absorbs his interest is the religious significance of human nature, its actual attitude towards God. That attitude is perverted. ' In me, I mean in my flesh, good does not dwell.' [4] Paul's view of human life is constantly described as ' pessimistic.' That is surely a misconception. It is true that he invariably emphasises the moral disaster which is the consequence of sin, but no man was ever more alive to the high possibilities of human nature when restored to that condition which was God's eternal purpose for mankind.[5] In all that he says of sin he speaks from the standpoint of the sincere Christian missionary who understands the needs of others because he has first grasped his own. For Paul, then, the ' flesh,' that is human nature apart from God, gives sin its material to work upon, so that the Law, even in its highest aspect as the revealed will of God, is made of no effect. In narrating his own inward conflict, which he has undoubtedly generalised, he lays stress on one feature of the situation, which, perhaps, stands out before him in clearer relief just because he has subsequently passed into a condition of spiritual freedom. That a man under the sway of sin should be confronted with a régime of moral prohibitions means resentment

[1] *E.g.* Isa. xxxi. 3 ; Ps. lvi. 4, etc.   See the scholarly discussion in Robinson's *Christian Doctrine of Man*, pp. 20-25.

[2] See esp. Capelle's article, ' Body (Greek and Roman),' *E. R. E.*

[3] Philo anticipates Paul in using σάρξ, ' flesh,' to denote the lower side of human nature as realised and felt in ordinary experience. But there is an important difference ; *e.g.*, in *Gig.* 40, Philo sets σάρξ and ψυχή in sharp antithesis, a usage never found in Paul.   But in the same treatise (§ 29) his usage is extraordinarily akin to Paul's regular contrast between σάρξ and πνεῦμα.   [4] Rom. vii. 18.

[5] Cf. Jülicher, *Paulus u. Jesus*, p. 51.

against such an order.[1] For sin is essentially self-will, or, in the words of 1 John iii. 4, ' lawlessness.'

Paul develops the account of his experience in the famous passage which may be summed up in the words · ' Not the good which I desire do I achieve, but the evil which I do not desire, this I do.' [2] The idea has found abundant expression in ancient literature. The words of Ovid are familiar : ' I see the higher course and approve it : the lower I follow ' (Metam. vii. 20).[3] The ground which the apostle here takes up reveals the nature of the course he had endeavoured to follow. Making all due allowance for the Christian standpoint from which he writes, it seems plain that he had approached God mainly as the supreme Judge of human action, and had been driven to recognise that he possessed no real merit on which he could count when face to face with the Divine Presence. Sin was too subtle and too strong for him. The very order which reminded him of God acted as an instigation to transgress. This was his personal experience and the experience, no doubt, of many. That it was by no means universal is evident from such outpourings of thankfulness for the Law as have been preserved in Psalm cxix.

Now the bitterness of his position was enhanced for Paul by the consciousness of those higher desires which protest against sin. ' I assent,' he says, ' to the law of God according to my inward man, but I see another law in my members opposing the law of my mind.' [4] Here we get a glimpse of Paul's idea of the constitution of human nature, which it is worth while examining in view of its bearing upon his whole conception of the Christian life.

(d) Human Nature

As has been already indicated, the basis of Paul's inter-

---

[1] Rom. vii. 7-11.   [2] Rom. vii. 19.
[3] An extraordinarily apt parallel to Paul's language occurs in Epictetus, ii. 26. 1: πᾶν ἁμάρτημα μάχην περιέχει. ἐπεὶ γὰρ ὁ ἁμαρτάνων οὐ θέλει ἁμαρτάνειν, ἀλλὰ κατορθῶσαι, δῆλον ὅτι ὃ μὲν θέλει οὐ ποιεῖ. See further parallels in Wetstein's N. T., ii. p. 57. It is doubtful whether such parallels justify the statement that Paul is here using Stoic expressions.
[4] Rom. vii. 22, 23.

pretation of human nature lies in the Old Testament.
There the primary aspects of the human personality are
described by the terms 'flesh' (*basar*), 'soul' (*nephesh*),
'spirit' (*ruach*), and 'heart' (*leb*). The most notable
feature about the Old Testament use of the term 'flesh'
for our discussion is that it often occurs with a psychical
and not mere physical meaning. That becomes almost
ethical in the group of passages quoted above, which
form the background of Paul's usage. But how far the
Old Testament is removed from the notion of the 'flesh'
as inherently evil is plain from such passages as Job iv.
17-19; xxv. 5, 6, in which 'physical frailty is used to
explain or to exculpate ethical imperfection.'[1] 'Heart' has
an extraordinarily wide range of application, not only possessing its physical sense, but associated with the activities
of feeling, intellect, and will. The same comprehensive
use of it (καρδία) is found in the New Testament, and is as
common in the Gospels as in Paul. As we shall see, however, the term 'mind' (νοῦς), which occurs several times
in the LXX as the rendering of *leb*, encroaches upon the
sphere of the 'heart' in the thought of Paul. 'Soul'
seems usually in the Old Testament to denote the principle of life in the individual, but is often extended to
embrace the emotional activities in particular, and sometimes, as might be expected, is almost a substitute for the
personal pronoun. Paul rarely uses ψυχή except in this
latter sense, following the LXX. Three or four times,
also in accord with the LXX, he employs it in the popular
sense of 'heart' or 'mind.' But in 1 Cor. xv. 45, where he
quotes the LXX rendering of Gen. ii. 7, εἰς ψυχὴν (לְנֶפֶשׁ)
ζῶσαν, he deliberately contrasts ψυχή with πνεῦμα, and it
becomes clear that in his view ψυχή, 'soul' stands for the
life of man as untouched by the spirit of God (πνεῦμα),
which he regards as God's special gift to the Christian
believer. While the noun is comparatively rare in Paul's
Letters, the adjective formed from it, meaning literally
'soulish' (ψυχικός), and translated 'natural' in the

---

[1] Robinson, *op. cit.*, p. 25.

Authorised Version, takes an important place. Some
scholars hold that Paul was influenced in his use of this
term by contemporary Hellenistic religion. The evidence
is altogether inadequate. But it is worthy of observa
tion that the adjective is used by the Jewish author of
4 Maccabees, who is certainly steeped in the current
popular philosophy, not in Paul's sense of the ' unspiritual '
as opposed to the ' spiritual,' but in that of ' belonging to
the soul ' as opposed to ' belonging to the body ' (4 Maccab.
i. 32 : τῶν δὲ ἐπιθυμιῶν αἱ μέν εἰσιν ψυχικαί, αἱ δὲ σωματικαί).
Philo, in accordance with his uses of ψυχή, employs the
adjective in all sorts of connections. In a few cases it
applies to the ordinary inner life of man, whether viewed
as physical or as the sphere of feeling and other forms of
consciousness. More often it occurs in the higher sense of
' spiritual,' which is totally alien to Paul.

Like *nephesh*, *ruach* meant in certain phases of its
development the ' breath-soul,' but in its earliest usage it
signified (*a*) the wind, (*b*) the stormier energies of human
life, (*c*) the influence from God which brought about
abnormal or ' demonic ' conditions in men. Probably
owing to this latter use, it came to connote a higher side of
the inner life than *nephesh*, closely associated with the
ruach of God Himself. Hence Paul uses ' spirit ' (πνεῦμα),
the word by which it is commonly rendered in the LXX,
for the Divine life kindled in man as well as for the Divine
Spirit which has kindled it, phenomena which must be
discussed at length in a later section. Occasionally, however, following what we have seen to be an Old Testament
usage, he employs ' spirit ' to denote the inner life without
special reference to its relation to God.[1] But the passage
which formed the starting-point of our present discussion
discloses further elements in his conception of the constitution of human nature. There [2] he uses the expressions
' the inner man ' and the ' mind ' (νοῦς) to describe that
part of the human consciousness, primarily his own, which

---

[1] See esp. Robinson, *op. cit.*, pp. 18 f., 26 f.
[2] Rom. vii. 22, 23. Cf. the use of νοῦς in the same sense in verse 25.

has an affinity with the will of God, which affords a point
of contact, so to speak, with Divine influences. This
confirms what was said above as to the error of calling Paul
a pessimist in regard to human nature. It is of interest to
note that Plato uses a phrase almost identical with that of
Paul, ' the man within,' [1] in distinguishing the power of the
rational consciousness from the lower capacities of the
soul, and the conception passed into Neoplatonism. But
here, as in the case of the cognate term in Paul, the ' mind '
($\nu o\hat{v}s$), we must be careful not to read into them the content
which they hold in Greek philosophy. At the same time,
it is quite possible that in selecting these words to describe
the power of rational (and moral) discernment belonging
to human nature, a carefully defined aspect of the inner
activity of man, Paul was more or less directly influenced
by the popular thought of his day.[2] This is certainly true
as regards his use of the term ' conscience ' ($\sigma \upsilon \nu \epsilon i \delta \eta \sigma \iota s$),
which ethical Greek philosophy took over from the popular
consciousness and which passed into the current ethical
terminology of that epoch.[3] This precise word is found
rather in popular writers than in philosophers, who pre-
ferred to use the corresponding verb. Probably Paul's
use of it [4] is practically identical with that current among
ourselves—the moral judgment which accompanies or
follows an action, as also the source of such judgment. As
Bonhöffer has instructively pointed out, the specifically
Jewish and Christian use of the term was differentiated
from contemporary philosophical usage by the fact that the
latter did not acknowledge ' a personal God towards whom
man recognises his responsibility.' [5]

---

[1] ὁ ἐντὸς ἄνθρωπος (*Repub.* ix. 589a). Paul's expression is ὁ ἔσω
ἄνθρωπος. His use of the same phrase in 2 Cor. iv. 16 seems to have the
more general sense of the ' spiritual ' as contrasted with the ' physical ' life.

[2] Cf. his emphasis on the intellectual element in νοῦς in Rom. i. 20, where
the verb νοεῖν describes the process by which the nature of God may be
comprehended. But Paul recognises that this faculty may be degraded
by misuse (Rom. i. 28, Eph. iv. 17) as well as raised to a higher level
(Rom. xii. 2, Eph. iv. 23). Philo uses νοῦς with a wide range of significance. See Hatch, *op. cit.*, p. 125.

[3] See an instructive note on the history of the term in Norden's *Agnostos
Theos*, p. 136, *n.* 1.   [4] *E.g.* Rom. ii. 15 ; 1 Cor. viii. 7, x. 25, etc.

[5] *Epiktet u. d. Neue Testament*, p. 157.

(e) *Origin of Sin*

In spite of the promptings of a better judgment, Paul, in his pre-Christian condition, was conscious of being mastered by the tyranny of sin. Sin had rendered the moral order exhibited in the Law ineffectual for enabling men to reach a right relation with God. The question naturally arises : How did Paul account for sin ? And it is easier to ask the question than to answer it. We have seen that while, as a fact of experience, he definitely associates sin with the ' flesh,' *i.e.* human nature in its existing constitution, there is nothing to suggest that in his view the ' flesh ' is inherently evil. Indeed, for Paul as a Jew, the bodily organism was the direct creation of God. On the basis of Gen. i. 27 he regards man as ' the image and glory of God.' [1] A factor has intruded to work disaster, to destroy the relation of harmony between man and his Creator. And the supreme evidence of this is death. Now the remarkable thing is that Paul repeatedly emphasises the connection between death and sin,[2] which was a familiar Jewish tenet, while apparently hesitating to speculate on the background of sin itself. In several passages, however, he plainly connects the entrance of sin into the world with Adam.[3] And, although no explicit statements are to be found on the subject, it is hard to resist the inference that theoretically Paul believed that in virtue of the solidarity of the race all sinned in Adam, and so shared in his penalty of death.[4] A similar conception is found in 4 Ezra vii. 118, a document belonging to the same century as Paul. But there the explanation is given that Adam, yielding to the ' evil impulse,' ' clothed himself with the evil heart,' [5] and this evil heart appeared in his descendants. Apparently the ' evil impulse ' was by many Rabbinic authorities identified with certain passions belonging to man as created

[1] 1 Cor. xi. 7.   [2] *E.g.* Rom. v. 12, 17.
[3] Rom. v. 12, 15, 18, 19 ; 1 Cor. xv. 21, 22.
[4] So also Prof. R. Mackintosh, *Christianity and Sin*, pp. 80, 81.
[5] 4 Ezra iii. 21.

which only became evil by his improper use of them.[1]
It is possible that Paul also held the doctrine of the 'evil
impulse,' and that it is represented by the 'other law' of
Rom. vii. 23. In any case both he and 4 Ezra are quite
clear as to the responsibility of the individual for his own
transgressions.[2] Thus the two conceptions stand side by
side. Man has a hereditary bias to sin, but he is responsible
for allowing that bias to overmaster him.

One passage occurs in which Paul refers to the deception
of Eve by the serpent.[3] Before Paul's time the serpent
had been identified with Satan. We know how here and
there the apostle reveals his consciousness of a dark world
of evil powers which beset human life and have the present
order under their sway, powers which will be abolished
before the final consummation.[4] They are led by 'the
ruler of the power of the air, the spirit at present working
in the sons of disobedience.'[5] To this hierarchy of
wickedness Paul assigns the gods of the heathen, who are
not gods but 'demons.'[6] Perhaps behind Adam's lapse
from the Divine image he recognises the influence of those
fallen spirits or their leader, who, in Jewish tradition, had
rebelled against the Divine authority.

After all, the apostle is chiefly concerned with sin as an
empirical fact. Theories of the origin of evil are secondary
for him, and belong to his Jewish heritage. Hence it is not
surprising that we have no clear data for connecting his
idea of mankind as sinning in Adam with his doctrine of
the 'flesh' as sinful. Indeed, it is conceivable, as Prof. R.
Mackintosh suggests,[7] that Paul came to formulate his
idea in this fashion as the result of his transforming
experience, in which the power of the Spirit vanquished
his evil desires, using the Old Testament term 'flesh' for
that earlier condition of helplessness on which he could
now look back as a condition for ever left behind.

---

[1] See Schechter, *Some Aspects of Rabbinic Theology*, p. 267.
[2] See Box's ed. of 4 Ezra, p. xlii.
[3] 2 Cor. xi. 3, in which reference is made to Gen. iii. 4, 13.
[4] 1 Cor. xv. 24, ii. 6 ; Col. ii. 15 ; Eph. vi. 12.
[5] Eph. ii. 2.   [6] 1 Cor. x. 20 f.   [7] *Expositor*, May 1913, p. 454.

(f) *The Significance of the Law*

If sin, then, makes conformity to the Law a futile effort, what is to be said of the Law itself ?   What does it mean ?   What is its value ?   Why is it there ?   Paul's precise estimate of the Law is exceedingly difficult to formulate, not owing to the lack of material, but because his theory and his experience have often come into collision, and because his attitude has been powerfully affected by his relations as a Christian missionary with Jews and Judaising Christians. So that his utterances regarding the significance which the Law possessed for him in his pre-Christian days can at no point be dissociated from the position which he had reached through his profound fellowship with Christ. For this reason we shall not attempt to divide our discussion of his attitude into clearly marked stages, although it may be possible to indicate more or less generally a certain process of development in his ideas.

Paul's religious life as a Pharisee under the Law had failed to give him peace with God, primarily because he saw no prospect of winning God's favour on legal lines.   Now it is true that there was room in Judaism for more than the contract-idea of religion.   The very possession of the Law was regarded as a gift of the Divine grace.   All its institutions symbolised the favour of the Most High to His chosen people.   The writer of Psalm cxix., whose reverence for the Law is so boundless, can count on the tenderness and loving-kindness of the Lord (vv. 77, 149).   And throughout the history of Judaism there were those who, regarding the Law as the revelation of the will of God, and alive to the spirit rather than the letter, cast themselves on the Divine mercy for help to be loyal to its claims.   But the evidence of the Gospels, and especially the criticisms pronounced by Jesus Himself, testify unmistakably that the legalism of the Pharisees at that epoch was in the main a religion, not of freedom, but of bondage.   And if Christian documents should be charged with prejudice, there is ample proof in the Rabbinic writings themselves that childlike trust in

the Divine grace and the abiding assurance of the Divine
love were overshadowed by a tormenting anxiety to obey
the letter of the Law, and so be able to stand before the
Judge in the awful day of reckoning. Plainly this was the
atmosphere in which Paul's earlier life was spent. His
pre-Christian endeavours are reflected in the quotation
from Psalm cxliii. 2, which he expands from his Christian
standpoint : ' By the works of the Law " no flesh shall be
justified." ' The words are echoed all through his Epistles.
They describe not theory but experience, even although the
apostle may have deduced a theory from them.

Yet it need scarcely be said that Paul did not start from
this position. The Pentateuch he regarded as divinely
inspired from beginning to end. There is no evidence that
he drew any distinction between the ritual and moral
elements of the Law. All was a revelation from God.
And, in a sense, he continues as a Christian to hold this
view. In the paragraph of autobiography which has
occupied us so often already, after showing that the very
existence and challenge of the Law provoked him to sin,
he deliberately declares : ' The law is holy, and the commandment holy and righteous and good ' ; and again :
' We know that the law is spiritual.' [1] These epithets
emphasise the intimate connection of the Law with God.
Now before his conversion, one of his most tormenting
problems must have been to account for the inability of
this divinely appointed scheme of things, as he regarded it,
to achieve its proper function of enabling men to become
righteous. The theory he found in the Law itself : ' He
that performeth these things shall live by them.' [2] Life,
which was a description of the sum-total of God's best gifts
in the Old Testament, awaited the man who satisfied this
high claim. Death, the loss of all that made existence
worth having, was the penalty of him who failed. And
Paul, with his abhorrence of compromises, with his demand
for truth, with his unflinching self-knowledge, felt compelled to rank himself with the failures. Probably, even at

---

[1] Rom. vii. 12, 14.   [2] Lev. xviii. 5 (qu. in Gal. iii. 12).

that time, he was conscious that his life in a body of flesh and blood, a life exposed to the influence of sense in all its seductive power, was somehow responsible for his failure. There is the ring of the old despair in the words : ' Wretched man that I am ! who shall deliver me from the body of this death ? '[1] They sound true to the original situation. What he then discerned as a fact, he wove later into a theory of the function of the Law. Already, as a Pharisee, he had discovered the horror of sin. When as a Christian thinker he began to reflect on the Law in the light of that discovery, he concluded that one purpose at least of its promulgation was to reveal sin in its true colours, to make sin as loathsome as possible to the man who was guilty of it.[2]

But if its task stopped there, the situation would be worse than ever. What advantage is it for a man to realise the awfulness of his sin, if he sees no means of escaping from it ? Possibly Paul had almost been driven to that position. It appears in 4 Ezra, which at so many points reveals affinities with the apostle : ' The evil heart has grown up in us which has estranged us from God, and brought us into destruction, and has made known to us the ways of death, and removed us far from life ; and that not a few only, but well nigh all that have been created.' [3] When, in view of his Christian experience, Paul asked himself, ' Of what value was this revelation of the essential meaning of sin through the Law,' the remarkable answer is given : ' It was intended to prepare men for the new disclosure of grace and love and power in Jesus Christ.' There is no more remarkable flash of insight in the Epistles than Paul's statement in Gal. iii. 24 : ' The law has been the slave in charge of us (παιδαγωγός) [4] with a view to Christ, that we might be justified by faith. And now that faith has arrived, we are no longer under the slave.' He has come to estimate the Law no more as an end in itself, but as a preparatory discipline for the individual, making him fully aware of

---

[1] Rom. vii. 24.   [2] Rom. vii. 13 ; Gal. iii. 19.   [3] vii. 48.
[4] The *paedagogus* was a slave of the household entrusted with the supervision and discipline of the child until he reached his majority. By far the most vivid picture of his functions is found in Plato, *Lysis*, 208 c.

his own helplessness in the presence of sin, and compelling
him to look for aid to One who is the medium of the very
might of God.

But Paul carries this conception a stage further. He
has evidently wrestled hard with the problem of the Law.
That need not surprise us, for it met him continually in the
course of his missionary labours. We usually allow his
work among heathens to overshadow all else in his career.
And we know from Gal. ii. 9 that he regarded that as his
principal obligation. But apart from the varied evidence
of the Epistles, which so constantly address themselves
to the Jewish consciousness, there is no reason to doubt
the report in Acts that he was accustomed to make the
synagogue the starting-point of his operations. It has
been supposed by some scholars that Paul could not have
criticised the Law before Jewish audiences in the earlier
period of his career.[1] To us it is inconceivable that a man
who, like Paul, was conscious of having passed out of a
condition of bondage into one of joyous freedom, could
avoid the discussion of so momentous an element in the
situation, when urging upon his fellow-countrymen the
claims of Jesus Christ. The further evolution in his conception seems indeed to have grown out of this environment. The Law, Paul declares, is not merely a preparatory
discipline, but a temporary phase in the religious history of
Israel.[2] Here the apostle takes up a bold position. With
remarkable insight he discovers in the Old Testament itself
a foreshadowing of that attitude towards God which has
been fully realised through Christ. It finds illustration in
the life of the patriarch Abraham, a classical name for
Hebrew religion. He is not oppressed by legal sanctions.
He is content to cast himself simply upon the gracious
promise of God (Gal. iii. 16-18). Paul dwells upon this
with enthusiasm. Promise and Law are, in a sense,
incompatible. Legalism works with the conception of a
contract between two parties. The religion of promise

[1] So J. Weiss, *op. cit.*, p. 169.
[2] Note the expression in Rom. v. 20 : ' The law came in as a side-issue
(παρεισῆλθεν).'

represents the unmerited grace of God (Gal. iii. 18-20).
Thus the apostle by the sheer force of his spiritual sensibility anticipates the discovery of modern investigation
that legalism was not the essential foundation of Old
Testament religion, but rather a phase of its development.

It may be frankly admitted that certain features in
Paul's estimate of the Law emerge as the result of keen
controversy with those Judaising Christians who insisted
that strict conformity to its provisions was compulsory for
all who would be *bona-fide* members of the Christian community. Here he meets them on their own ground,
availing himself of Rabbinic traditions and exegesis to press
home the secondary character of the legal dispensation.
Thus, in Gal. iii. 19, he speaks of the Law as ' transmitted
by angels ' in contrast with the promise which was ' freely
given by God ' (ver. 18). The words seem to have in view
a Jewish tradition, found also in Acts vii. 53, Heb. ii. 2,
the LXX text of Deut. xxxiii. 2, and Josephus, *Antiq.* xv.
136 (ed. Niese), that the angels were concerned in the
communication of the Law to Israel.[1] Obviously the
tradition was intended to enhance the glory of the scene
at Sinai. Paul boldly inverts its significance for the sake
of emphasising the inferiority of the legal dispensation,
and he is followed in this interpretation by the writer to the
Hebrews.

The climax of this critical estimate of the Law appears
in his latest writings. His ripening experience of all that
is involved in Christ and Christ's salvation detaches him
more and more completely from his original standpoint.
As he reflects on the manifold bearings of the new relationship to God, which is a constant wonder to his soul, whatever savours of legalism becomes utterly irksome to him.
The only law he feels at liberty to recognise is the law of
Christ, which is love in its widest sense. When, therefore, from his new point of vantage, which commands
ever-widening horizons, he looks back on that condition
of painful servitude under which his spirit had chafed, he

---

[1] See Dibelius, *Die Geisterwelt im Glauben d. Paulus*, pp. 26-28.

seems to lose sight of any Divine purpose in that phase of the old order, and simply exults over its abolishment by Christ. The Law now appears to him as a positive barrier between the soul and God, which has had to be torn down. ' He cancelled the regulations that stood against us—all these obligations he set aside when he nailed them to the cross, when he cut away the angelic rulers and powers from us, exposing them to all the world and triumphing over them in the cross.' [1] Here it appears as if the ' angels ' whom he had introduced in Gal. iii. 19 as symbols of the inferiority of the legal dispensation, are identified with the realm of evil spiritual forces which dominate the present age. A foreshadowing of such identification is found in Gal. iv. 3, 8-10, where the sway of legalism over the Jews is set in parallel with that of ' elemental spirits ' (στοιχεῖα) over heathen. And he returns to this parallel in the paragraph immediately following the important passage from Colossians quoted above, thus indicating that it belonged to the permanent background of his reflection upon the significance of the Law.[2]

At this point we are confronted with a fact which has often been ignored. Warneck has most suggestively pointed out the essential legalism of heathen religions, and goes the length of saying that there is no graver peril in immature mission-communities than the desire to win God's favour by the performance of good deeds.[3] Hence, in guarding his newly won converts from the obligations of the Law, he was not merely concerned that they should be saved from a false conception of Christianity, but he was thoroughly alive to the fact that there was deeply rooted in their natures the very tendency to make religion a thing of rules and forms which he felt to be the paralysis of Judaism. So that the emphasis which he lays on the freedom of the spirit in relation to God has a direct bearing on the mental drift of heathen-Christians as well as on the

[1] Col. ii. 14, 15 (M.).
[2] Col. ii. 20-23. Cf. Eph. ii. 15, where the Law is represented as the basis of that enmity which kept Jew and Gentile apart.
[3] *Paulus im Lichte d. heutigen Heidenmission*, pp. 301-311.

hereditary religious training of Jews. For both alike, Christ is the ' end ' of the Law to every one who believes (Rom. x. 4).

(g) Paul's Relation to the Sect of the Nazarenes

The sketch which has been given of Paul's estimate of the Law casts a flood of light on his pre-Christian position. Allowing for all those elements in it which have been elaborated in the course of keen controversies with opponents, and their adaptation to the needs of heathen converts, no one can be blind to the ineffaceable mark which his mental confusion and dispeace under the Law had left upon his spiritual nature. As we have seen, his tormenting doubts of his own position urged him on to ruthless persecution of the sect who worshipped the crucified Jesus as the Messiah of God. But his contact with Christian disciples must have had real significance for the direction of his thought. It is true that his hatred would blind him to much that he might have learned regarding Jesus and His claims. But it is impossible to suppose that a man of his penetration of mind and earnestness of purpose should remain ignorant of the fundamental positions which were being taken up by the disciples of Christ in Jerusalem. The chief of these was the Messiahship of the crucified Jesus, who, His followers with one accord alleged, had been raised from the dead, and had manifested Himself to many of them. Paul would at least hear the common report of Jesus' career. He would be aware of the impression which this Teacher had made upon men and women who still retained their connection with the Temple-worship and the Law. He must necessarily have inquired into some of the reasons for such an impression. But we can go further. The book of Acts makes it perfectly clear that the young Rabbinic scholar, Paul, was an accomplice in the murder of Stephen, and that that event was the starting-point of his relentless crusade against the sect of the Nazarenes. But these schemes were not the impulse of a moment. An interesting note preserved in Acts (vi. 9) reveals as their background a hot religious controversy between Stephen, who was no doubt a Hellenist, and certain of his Hellenistic fellow-countrymen who had synagogues of their own at Jerusalem. Some of his opponents are described as Cilicians, and there can be little doubt that Paul was one of them. The charge they brought against the Christian leader was that he was constantly speaking against the Temple and the Law. Probably the writer of Acts is justified in calling this charge false, for the Christian community was still loyal to both these institutions, and Stephen could not have occupied the place he did if he were at variance with his fellow-disciples on so vital a question.[1] But the wording of the accusation, 'We have heard him say that Jesus the Nazarene will destroy this place and alter the customs handed down to us by Moses,' suggests that Stephen had grasped the inner significance of the teaching of Jesus, and that he had begun to show the same antagonism as his Master to the pedantries of formal worship and observance which played so important a part in the Judaism of the day. He had become alive to the hollowness of much that passed muster as piety, and he saw plainly that it was Jesus' criticism of this pseudo-obedience which had sent Him to the cross. Now the controversy between Stephen and his fellow-Hellenists must have turned upon such matters. In the course of it, Paul would inevitably be brought face to face with positions taken up by Jesus. And the very fact that the meaning of the Law was involved would kindle his interest with a unique intensity. We have no data from which even to surmise the point of view adopted by Stephen, for the main drift of his speech before the Sanhedrim, as reported in Acts, is concerned with Moses as pointing forward to Christ. But if we recollect that Paul was in the throes of a spiritual struggle which chiefly arose from his consciousness of the inadequacy of legalism, and then realise that there was presented to him a new

[1] See Feine, *Theologie d. N. T.*, p. 228.

estimate of the Law as adumbrated by Jesus, we can
picture a further undermining of the very bulwarks of his
religious position, and, alongside of this, a passionate
attempt to convince his own mind, in spite of doubts that
could not be laid, by plunging into a course which asserted
by deeds and not words the validity of his inherited beliefs.
Johannes Weiss has attempted to show that Paul, in all
likelihood, must have seen Jesus in Jerusalem.[1] There is
nothing impossible in the hypothesis, although it is most
precarious to base it on 2 Cor. v. 16, of which, in our
judgment, Weiss gives a quite erroneous exegesis. What
he is concerned, however, to prove is that before his
conversion Paul had a clear impression of the historical
Jesus, both as regards His personal characteristics and
His remarkable claims. And certainly the experience,
whatever in it may elude all ordinary investigation, can
be more readily comprehended on this hypothesis. We
know what horror the notion of a crucified Messiah must
have struck into Paul's mind. We know that the attempt
to vindicate such a position must have seemed to him
the most appalling blasphemy, and urged him on the more
furiously in his persecuting ardour. Yet, beside this cari-
cature of his nation's hope, there would stand the figure
of Jesus of Nazareth, who had pitied the outcast and
welcomed little children. He had indeed pronounced
solemn woes on Pharisaic formalism and hypocrisy, and
His denunciations went to the heart of legalism. But He
had also called up visions of a new spiritual ideal, whose
fascination at least it would be hard for any earnest soul
to evade. Nor would it count for little that His followers
were willing to face shame and death for His sake, and that
in their sorest trials they remained true to that spirit and
temper which they had learned from their Lord. Of these
things Paul must have been a frequent witness. Can we
doubt that his confusion deepened, that it became ' hard for
him to kick against the goads ' (Acts xxvi. 14) ?

[1] *Paulus u. Jesus*, pp. 22-31.

D

CHAPTER III

ST. PAUL'S CONVERSION

(a) A Revelation of Jesus as Risen

THE story of Paul's conversion belongs to his biography. What concerns us here is its significance for his theology.

When the zealous Pharisee embarked on his crusade of persecution, his feelings were shocked by the mingled blasphemy and folly of the disciples of Jesus in claiming that their crucified Master was proved to be the Messiah by His resurrection from the dead. It was the inevitable result of teaching which appeared to be a disparagement of the Pharisaic position and a disintegration of those beliefs which were the pride of national tradition. The claims of patriotism demanded that such deadly heresy should be extirpated. But we have seen that the champion of legalism at this critical moment was far from being satisfied with his own religious attainment. A conflict between the actual and the ideal raged within him, which the Law seemed powerless to allay. He knew something by hearsay of Jesus of Nazareth. He could not be grouped with those revolutionary pseudo-Messiahs who made a momentary sensation in times of political ferment. The echoes of His teaching which had come to Paul's ears suggested a man of balanced nature, spiritual enthusiasm, and moral sincerity. And the aspect of His followers confirmed the report. Their only fanaticism was mutual love. There was no sign of scheming for personal aggrandisement. They did not seem to lean on outward force. A contagious gladness possessed them, and this no spasmodic emotion, but an abiding spirit which kept them calm and courageous even in the presence of death.   And all their joy and hope they attributed to the grace of their risen Lord, who was exalted to Divine power, and should soon return to perfect their salvation and subdue the world to God.

We can only form conjectures as to the condition of thought and feeling which was the resultant of these conflicting groups of forces.   Such conjectures are as likely to be erroneous as accurate   Some scholars go the length of imagining that Paul the Pharisee had reached the point of asking himself, ' Have these Nazarenes found the truth ? Has the crucified Jesus indeed manifested Himself to them ? Has God vindicated His claims in this marvellous fashion ? ' All that may reasonably be inferred is the existence of a silent preparation in the soul of this restless seeker after God.   To attempt to define its psychological stages, as, e.g., Holsten has done,[1] is to read an artificial construction into the mysterious processes of that elusive realm which we call personality.

The apostle himself makes no reference to a silent process which culminated in the revelation of Christ to him as risen and exalted.   For him the crisis was altogether sudden and wonderful.   ' It was God, who said, Light shall shine out of darkness, that shone in my heart.' [2]   That is to say, what remained with him as the supreme impression was the unexpected transformation of his religious experience by the instrumentality of God.   It is of little value to discuss the precise nature of this epoch-making event.   To us it seems futile to regard it as the mere visionary product of the highly agitated mental condition of Paul the Pharisee. The conditions of receptivity were of course present.   But the vision had a content which Paul had not created.   There were Divine forces at work for one of the crucial ends in the history of God's self-manifestation to men.   ' He who set me apart from my birth and called me through his grace was pleased to reveal his Son in me that I might preach him

---

[1] *Das Evangelium d. Paulus*, Teil II., 1898.
[2] 2 Cor. iv. 6.   One feels sure that Dr. Moffatt is right in translating ἡμῶν here by ' my.'

among the heathen.' [1]   It is noteworthy that Paul never
dwells on the abnormal aspect of the event. He is exclusively concerned with its religious significance and value.
The standpoint from which he views it is made perfectly
clear by his statement in 1 Cor. xv. 8 f. The subject of this
chapter is the reality of the resurrection of Christ as an
evidence for that of Christians. After mentioning various
manifestations of the risen Jesus to disciples, he concludes :
' And last of all he appeared to me also, the untimely born.
For I am the least of the apostles, unworthy even of the
name of apostle, because I persecuted the church of God,
but by the grace of God I am what I am.' That is invariably the note of his experience, the Divine condescen-
sion and mercy to one who had no claim whatever upon
them. What moves his soul is the loving hand stretched
out to arrest him in his folly, the hand of Christ by which
he was grasped.[2]

In this crisis Paul passed into a new world. All his
religious values were changed. ' What things were gain
to me, these I have counted loss for Christ.' [3] His national
prerogatives, his long and careful training, his pride as an
expert in the Law, his reputation as a Pharisee, his prospects
as a leader in the religious life of his people—everything
was sacrificed on the altar of devotion to Christ. Perhaps
the most fundamental aspect of the transformation is that
which is conditioned by the apostle's overpowering conviction of the Divine grace, referred to above. Henceforward God is not primarily the Being who sets up a
standard which must be conformed to, who demands an
obedience which must be painfully attained. He is rather
the generous Giver, who furnishes the trusting soul with all
the equipment necessary for realising its highest life. The
Divine revelation which Paul has received is indeed in a
real sense new knowledge, but, to a still greater degree,
new power. That involves a fresh moral impetus, which is
above all else directed by the dominating impulse of love,

[1] Gal i. 15, 16. For a discussion of Paul's vision which keeps in view
all its aspects, see Olschewski, *Die Wurzeln d. paulin. Christologie*, pp.
25-29.   [2] Phil. iii. 12.   [3] Phil. iii. 7.

the reflection and product of the redeeming love of God in Christ.

Before we examine the factors emerging from Paul's conversion-experience which were normative for his religious thought, let us endeavour to get a firm grasp of the immediate consequence of the event for his position. Plainly he became convinced that *Jesus was risen and living*. The extraordinary vividness of his conviction is evident from the casual manner in which he is able to introduce it into a practical discussion. ' Have not I seen Jesus, our Lord ? ' he says to the Christian community at Corinth, in a context where he urges them to practise self-denial, as he, an apostle, has invariably done.[1] His language is note-worthy. It is *Jesus* who has been revealed to him. The name which he uses illuminates his standpoint, and it is significant that in the three accounts of the incident in Acts, Jesus, and not Christ, is the designation employed.[2] The fact reminds us of an extremely important consideration. The Being with whom he has come into relation is no mere abstraction. There could scarcely be a more glaring misconception than that of Bousset : ' The Jesus whom Paul knows is the pre-existent supra-mundane Christ.' [3] There is no evidence to show that Paul had already in his mind the clear-cut conception of a Heavenly Man, pre-served by the Divine wisdom to be revealed at the proper time for the performance of Messianic functions. There is no ground for supposing that with this apocalyptic idea he vaguely associated the name of Jesus of Nazareth, in whom, as a historical person, he had no genuine interest.[4] Even when he describes the Risen One, who had appeared to him as Christ, he is not speaking of the Messiah *in vacuo*. As a matter of fact, he constantly uses the name ' Christ ' of the earthly Jesus.[5]

---

[1] 1 Cor. ix. 1.

[2] We do not leave out of sight the fact that Paul uses ' Christ ' about twelve times as often as ' Jesus.' See the interesting discussion of the ' Names ' of Christ in Paul's Letters in Feine's *Jesus Christus u. Paulus*, pp. 21-45.   [3] *Kyrios Christos*, p. 144.

[4] So Brückner, *Die Entstehung d. paulin. Christologie, e.g.* pp. 30 ff., 93 ff.

[5] *E.g.* Rom. v. 6, vii. 4 ; 2 Cor. i. 5, etc.

Everything really turns on the recognition that it was
Jesus, against whose cause he had plotted and acted, who
was revealed to Paul. Already for the persecutor He was
a figure warm with life. Paul was acquainted with the
main features of His character. He knew something of the
import of His preaching. He was fully aware of the extraordinary impression of their Master which His followers
retained. He had seen how their lives were shaped by
contact with Him. And they claimed to have His presence abiding with them, the presence of the risen Lord.
It was all true. He had overcome death. The significance of His victory was overwhelming. All that He had
taught of God was true. For God had vindicated Him in
this astounding fashion. His attitude towards legalism
was the right attitude. His conception of the Kingdom
of God was alone valid. His ideals for living were stamped
with Divine authority. He was the promised Messiah.
This was in some ways the most stupendous fact of all.
The hope around which the most eager yearnings of the
Pharisee had circled was virtually realised. The new era
had dawned. Operations of God were in motion for which
the centuries had been waiting. There was no limit to
that which might be expected. Christ must return to
complete the Divine purpose, but the purpose was as good
as accomplished, because the pledge of it was already a
reality. Men could feel the stirring of the Spirit of God
in their hearts. Their disobedience had not alienated the
Divine love.

The supreme obstacle in Paul's mind was taken out
of the way. A suffering Messiah had never been con-
templated by Jewish religion. From first to last his career
must be one of glory and triumph. But crucifixion was
more than suffering. It meant degradation and a curse.
We cannot tell what confusion the cross of Jesus had
wrought in the soul of this Pharisee, as he caught gleams
of illumination and then sank back into grosser darkness.
But in the light of his new experience his unerring religious
instinct taught him that the cross was not a tragic accident :

that it was wrought into the very texture of God's self-revelation to men. And so he wrestled with its mystery on every side, endeavouring to express by analogies based on the Old Testament, by thought-forms of the Judaism in which he had been reared, and by daring constructions of his own speculative power, the ineffable significance of the crisis in which the love of God at its highest met the sin of men at its worst.

We must, however, guard against the idea that the chief effect of his conversion on Paul was the reshaping of intellectual positions. That is the element in his experience which is easiest to account for and to describe. But behind that lay the recreated attitude towards God. Not the God he had worshipped in Judaism, not even the God that might be approached through the prophets of the Old Testament, but the God who was interpreted by Christ. Here we touch the heart of the situation. But it lies so deep that we need not attempt to fathom it. We can only say that in this contact with the Divine, Paul became aware of the real meaning of God, not as a mental judgment or conclusion, but as the assurance of love and redeeming power. A sick man may read with interest a scientific description of the symptoms of returning health. But there is a world of difference between that interest and the actual experience of new vigour and power of action. The personal quickening came first in Paul's case : removal of barriers, access to God, understanding of His nature, complete and joyful trust in His grace and love, the sense of victory over sin, power to live as a son of the Father, and, resulting from this, a fresh vision of duty and responsibility. Nothing could be more characteristic of the meaning of his conversion for Paul than the relation to Christ on which he enters. Much later in his career he says : 'For me to live is Christ.' [1] But this attitude began with the crisis. Whatever other elements may be involved in his favourite designation of Christ as ' Lord,' the *personal* stands in the forefront. To Christ he makes over his life in all its parts

[1] Phil. i. 21.

and possibilities. No other power can contest that sovereignty. He is Christ's ' slave ' (δοῦλος),[1] to do and to suffer all that his Lord may appoint. He exults in being led a captive in Christ's triumphal procession.[2]

(b) A Call to Service

It is a remarkable fact that in the two classical passages in which he refers to his conversion, Paul directly associates the event with a call to service. In Gal. i. 15, 16, he describes the purpose of the revelation of Christ to him as involving a mission to the heathen. And in 2 Cor. iv. 6 he declares that the light of God had shone within his heart ' to illuminate men with the knowledge of God's glory in the face of Christ ' (M.). Some scholars, notably Sir William Ramsay,[3] have laid much stress on the idea that, from his earliest days, Paul's ardent ambition was to win the Roman Empire for Judaism, and that as a Christian he simply carried forward on new lines the bold plan which he had long before conceived. There is nothing impossible in the hypothesis. But we prefer to follow the apostle's own indications and to trace his missionary enterprise among heathen peoples to the intrinsic nature of his great spiritual discovery.

Much discussion has turned on the question, ' At what point in his Christian career did Paul resolve to preach his Gospel to the non-Jewish world ? ' In the story of his self-defence narrated in Acts xxii., mention is made of his conviction of having received a Divine commission to be Christ's ambassador to the Gentiles at a time when he was absorbed in prayer in the Temple at Jerusalem. In his address before Festus and Agrippa this commission is immediately connected with his experience on the Damascus road. The first reference to his mission-work among Gentiles is probably that in Acts xi. 25 f., where Barnabas is described as having gone to Tarsus and brought

---

[1] Rom. i. 1; Gal. i. 10; Phil. i. 1.   [2] 2 Cor. ii. 14.
[3] See, e.g., his interesting essay on ' The Statesmanship of Paul ' in *Pauline and Other Studies*, pp. 49-100.

Paul thence to Antioch, where a vigorous Christian propaganda had already been begun. These reports are, of course, much later than the events they record, and the traditions of Paul's earlier movements were no doubt vague enough. In our judgment the details of the apostle's procedure are of far less importance than the principles by which they were regulated. It seems an extraordinarily meagre interpretation of the facts to suppose that Paul's splendid realisation of a universal Gospel was bound up with his new view of the Messiah as ' the Heavenly Man.' [1] It surely lies in the very essence of the religious experience which changed his life. Whether he saw all that this involved for his own vocation from the beginning, or whether that emerged somewhat later as the result of earnest reflection, is a matter of secondary importance. The vital consequence of Paul's meeting with the risen Christ was a new experience of God, and, on the basis of that experience, a new relation to God. We must discuss the situation fully in a later section.

Meanwhile it may be noted that for Paul the demand for conformity to legal requirements, which he had looked upon as a Divine demand, vanished out of sight. The idea of attaining the approval of God by a laborious process of meritorious actions had been transformed into the assurance that God was there, waiting to reveal His love in generous fulness to the soul that was willing to trust Him. But this attitude of faith had nothing to do with national prerogatives. These Paul had found to be a positive barrier to real inward peace with God. And the love of God which was interpreted to men in Christ was infinitely larger than any hereditary privileges. It yearned for man as man, apart from race or class or sex. ' There is no longer Jew or Greek, there is no longer slave or freeman, there is no longer male or female. For you are all one in Christ Jesus.' [2] Here was an amazing revolution in religious outlook. There was nothing like it in the ancient world. And its significance possessed Paul as a consuming

---

[1] So Holtzmann, *op. cit.*, ii. p. 70.　　　[2] Gal. iii. 28.

passion. What truth in the universe could be compared
to this ? What must it mean for any one to reach the
conviction that God was calling him into His family, eager
to bestow upon him all the wealth of His Divine resources ?
Paul felt with his whole soul that it had made him a new
creature. And in that experience he was aware of a constraint from God laid upon him to proclaim the good news
everywhere. ' Necessity is laid upon me : yes, woe is to
me if I do not preach the Gospel.' [1] It was the one way
in which he could discharge his unspeakable debt to Jesus
Christ.

Paul invariably associates his apostolic labours with a
Divine purpose and call. The all-important description
of his conversion in Gal. i. 15, already cited, lays particular
emphasis on God's choice of His instrument, and its form
suggests that Paul had in his mind the account given by
Jeremiah of his call to the prophetic office.[2] The Old
Testament recognises no second causes. All events are
referred directly to Divine causation. But in Paul's case
there was something more than a traditional belief. He
was profoundly conscious of the antagonism between
past and present in his history. And yet that past, with
its bondage and dissatisfaction, had been preparing for
what followed. He had been ' kept in strict ward with a
view to the faith which was destined to be revealed.' [3]
Then, at what appeared to his reflection the most unlikely
moment, when he was at the height of his persecuting fury,
he was brought to a sudden halt by a force blended of
love and wisdom and power. He felt it to be Divine,
and as he could never hold an atomistic view of history,
he was persuaded that from the very beginning, all unconscious as he was, the Divine hand had been shaping
his career for that decisive epoch in which the veil was torn
from his eyes, and the truth flashed upon him in the
personal manifestation of the Son of God. This persuasion
became regulative for the entire course of his life. A chief
effect of it may be designated his *apostolic consciousness*.

[1] 1 Cor. ix. 16.   [2] Jer. i. 5.   [3] Gal. iii. 23.

He believed intensely that he had been set apart to declare the good news of Christ to the heathen.[1] His descriptions of this vocation are very instructive. His highest title is 'apostle,'[2] the delegate of Jesus Christ, a name perhaps used by the Master Himself. He is a 'servant of Christ' and 'a steward of the mysteries of God.'[3] He can write to the Romans 'with a certain freedom, in virtue of my Divine commission as a priest of Christ Jesus to the Gentiles in the service of God's Gospel.'[4] On the basis of this same commission, he has laid the foundation of the spiritual house at Corinth as 'a skilled master builder.'[5] God has fitted him for being the minister of a new covenant.[6] On Christ's behalf he comes as an ambassador, as if God were urging men through him.[7] To him the Divine secret has been revealed that Gentiles are to share with Jews in the promises of God.[8] Therefore, if we are to form any true conception of his general standpoint, we must keep in mind this 'apostolic consciousness.' To this must be attributed the tone of grave authority which he assumes in writing to Christian communities, a tone which imparts a peculiar dignity even to his language and style, and marks off his Epistles completely from those colloquial documents with which they have so often been compared. The high claims which he constantly makes do not rest on a love of power or confidence in his own judgment. None of the great figures in human history was more conscious of weakness. 'I carry this treasure' (of the Gospel), he says, 'in a frail vessel of earth, to show that the transcending power belongs to God, not to myself.'[9] But the work which God has entrusted to him is a matter of life and death. And he will run the risk of appearing egotistic to save his beloved converts from error. 'I wish,' he begs of the Corinthians, 'that you would put up with a little " folly " from me. Do put up with me, for I feel a Divine jealousy on your behalf.'[10]

---

[1] See esp. Rom. i. 1-5; Gal. i. 16.
[2] E.g. 1 Cor. ix. 1.
[3] 1 Cor. iv. 1.
[4] Rom. xv. 15, 16 (M.).
[5] 1 Cor. iii. 10.
[6] 2 Cor. iii. 6.
[7] 2 Cor. v. 20.
[8] Eph. iii. 2-9; Col. i. 25-27.
[9] 2 Cor. iv. 7 (partly M.).
[10] 2 Cor. xi. 1 (M.).

Was there ever penned a more amazing document than
2 Cor. x.-xiii. ?   For the spiritual health of this community
he feels compelled to defend his position against unscrupulous
men who were working hard to undermine their confidence
in him.   It hurts his sensitive feeling to assert his claims
upon their respect.   ' I am mad to talk like this,' he inter-
jects, in the course of his statement.[1] But the climax of
this marvellous self-revelation, in which every thought and
emotion can be tracked as they pass over his soul, brings out
the genuine attitude of the devoted, self-forgetful pastor
and teacher : ' I am glad to be weak if you are strong.' [2]
Hence all charges of arrogance and presumption are simply
due to a misunderstanding of the ground which the apostle
occupies.   From first to last he is conscious of being the
' spokesman of Christ.' [3]

(c) His Election

This ' apostolic consciousness ' of Paul means, as we
have indicated, his conviction that God has chosen him for
a high vocation.   But if we think at all of choice in connection with God, it cannot be conceived as something
casual, but as belonging to His eternal vision of things.
So we are confronted with Paul's idea of Election, the main
significance of which has constantly been misconceived
owing to the emphasis being placed on the wrong element in
it.   We know how, in the Old Testament, the people of
Israel, from their remarkable experience of the goodness of
God, concluded that He had specially chosen them for His
favour from among the nations.   And the great prophets
like Amos find in that position not a reason for self-
satisfaction or slackness of effort, but for a deeper sense
of responsibility.[4] Paul also starts from personal experience.   The wonder of God's grace to him in Christ has overpowered him.   What does it mean ?   As we have seen,
his destination for a special function in the all-wise plan of

---

[1] 2 Cor. xi. 23 (M.).   [2] 2 Cor. xiii. 9 (M.).
[3] 2 Cor. xiii. 3 (M.).   [4] Amos iii. 2.

God. But that forms part of the profound experience
which he calls his salvation. Such an experience cannot
be a mere accident. It must go back to God's eternal
purpose. It is involved in God's thought for the world.
That thought must sooner or later be realised. And so when
Paul feels the inadequacy of his service and shrinks from
presenting so faltering an obedience to the all-holy Father,
his soul is cheered by the assurance that the God who has
taken such pains with his life will not allow that life to
fail. Human weakness does much to hamper the progress
of the Divine operation. But Paul is convinced that what
God has begun He will carry out to the end.[1] 'Faithful
is he who calls you : he will also perform it.'[2] The loving
effort which God lavishes on winning a life for His service,
Paul describes as His 'call.' Those who respond to it
thereby prove themselves to be the objects of His choice.
And they are able to realise that while they work out their
own salvation with fear and trembling, God Himself is
behind and in the process, by His gracious disposition
towards them enabling them to achieve their desire without
failure. What of the other side of the picture ? Has God
deliberately and in His eternal purpose excluded some
from His salvation in Jesus Christ ? The apostle was too
whole-hearted a missionary to act at any time on that
assumption. As Jülicher admirably puts it : 'He never
said to any one : You have been made hard of heart, you
have been destined to unbelief and destruction : there is
no use wasting my energy in trying to win you over :
there is no use wasting love on you. . . . For Paul's
practical piety both propositions alike stand firm : I myself
am responsible for all my sins : all that is good in me is the
gift of God's grace.'[3] The misconception referred to is
due to the prominence given to the theoretical discussion
of Rom. ix.-xi. There the apostle is face to face with the
serious problem of the rejection of Christ by the Jewish
people. It fills him with perplexity. What can it mean ?
Has the purpose of God for Israel been defeated ? To

[1] Phil. i. 6.   [2] 1 Thess. v. 24.   [3] *Paulus u. Jesus*, p. 45.

begin with, he endeavours to show from what actually
happened in the history of the nation that, far back in the
past, religious distinctions revealed themselves between
various families, Isaac and Ishmael, Esau and Jacob.
And he ends by pointing out to his Gentile readers that, as
it is, a remnant of the chosen people have entered the
promised blessedness, and by disclosing his conviction that
one day ' all Israel will be saved.'   But in the course of
his argument he tries to account for the actual circumstances of the case by the Pharisaic theory that God has
mercy on whom He pleases and makes stubborn whom He
pleases.   This is plainly to ignore the moral conditions of
the Divine activity.   For, as Dr. Denney has tersely put
it in his comment on Rom. ix. 20, which compares God's
relation to man with that of the potter to the clay, ' A
man is not a thing, and if the whole explanation of his
destiny is to be sought in the bare will of God, he *will* say,
Why didst Thou make me thus ?   And not even the
authority of Paul will silence him.' [1]

(d) The Bearing of his Vocation on his Theology

As Paul's consciousness of a direct call from God gave
stability to his faith, so the purpose of that call absorbed
his practical interest.   In attempting to estimate his
religious thought, it is needful to bear in mind that it took
shape on the mission-field, and that its most important
features were to a large extent determined by missionary
experience.   However meagre our knowledge of Paul's
earlier Christian career, it is plain that from the first he
became a preacher of the Gospel.   So there was probably
no period in his Christian life in which he was not testing
the validity of those truths which appeared to him fundamental.   It was pointed out in an earlier paragraph that
he would naturally attach supreme value to the convictions
which had sprung out of the crisis of his conversion.   He
would be constrained to believe that the particular revela-

[1] *Expos. Greek Test.*, ii. p. 663.

tion of God in Christ which had brought peace and joy to his own soul must be equally effective in the lives of others. Jesus Christ would always be the centre of his message. But obviously he had, as a Christian missionary, to deal with divergent types of men. Although he regarded the heathen communities of the Empire as his peculiar sphere, his heart yearned for his brethren in Judaism, and especially for Jews of the Dispersion like himself. Now, in this case, he had a wide basis of common belief from which to start. There was the one living and true God to whom they and he alike did reverence. There was the conviction of a future Judgment in which men should be recompensed according to the actual issue of their earthly life. There was the hope of a new order of things, associated with the manifestation of the Messiah, in which those declared righteous by God should enter upon a condition of eternal blessedness. And he could count on an acknowledgment from his Jewish audiences of a moral standard which placed them on a far higher level than that of heathenism. But Paul had to enlarge the conception of a righteous and holy God by emphasising that grace and love which through Christ had come to be for him the truest expression of the Divine character. He had to turn the hearts of his fellow-countrymen from the attitude of trembling uncertainty in which they stood towards the decision of God upon their conduct, and to persuade them that in union with Christ, the union reached through faith, they could even now become assured of God's forgiveness for Christ's sake. He had to urge that their painful efforts to win merit in God's sight were rendered needless by the wondrous exhibition of the very meaning of God in the cross of His Son. So that his central doctrine of Justification by faith is not a scholastic abstraction, formulated to round off an artificial theory. It is, as Luther discovered later, an attempt to express in limited human terms what is most vital in the Gospel of Jesus Christ. It was impossible for him, however, to show the real value of this new attitude to God without revealing the inadequacy of the old. Hence

his constant criticism of Pharisaic legalism, the religious
attitude which had kept his own soul in a state of unrest.
This criticism comes into the forefront of his Epistles,
because Jews and Judaising Christians regarded Paul's
independence of the Law both as treachery to the Divine
revelation and as a serious peril for morality. In the case
of the former, of course, it was only one of several formid-
able barriers between them and the new faith. But as
regards the latter, Paul felt that their Christian position
was vitiated in its very foundation by their failure to
recognise that it meant the exchange of codes of regulations
for the free and joyful inspiration of the Spirit of God.
When they endeavoured to force their view upon converts from heathenism, he did not hesitate to charge them
with falsifying the Gospel of Christ.

The Messianic Hope was a burning question in Judaism
when Paul became a follower of Jesus. Nothing produced
upon him a more profound impression than the discovery
that in Jesus all the promises of God were fulfilled. He
retained much of the Jewish eschatology associated with
the consummation of the Kingdom of God, but even this
was powerfully affected by the recognition that in a real
sense the new epoch had already broken in, that Christians
were living among the powers of the world to come. The
pledge of this was their actual experience of the Spirit.
He did not require to inculcate morality in the ordinary
sense upon his Jewish brethren. But he had to make plain
to them that the presence in their lives of the Divine Spirit,
which was God's answer to their faith, was a much more
stable basis of worthy conduct than any formal attempts
to comply with a legal standard.

Probably Paul's method of approach as a Christian
missionary to Jewish audiences would to a large extent
appeal to those ' God-fearers,' [1] who formed groups of
earnest inquirers in many Jewish synagogues, and who
were already influenced by the idea of one righteous God,

[1] Regularly described as οἱ σεβόμενοι τὸν Θεόν in Acts. Moffatt translates ' devout proselytes.'

a moral life, and a future day of retribution. When, however, he came to deal with Gentiles, he could not as a rule take these fundamental positions for granted. First and foremost in that ancient Hellenistic world stood the need of Redemption. It is true that this took the form of a yearning to be liberated from the crushing tyranny of Fate or of those elemental spirits whose malice was everywhere feared. Men were burdened with a sense of helplessness rather than of sin. They believed in supernatural powers, but merely to be suspicious of them. Paul proclaimed to them the cross of Christ as a demonstration of that ineffable Divine love which was incarnate in the Saviour, as an exposure of human sin at its darkest in rejecting the gracious appeal of God, and as an exhibition of the Divine righteousness in virtue of which all contact with sin means suffering. The cross of Christ is his central theme. For he knows by experience that it constitutes the most powerful summons to repentance. God is there in His love and holiness, condemning sin, and offering deliverance in Christ to the sinner. But this fundamental Gospel of the apostle bore directly on the heathen attitude of fear towards the mighty powers that towered above them. God was no longer blind force or inscrutable cunning. He was presented in gracious guise as the loving Father, the Father of the Lord and Saviour Jesus Christ. He was brought near to them in His dear Son, the Redeemer. And their contact with Him meant inspiration with new life and power. They were not abandoned to the passing effects of magical ceremonies and mystic initiations. They were equipped with the very qualities which gave them the victory over sin and temptation. The whole armour of God was placed at their disposal in virtue of their surrender to Christ. Now this power imparted to them through the Divine Spirit was to find expression, not in fitful outbursts of enthusiasm like the frenzy of heathen orgies but in the channels of daily behaviour. Love, joy, kindness, purity, lowliness, trustworthiness, self-control—these were the genuine fruits of the Spirit. It is plain from

E

the evidence of the Epistles that Paul spared no pains in the ethical training of his converts. And perhaps nothing proved more effective in morally immature communities than his announcement of a day in which God should judge the secrets of men by Jesus Christ. This day was coincident with the return of Christ and the complete inauguration of that age in which God's rule should be supreme. The thought of its approach, the conviction that the dark night was already receding before the dawn, formed a powerful incentive to sobriety of life and watchful self-control. Idolatry, sensuality, strife, untruthfulness, fraud—how could a soul soiled by such stains appear in presence of the spotless purity of Christ ? So that Paul's emphasis on the Parousia is not a piece of mere eschatological scenery, but a powerful appeal for Christian living.

We have already seen that the constantly recurring discussions of legalism in the Epistles had a much wider application than to Jewish or Jewish-Christian communities. They were thoroughly relevant to the traditional subjection of heathen peoples to innumerable rites and customs, which usually had little ethical significance. Therefore the proclamation of an inward freedom of the spirit as the very kernel of religion, while possessing its own dangers, as Paul well knew, meant a welcome liberation from a routine which was irksome in proportion to its lack of value for spiritual needs.

The unerring moral perception revealed in Paul's selection of truth to be set forth is attested on every mission-field. The aspects of Christian faith and morality which he never wearies of commending are precisely those which the modern missionary finds most effective.[1] This must be borne in mind at a time when so much stress is laid on the chasm which separates Paul's religious ideas from ours. Unquestionably his theology has primarily in view those who, through the crisis of conversion, have come over from heathenism to Christianity, and it was shaped at the outset in the throes of a parallel experience of his own. Such a

---

[1] See esp. Warneck, *op. cit.*, pp. 81-122, 287-339.

course cannot be postulated as normal. But we must beware of forgetting that the elemental things in religion are strangely persistent. And there is rich significance in Harnack's observation that all the great movements of spiritual renewal in the history of the Church may be traced to a fresh discovery of the meaning of the Gospel of Paul.

CHAPTER IV

THE NORMATIVE INFLUENCE OF ST. PAUL'S CONVERSION ON
HIS RELIGIOUS THOUGHT

(a) *Jesus the Conqueror of Death*

ENOUGH has been said to make it perfectly clear that
Paul's entire conversion-experience circled round the
person of Jesus. Henceforth he was persuaded that his
function in the world was to bring his fellow-men into touch
with those supreme benefits which, through Jesus Christ,
had transformed existence for him. This epoch-making
change affected every feature of his religious outlook.
His view of God, his Messianic expectation, his eschatology,
his relation to the Law, his moral ideal—all were directly
modified in the light of the decisive revelation which had
come to him. Truly old things had passed away ; new
things had come to be.[1] It is plain, therefore, that his
religious thought will be, primarily, the result of reflection
upon these new things. So that we ought to be able to
discover the main drift of his theology by examining the
convictions which were borne in upon his mind by his
conversion.

Paul, as we have noted, must have been familiar with
the common faith of those Christians whom he harassed.
For them everything turned on the assurance that Jesus,
who had been crucified, was risen. There was no belief
comparable to this in the history of Jewish religion, and
its sheer daring must have impressed a mind like Paul's,
more especially as it was associated with one who had died
a death of shame. The crucifixion of Jesus by itself put

[1] 2 Cor. v. 17.

an end for ever to all Messianic claims and hopes. But if He could not be holden of death, no dignity could be too honourable for Him. The suggestion was monstrous. And Paul must often have fallen back on its incredibility, when his opposition to the Nazarenes required reinforcement. But it was this Jesus who laid hold of him, who claimed his life, who made him a new creature. Astounding readjustments of religious ideas were needful in every direction, as soon as he had opportunity to make them. These readjustments form the subject of our investigation. But the presupposition of them all is *Jesus as the conqueror of death.*

The central place of this conviction in Paul's mind is evident from the stress which he lays upon it in crucial passages of his Letters. Thus in the opening words of the Epistle to the Galatians, a document intended to lay bare the essence of his Gospel, when linking together the name of Jesus Christ with that of God the Father, he attaches to the latter the description, ' who raised him from the dead.' [1] That is to say, in his new discovery of the mind and purpose of God, the most amazing element was the resurrection of Jesus Christ. The idea is elaborated in his famous statement regarding Jesus Christ in the introduction to Romans : ' Born of the seed of David by natural descent, and installed as Son of God with power in virtue of the Spirit of holiness as the result of resurrection from the dead.' [2] Here is a compendium of Paul's Christology, and it illuminates what he conceives to be the bearing of the resurrection on the person of Christ. The resurrection has put the seal upon His supreme dignity as Son of God, with all that that involves for His relation to men. He is now exalted to the highest place that heaven affords. It is no arbitrary process, for it is the operation of that Spirit of holiness which was the controlling principle of His nature, and which death could not quench. But for Paul, the practical consequence of this crowning event in the experience of his Lord and Master is paramount. In

[1] Gal. i. 1.   [2] Rom. i. 3, 4 (partly M.).

one of the most intimate of all his self-revelations, he
declares how he has spurned all that he once had valued
in order to know Christ ' in the power of his resurrection
and the fellowship of his sufferings.' [1] The basis of a
genuine heart-to-heart knowledge of Christ is His risen life.
The later development in the Johannine literature is the
elaboration of Paul's position : ' He who possesses the
Son possesses life.' [2]

These passages suggest the main significance of Paul's
conviction that Jesus has conquered death. (1) The resurrection is God's vindication of all that Christ has been
and has done. His career is shot through with a Divine
purpose. What seems tragic failure can be estimated in
its genuine meaning, when viewed in the light of its
consummation. Christ's earthly life, Christ's death of
shame, cannot be understood apart from His resurrection
which involves His exaltation. It is very noteworthy that
when Paul thinks of His human experience, it is as an
element in His humiliation (*e.g.* Phil. ii. 7 ; 2 Cor. viii. 9),
that humiliation whose climax is the cross (Phil ii. 8).
All this leads up to His supreme dignity as Son of God with
power. That is the complement of His voluntary self-
renunciation : ' Wherefore also God highly exalted him
and gave him the name which is above every name '
(Phil. ii. 9). (2) All that has been said implies that for
Paul the resurrection forms an integral part of God's
redeeming operation. Not only may such an impression
be drawn from the association of ideas in Phil. iii. 10 and
from Gal. i. 1-4, where the resurrection is plainly connected
with Christ's redemption of men, but the fact is emphasised
in the highly compressed statement of Rom. iv. 25 : ' Jesus
who was " delivered up for our trespasses " [3] and raised
that we might be justified.' This is one of those characteristically Pauline passages in which the death and resurrection of Jesus Christ are regarded as inseparable co-
efficients of the same mighty achievement. The words

must not be parsed, but interpreted in their broad significance. They do not suggest that the cross meant one thing and the resurrection another. For Paul the cross is unintelligible apart from the resurrection, and the real import of the resurrection becomes clear only in the light of the cross. The words mean, to quote Dr. Denney's apt comment, ' that we believe in a living Saviour, and that it is faith in Him which justifies. But then it is faith in Him as One who not only lives, but was delivered up to death to atone for our offences. He both died and was raised for our justification : the work is one and its end one.' [1]   Here Paul interprets the death of Christ from his experience of the risen Lord. (3) But the revelation of Jesus as the conqueror of death meant for Paul immediate contact with the forces of that higher order which was destined to replace ' this present evil age.' He felt that the coming era of blessedness, so long and wistfully yearned for, was at the door. He speaks of himself and his fellow-Christians as those ' whose lot has been cast in the closing hours of the world.' [2]   The reign of Messiah has begun with the exaltation of Jesus. New powers are being liberated from the unseen, of which Paul is intensely conscious. The risen Lord dwells in the souls of His faithful disciples.[3] The love of God has been poured forth in their hearts through the Holy Spirit given to them.[4] This confidence in the dawn of the new epoch of God's dominion must inevitably kindle high hopes and enthusiasms. Already the apostle can say : ' Our commonwealth is in heaven, from whence we eagerly look for the Saviour.' [5] The corollary of such high confidence is to be found in the injunction : ' Seek the things where Christ is seated at the right hand of God . . . for you died and your life is hidden with Christ in God.' [6] (4) We know how sorely hampered Paul felt himself to be by the burden of physical life. What he calls his ' earthly tent ' [7] he makes responsible for much of the failure of his spiritual life. And he therefore sighs after that existence in

---

[1] *E. G. T.*, ii. p. 622.   [2] 1 Cor. x. 11 (M.).   [3] Gal. ii. 20.   [4] Rom. v. 5.
[5] Phil. iii. 20.   [6] Col. iii. 1, 3.   [7] 2 Cor. v. 1.

which his mortal element shall be swallowed up by life.[1]
The risen Christ is for him the pledge of perfected being.
' If the Spirit of him who raised Jesus from the dead dwell
in you, he that raised from the dead Christ Jesus shall also
make alive your mortal body through his Spirit dwelling
in you.' [2] Christ is the first-fruits of those who have
fallen asleep.[3] His victory over the grave is the demonstration that a triumphant life awaits all who have entered
His fellowship.

(b) The Significance of the Cross

For Paul, as we have observed, the significance of the
cross was bound up with the conviction that Jesus Christ
had conquered death and was alive for evermore. The fact
of a crucified Messiah was placed in a new perspective by
His exaltation. Crucifixion in this case did not involve
the curse of God. Jesus had been revealed as the
Chosen of the Divine love. Now the early chapters of
Acts reflect the emphasis which was laid by the primitive
Christian community on the human malice which brought
about the cruel death of Jesus.[4] But if we are to appeal
to them as evidence for such a conception, we must also
recognise that they trace the event to the deliberate purpose
of God;[5] and associate it with the forecasts of the prophets.[6]
The description of Jesus in these chapters as the ' Servant '
of God [7] at once suggests the famous ' Songs of the Servant '
in Deutero-Isaiah. There an Old Testament basis is found
for the doctrine of a suffering Messiah. We cannot be sure
at how early a date this Old Testament foreshadowing was
used to interpret the Passion of Jesus. Considering the
authoritative place which the Scriptures held in the consciousness of Jewish Christians, a place all the more unique
now that they were being persecuted by the Pharisees and
so would be detached from the oral tradition, we are obliged
to suppose that almost from the beginning they must have

---

[1] 2 Cor. v. 4.   [2] Rom. viii. 11.   [3] 1 Cor. xv. 20.
[4] E.g. iii. 13, 14 ; v. 30, etc. [5] E.g. ii. 23 ; iv. 28, etc.
[6] iii. 18.   [7] ὁ παῖς, iii. 13, 26 ; iv. 27, 30.

eagerly studied the Old Testament for light upon the new circumstances in which they found themselves. Whether Paul, before his conversion, had ever been led to examine the data, must be a matter of mere conjecture. But as soon as he had entered into fellowship with the risen Christ, the cross, although no longer a scandal, must have appeared an enigma. As a loyal monotheist, he was compelled to assign it a place in the Divine order. But innumerable questions would present themselves. The event was a startling reversal of Jewish ideas. The Messiah was the very symbol of triumph, and this had been degradation. Yet Jesus was sinless. Why should the Holy One of God undergo so appalling an experience ? To estimate the full significance of such a problem for Paul, we have to remind ourselves that for a Jew death was the emblem of separation from God. It marked the disastrous issue of that taint of evil which had poisoned human nature from the first. The wages of sin was death. What could this mean for God's Vicegerent ? It is far from sufficient to say that it was the necessary transition to a state of glory and exaltation.[1] Paul's strenuous mind would demand some profounder answer than that. And the answer must be more than the device of a skilful apologetic. We may readily admit that Paul had to interpret the significance of the death of the Messiah to other minds than his own. But surely Jülicher's view of the situation is superficial when he declares that 'Paul . . . was obliged . . . to transform the " folly " [of the cross] into wisdom.'[2] Paul felt, like every unprejudiced thinker who has faced the facts, that there was something stupendous in the experience of Calvary, something that unveiled a realm of spiritual realities which almost blinded the mental vision of men with excess of light. And we know how he exhausted the resources of metaphor and analogy in trying to express that intuition of the Divine nature which had flashed upon his soul from the cross of Jesus Christ.

---

[1] So, e.g., Weizsäcker, Apostol. Zeitalter, p. 111.
[2] Paulus u. Jesus, p. 65.

We cannot help thinking that the clue to his many-sided conception of the death of Christ is to be found primarily in his conversion-experience. Whatever else in it subdued his nature, first and foremost was his impression of unspeakable grace. That was the atmosphere into which he had been transferred by his wonderful contact with the risen Jesus. The bitter persecutor had been laid hold of from sheer compassion. A love too deep to comprehend had come to his aid in the midst of bewildering struggle. The whole relation of God to men was encircled with mercy. Need we be surprised that this liberated soul attained to the spiritual height of the Old Testament prophet's estimate of God ? ' In all their affliction he was afflicted, and the angel of his presence saved them : in his love and pity himself redeemed them : and he bare them and carried them all the days of old.' [1] It was surely his fresh impression of the meaning of God as discovered in the living Christ which prompted him to look for the secret of the cross in the depths of the Divine love. We misconceive Paul's standpoint entirely if we try to account for his interpretation of the death of Christ as the effort to resolve by an ingenious process of dialectic a problem which refused to square with ordinary facts. And it is easy to ascribe too much importance to the influence of information concerning Jesus which had reached him in his Pharisaic days, or to the counsel of Christian believers who assisted this strange convert in the first moments of his new life. We would by no means undervalue such factors in the situation.[2] Nothing prevents us from supposing that Paul had heard of Jesus' wonderful way with outcasts and sinners. And unquestionably real light would be shed upon the mystery when he learned from his Christian brethren the pathetic story of the Last Supper, and was told of Jesus' remarkable words concerning a ' new covenant,' a new relation of men with God, to be inaugurated by His death. Paul was already conscious of this new relation. It had

---

[1] Isa. lxiii. 9.
[2] See J. Weiss, *op. cit.*, pp. 345, 346.

brought joy and peace to his soul.   Its foundation could be
nothing else than the boundless love of God.

(c) *The Messiah (Son of God)*

Paul's conviction that Jesus was risen carried with it
the acknowledgment that He was the Messiah of God
Jesus' life and teaching had involved this high claim, and
from the outset His followers had placed it in the forefront.
We have seen the serious issue which confronted an ardent
Pharisee like Paul when he faced the situation.   Jesus
had shown an attitude of laxity towards such vital elements
of the Jewish system as the Sabbath laws and the regulations concerning purification.   But the fulfilment of the
Messianic Hope of Israel depended on strict loyalty to the
authoritative standard.   This teacher of heresy had only
met his deserts when he was condemned to the most
degrading penalty that could be inflicted, that of death
by crucifixion.   We can only grasp Paul's estimate of the
Christian movement if we try to realise that for him, as for
all devout Jews, every ideal worth living for was summed up
in the Messianic Age.   In his religious earnestness he had
yearned and prayed for the advent of that era.   His bold
imagination had often pictured the bliss of the final deliverance.   He had studied the forecasts of prophets and
psalmists.   In thought he had beheld the foreign domina-
tion broken, and the chosen people fulfilling their function
as a light to the nations.   Iniquity was purged and
righteousness was triumphant.   As he looked on the prosaic
reality of Jewish religion, this glorious vista must have
seemed remote enough.   But a worse thing had happened.
The Nazarene and his followers were bringing the national
Hope into contempt.   Their assertions were horrid blasphemy.

It is against the background of his earlier position that
the full significance of his new conviction becomes evident.
The glory of Messiahship in no way fades when the office
is assigned to Jesus.   Paul never loses sight of the fact

that the revelation of Messiah means the climax of God's wonderful dealings with His people. He is true to his former expectations when he says of Jesus Christ : ' In him is the " Yes " that affirms all the promises of God.' [1] He cannot conceive any manifestation of the Divine purpose which will surpass that which he has received in the risen Jesus. But it is plain that his Messianic expectations were profoundly modified by the actual experience through which he passed. Johannes Weiss has suggestively pointed out that there are only a few places in Paul's writings where the constantly recurring term ' Christos ' can be translated ' Messiah.' [2] The expression ' Jesus the Christ ' is never found. These phenomena indicate that the reality of the personal Jesus has absorbed the Messianic functions. It is the living Person who has impressed the soul of Paul—we may almost say, the personal Saviour. The Messiah *quâ* Messiah was to the Jewish mind a public functionary. His office was conceived in terms of kingship. He was set apart for judgment. Hence kingly attributes were usually ascribed to him : righteousness, justice, wisdom, power.[3] For Paul and the early Church the centre of gravity is shifted. They have not to deal with an august, remote Being, whose character is composed of abstract ideals. ' Christ ' has for them become the name of a historical Person. And this historical Person is the embodiment of grace and lowliness and love. For those who had companied with Jesus in the days of His earthly ministry that impression had transcended all others. Paul had caught many glimpses of it while still a persecutor. But now, as the result of his amazing experience of the risen Jesus, it was imprinted for ever on his soul. In the light of it, the Messianic redemption is for him transfigured. It is transferred to a new level. No longer can it mean the deliverance of the nation from an alien yoke, as a reward of faithfulness to their covenant with God. Salva-

---

[1] 2 Cor. i. 20 (M.).

[2] *E.g.* Rom. ix. 5 : perhaps also in the phrase, ' the Gospel of Christ ' ; possibly in Rom. x. 6, 7 ; 2 Cor. v. 10. See J. Weiss, *op. cit.*, p. 350.

[3] *E.g.* Isa. xi. 1-5.

tion is once for all released from national categories. The very significance of Paul's contact with Christ gives it a universal bearing. He has found in the risen Lord the source of spiritual power, of victory over sin and failure. Hence redemption belongs essentially to the spiritual life. It has no concern with material conditions, except in so far as these are evil. The Messiah is He who can rescue from sin, who can deliver from that Divine ' wrath ' which is the reaction of God's holiness against all that is vile.[1] But the transformation of the Messianic Hope goes deeper. As has been hinted, the notion of reward falls into the background. Paul had honestly faced the facts as a Pharisee, and had been compelled to acknowledge in the secret place of his heart that if God were to reckon with His people on the ground of merit, the promised redemption must still remain a dream. The crisis in his own life flashed upon him an extraordinary discovery. God had not waited for him to win salvation. He was not left to purchase the boon of inward peace with the price of a laborious obedience. God in His infinite grace had anticipated his action. Like the father in the Parable of the Lost Son, He had gone to meet him while still far off. He had plied him with love and mercy; He had offered him the gift of new life. He had shown Himself on the side of frail human nature, appealing to men to enter His fellowship through Jesus Christ.

Here is a complete revolution in eschatology. We shall have to examine its implications in the case of many of Paul's fundamental ideas. Meanwhile let us note its general bearings. It is easy to show how much of the eschatological apparatus of Judaism Paul retained as a Christian apostle. In his earliest Letters he portrays the Second Advent of Christ in typically Jewish colours. Its accompaniments are the shouts of archangels and the sounding of trumpets. It is the signal of doom for those who refuse to listen to the Gospel of the Lord Jesus. Those who have fallen asleep in Christ shall rise from their graves

---

[1] 1 Thess. i. 10.

to meet Him.[1] In later documents he employs the same
type of imagery. In depicting the consummation of the
Kingdom of God, he sketches, though with great restraint,
the sequence of events at the Parousia. After the resurrection of His followers, Christ abolishes all opposing forces,
and among these Paul includes the vast hierarchy of evil
powers who enslave human destiny and contest the
supremacy of God over men. Death itself is annihilated,
and finally the Son delivers up the Kingdom to the Father,
' that God may be all in all.' In the resurrection flesh and
blood shall have no part. Both living and dead will be
clothed with an incorruptible spiritual organism, ' in a
moment, in the twinkling of an eye, at the last trumpet-
call.' [2] In a passage of extraordinary intimacy, Paul
reveals his eagerness to exchange ' this earthly tent ' for
his ' heavenly habitation,' and his dread of being ' naked '
at the hour of death.[3] The language and imagery which
he uses have numerous parallels both in the prophets and
the apocalypses, as well as in the apocalyptic discourses of
Jesus. We have already noted what strong emphasis he
lays upon the future Judgment, and how he urges the
nearness of the Parousia as a motive for self-discipline
and watchfulness of life. Apart altogether from traditional
pictures of the Last Things, which are strangely persistent
in all religions even after the beliefs which they originally
embodied have begun to fade, there remains a genuinely
eschatological strain in Paul's religious outlook. He
yearns for the consummation of God's dominion over men
and the universe. He yearns for the extirpation of all the
forces of evil, which he conceives as an army of spirits
mustered under ' the ruler of the power of the air, the spirit
which is at present working in the sons of disobedience.' [4]
He longs for the spiritual attainment which will be the
outcome of liberation from the trammels of a body of flesh.
For him the future means perfect conformity to the image

---

[1] 1 Thess. iv. 15-17; 2 Thess. i. 7-10.
[2] 1 Cor. xv. 22-28, 50-52.   [3] 2 Cor. v. 1-4.
[4] Eph. ii. 2 ; cf. Col. i. 13, Eph. vi. 12.

of Christ : participation in that 'glory' which constitutes
the Divine essence. And so when he deals with Justification
he invariably keeps in view the final stage, when his salvation will be completed. Indeed, no more typical statement
of the Pauline position could be cited than that of Gal. v. 5:
'We by the Spirit as the result of faith eagerly expect the
righteousness we hope for.' But while all this is true, we
must assign its proper place to the complementary aspect
of Paul's religious thought. The future has, in a very real
sense, become present. Fundamentally, that which it has
to offer is given already in Christ to the trustful heart.
In principle the Christian has begun to participate in his
glorious heritage. Already he possesses the love of God
which is in Christ Jesus his Lord, and nothing shall ever be
able to rob him of his priceless possession.[1] This consciousness that he had virtually entered upon the coming Age of
apocalyptic expectation meant an entire readjustment of
the older Hope, and marked off Paul's outlook from that
of Jewish Messianism. In a real sense, the Messianic rule
was present, attested by signs and wonders and all the
gifts of the Spirit. The new condition could not be compared to the old. The resurrection and exaltation of Jesus
were the proof that the 'rulers of this world had been
vanquished.' Believers might still appear a feeble folk
in the midst of 'a crooked and perverse generation,' but
their light was visible in the surrounding darkness.[2] The
whole creation was eagerly waiting for the complete
revelation of the sons of God. When Christ, who was their
life, should appear, they also would appear with Him in
glory.[3]

Perhaps enough has been said to bring out the unique
character of Paul's conception of Jesus as Messiah. And it
certainly refuses to tally with some theories much in vogue
at the present time. Prominent scholars like Wrede,
J. Weiss, and others have argued that the foundation of
Paul's Christology is to be found in his pre-Christian view
of Messiah. Taking their stand mainly upon the apocalyptic

[1] Rom. viii. 35-39.   [2] Phil. ii. 15.   [3] Col. iii. 4.

pictures in 1 Enoch [1] and 4 Ezra,[2] they hold that the
heavenly being there portrayed, to whom was committed
the function of judgment, may be regarded as representing
the current Messianic doctrine of Judaism.[3] But the
evidence is highly conflicting. In the *Psalms of Solomon*,
a Jewish work of the first century B.C., and also a product
of the Pharisaic party, there is no trace of such a conception. It adheres to the common view that the Messiah
should be a prince of the house of David.[4] There is no
proof that the other notion was widely diffused. Mr.
G. H. Box refers it to some ' probably small apocalyptic
circles,' while ' the orthodox Rabbinic view . . . accepts an
earthly national Messiah, the son of David, and sometimes
affirms for him an earthly pre-existence (*e.g.* that he has
already been born but is in concealment, awaiting the time
of his manifestation).' [5] Paul's actual language seems to
coincide, as we might expect, with the usual Rabbinic
position, for in Rom. i. 3 ff., when describing the Son of God,
who is the subject of his Gospel, he emphasises His Davidic
descent, omitting all mention of heavenly origin, and
pointing to His exaltation as the decisive moment in His
Messianic career. There are, of course, important passages
which refer to His pre-existence. But it is not necessary
to find the origin of the idea in that strain of Jewish
apocalyptic tradition which may plausibly be referred back
to the early myth of the ' archetypal Man.' Pre-existence,
in some sense, must belong to One who is placed on the
side of Deity. The artificial nature of the attempted
analysis of Paul's Christology appears from the fact that
the keenest advocates of this view declare the whole period
from the Incarnation to the Parousia to be a mere episode
for Paul's mind.[6] Such a hypothesis, even in the light of the
facts already examined, is scarcely worthy of refutation.

But while Paul has not constructed his Christology on

---

[1] Esp. chapters xlvi., xlviii., lxii.   [2] Chap. xiii.
[3] *E.g.* Wrede, *Paulus*, p. 86 f.; Brückner, *Die Entstehung d. paulin.
Christologie, passim*; J. Weiss, *Christus*, p. 18 f.
[4] See *Pss. of Solomon*, xvii., xviii.
[5] *The Ezra Apocalypse.* p. 284.
[6] This does not apply to J. Weiss.

these mechanical lines, its super-human implications appear in his frequent use of the designation, *Son of God*. We might naturally be disposed to look for the root of the idea in the Old Testament. And we know the central place occupied in early Christian thought by Ps. ii. 7 (LXX): 'The Lord said to me, Thou art my son, I have to-day begotten thee.' When it is observed that the succeeding sentence of the passage runs : 'Ask of me, and I will give the heathen as thine inheritance,' we can easily realise the force of its appeal to Paul. This description of Messiah does not stand alone. In Ps. lxxxix. 28 (LXX) God declares : 'I will also make him my first-born, exalted in presence of the kings of the earth.' And Ps. cx. 3 (LXX), where again the ' begetting ' of the chosen king is a feature, was very familiar to the primitive Church. The title ' Son ' appears also in several apocalypses as applied to the Messiah of God. This usage has obviously an official character. To be the chosen of God is to stand towards Him in a special relation. It may be legitimate to refer for a parallel to the ancient Oriental designation of kings as ' sons ' of God.[1] But the comparison does not shed much light on Paul's conception. A remarkable affinity is discernible between the Old Testament Messianic application of the title and such statements of Paul as Rom. i. 3, 4 : ' His son, born of the seed of David by natural descent, and installed as Son of God with power in virtue of the Spirit of holiness as the result of resurrection from the dead.' Here the installation as Son of God with power is directly equivalent to the ' supreme exaltation ' of which Paul speaks in Phil. ii. 9 as bestowed upon Christ by God as the result of His humiliation. There is an enhancing of His position in the universe. He is henceforth ' Lord,' with a right to universal dominion and universal adoration. Of special value for the comprehension of Paul's idea is his description of Christ as ' the image of the invisible God, the first-born of the whole creation.' [2] Here, unquestionably, he has in view what must be called a ' metaphysical '

---

[1] See J. Weiss, *Christus*, pp. 19-21.　　　[2] Col. i. 15 ; cf. Heb. i. 3.

relationship. It represents something more than perfect
mutual understanding, completely reciprocated love. But
even in the incidental references found in the Synoptic Gospels to the unique relation between Jesus and His Father,
while we may be content with formulating it in ethical
terms, we are all the time conscious that reflection cannot
stop there, although it has no instrument adequate to
interpret the phenomena.

As a matter of fact, Paul does not speculate in this
mysterious realm. To trace his use of the title ' Son of
God ' to a mythological tradition which had come down
from polytheistic religions, but had been gradually purged
of its mythological character by monotheistic influence and
philosophical abstraction, is altogether gratuitous.[1] It does
not, indeed, seem enough to say, with Weinel, that our
phrase, ' Son,' following a common Semitic usage, merely
denotes ' belonging to.' [2] We believe that here, as elsewhere, Paul's religious experience lies in the background.
The wonderful Person who had laid hold of him so graciously
and transfigured his whole being must belong to a sphere
above humanity. The Christian tradition had probably
already associated the term ' Son ' with Jesus' self-consciousness. Its use accorded with the apostle's strict monotheism. He never called Jesus God. ' Son of God '
assigns Him to His proper sphere of being. Without
speculative attempts at definition, it suggests His oneness
with the Father.[3]

(d) The Lord

Johannes Weiss remarks with truth that ' early-Christian
religion is contained in germ in the formula, our Lord
Jesus Christ.' [4] We cannot precisely determine how the
title ' Lord ' came into currency. In Acts ii. 36 Peter is

---

[1] See J. Weiss, *Christus*, pp. 36, 37.

[2] *Paulus*, p. 251. He compares Matt. xii. 27, viii. 12, xiii. 38, etc.

[3] Bousset is inclined to think that the phrase was a creation of Paul's
own, the product of religious reflection rather than of the worship of the
Church (*Kyrios Christos*, pp. 181, 182). The evidence of the Synoptics,
even when estimated critically, seems to favour the view in the text.

[4] *Christus*, p. 24.

reported as saying, ' Let all the house of Israel know that God made him both Lord and Christ, this Jesus whom you crucified.' Plainly the title is here connected with His exaltation, and that idea seems always to lie in the background of its use. The writer of Acts links it with a famous Messianic passage, Ps. cx. 1 : ' The Lord said to my Lord, Sit on my right hand, until I make thine enemies a footstool for thy feet.' And there can be little doubt that this passage was a most important factor in the formation of the usage. But for Paul at least it is far more than a synonym for Messiah. Possibly the same thing is true for the early Church as a whole. It is certainly significant that the translators of the LXX, in all likelihood Egyptian Jews, rendered the Old Testament ' Jahweh ' by Κύριος, ' Lord.' No doubt in so doing they were influenced by the fact that in the Hebrew text of the Old Testament the Tetragrammaton was pronounced as *Adonai*, a Semitic title of deity which was a more or less accurate equivalent of Κύριος. In any case, their action gave the claims of the God of Israel a world-wide bearing.[1] For the peoples of the Hellenistic epoch were familiar with the Divine significance of Κύριος. It was a typically Oriental title. It was constantly used of characteristically Oriental deities, such as the Egyptian Isis, Osiris, and Serapis.[2] In the first century it was quickly taking its place as the designation of the deified Emperor, and thus becoming the central term of the Imperial cult.[3] Its application to Christ was all the more significant from its Hellenistic atmosphere, and especially from its intimate association with the cult of the Cæsars. The impression which it made upon heathen-Christians is strikingly brought out by a passage in the *Acts of the Scillitan Martyrs* (1-2),[4] where Speratus contrasts Christ as *imperator noster* (' our Emperor ') with the *dominus noster imperator* (' our Lord

[1] See Deissmann, *Die Hellenisierung d. semitischen Monotheismus*, p. 14.
[2] See Bousset, *op. cit.*, p. 118.
[3] See the examples *sub voce* Κύριος in Dittenberger's *Orientis Graecae Inscriptiones Selectae.*
[4] Quoted by Lietzmann on Rom. x. 9.

the Emperor') of the Roman proconsul, and another (6)
in which he declares : ' I refuse to acknowledge the Empire
of this world . . . I acknowledge my Lord who is Emperor
of the kings of all nations.'

Possibly Hellenistic practice as well as the usage of the
LXX had some influence in the regular ascription of the
term ' Lord ' to the exalted Christ. Yet the appearance of
the Aramaic formula *Maran atha*, ' Lord come ' (1 Cor.
xvi. 22), forbids us to distinguish between Palestinian and
Hellenistic Christianity in regard to the use of Κύριος.[1]
The same consideration prevents us from accepting Bousset's
hypothesis that Κύριος, as applied to Jesus, means primarily ' the Lord who presides over the community-life of
Christians, as that life is unfolded in the public worship of
the Church, *i.e.* in the cult.' [2] Perhaps this conception
may have formed an element in the situation. Full force
must be assigned to such important phrases as ' calling
upon the name of the Lord,' [3] which may be taken as a
brief description of Christians, and referred to the attitude
of the community assembled for worship. But the personal
relationship involved in the designation must be placed in
the forefront by any careful student of Paul. Here the
influence of the Old Testament becomes apparent. Passages
like Ps. cxvi. 17 (LXX), ' O Lord (Κύριος), I am thy bond
servant (δοῦλος),' give a partial clue to Paul's standpoint.
Corresponding to the position of Jesus as Lord is his own
as devoted slave. Again and again he calls himself by this
name.[4] It is no conventional description, but suggests
how large and profound is the relationship between his
Lord and himself. It implies surrender, obedience, reverence, trust, grateful love. Accordingly, whether Paul was
indebted to the Christian community for this conception
or not, he has, at least, made it completely his own. He
uses it as the vehicle for expressing what he feels about

[1] Bousset's attempt to restrict the formula to Antiochene Christianity
(*op. cit.*, p. 103, note 3) is quite unconvincing.
[2] *Op. cit.*, p. 105.
[3] *E.g.* 1 Cor. i. 2 ; Rom. x. 12 ; Acts ix. 14, 21.
[4] *E.g.* Rom. i. 1 ; Gal. i. 10.

Christ. And the feeling is the direct transcript of his conversion-experience. Christ is for the apostle pre-eminently ' my Lord.' [1] So that with equal right we may derive its cult-association from its personal significance. This is evident from statements found in Paul's Letters. Thus, in 1 Cor. xii. 3, he declares : ' No one can say Jesus is Lord but by the Holy Spirit.' Here is a process of transition from the personal to the public confession. Yet, however fundamental the ascription of lordship to Jesus may be for the life of the community, it must have its roots in the inward discovery of the soul. In Paul's case, that has as its issue union with the living and exalted Lord.

But the idea of exaltation in Paul's use of the title must be specially emphasised. It was as the exalted One that Christ revealed Himself to the Pharisee. And that note may always |be heard when Paul speaks of Him as Lord. The most important material for the elucidation of this conception is found in Phil. ii. 9, 10 : ' Wherefore (i.e. as the issue of His lowly self-renunciation) God highly exalted him and gave him the name which is above every name, that in the name of Jesus every knee should bow, of things in heaven and things on earth and things under the earth, and that every tongue should confess that Jesus Christ is Lord, to the glory of God the Father.' Plainly, in this passage, the ' name above every name ' is that of ' Lord.' What this meant for a devout Hellenistic Jew may be inferred from such Old Testament declarations as Isa. xlii. 8 (LXX) : ' I am the Lord (Κύριος ὁ Θεός), this is my name.' And the background of Paul's thought in the passage quoted appears in Isa. xlv. 23 (LXX) : ' I swear by myself . . . my words shall not be turned away, that to me every knee shall bow, and every tongue shall swear (some good authorities read ' confess ') by God ' (an excellent authority reads ' the Lord '). As in the case of the designation ' Son of God,' Paul, in this affirmation of His lordship, deliberately assigns Jesus to

[1] Phil. iii. 8.

the sphere of the Divine. Apart from the judgment of
the Christian community which he has entered, he makes
this ascription as the result of his personal experience.
It is scarcely needful to point out that for ancient thought
the giving of a name carried with it the imparting of all
the name stood for. The Old Testament use of ' Lord '
implies the right to universal worship and dominion: that
which is due to Jahweh. With all these considerations
before his mind, Paul does not hesitate to call Christ the
Lord. But it is instructive to notice that the final goal
of the lordship of Christ is ' the glory of God the Father.'
Paul never deserts his monotheistic position. And perhaps
J. Weiss is justified in suggesting [1] that he welcomed the
possibility of using the term ' Lord,' which for him expresses Christ's position of equality with God in the eyes
of men and His right to universal adoration, while, at the
same time, the name of ' God ' is reserved for the Father
to whom even Christ shall one day deliver up His dominion,
' that God may be all in all.' [2]

(e) The Spirit

In the most explicit account of his conversion which
Paul gives in his Epistles, he speaks of the gracious purpose
of God to reveal His Son ' in me.' [3] Whatever may have
been the objective circumstances of the revelation, the
permanent gain for the apostle is something spiritual, the
fellowship of his spirit with the Divine life in Jesus Christ.
Hence he can describe Him as ' life-creating spirit.' [4] And
the gift of new life or power is for him the supreme token
of God's operation in his personal experience. So from this
time forward the decisive criterion for the Christian life
is the reception of the Spirit. When he desires to bring
his erring Galatian converts to the touchstone of fundamental realities, he asks them : ' This is the only thing I
wish to find out from you : Did you receive the Spirit as

[1] *Christus,* p. 26.   [2] 1 Cor. xv. 28.
[3] Gal. i. 16.   [4] 1 Cor. xv. 45.

the result of observing the Law, or was it because of the hearing which your faith gave to the Gospel ? ' [1] The one vindication of his preaching which he submits to the intellectually restless Corinthians is the ' demonstration of the Spirit and of power.' [2] How are we to estimate this standpoint of the apostle ?

It is noteworthy that in the earlier narratives of the Old Testament, phenomena of an abnormal or ' demonic ' nature were usually referred to the ' spirit ' or ' breath ' of God. Probably this explanation represents an advance on some primitive animistic theory. Thus, Samson's extraordinary physical strength (Judges xiv. 6) and the technical skill of Bezaleel the artificer of the Tabernacle (Exod. xxxv. 30, 31) are ascribed to the Spirit of God. As might be expected, a similar origin is presupposed for the ecstatic experiences of both earlier and later prophecy. The former were apparently more physical than spiritual in character (see, e.g., 1 Sam. x. 10). This, possibly, was the reason why famous prophets like Isaiah and Jeremiah did not associate their prophetic utterances with the ' Spirit ' of God. The idea may still have borne traces of its more primitive unethical features. In the case of Ezekiel, however, whose career gives evidence of a marked pathological element, the conception of the Spirit of God comes into prominence (e.g. ch. xi. 1, 5, 24), although he also more frequently speaks of the ' hand ' of the Lord. In a few places, endowment with the Spirit is associated with special service in God's Kingdom (e.g. Isa. xi. 2), and occasionally its value is emphasised for the needs of the religious life (e.g. Ps. li. 11 ; cxliii. 10). In the Wisdom-literature of Israel, its place is taken by the semi-personalised conception of Wisdom, represented as God's instrument in creation and the channel of Divine energy to the universe. The relation of the two allied conceptions will meet us again when we examine Paul's view of the cosmic significance of Christ. In Rabbinic theology, the ' Spirit of holiness ' is the equipment of specially gifted

[1] Gal. iii. 2.　　　　　　　　　　　[2] 1 Cor. ii. 4.

teachers. Of more importance for our purpose is the
eschatological expectation that the Messianic Age should
be marked by an extraordinary visitation of the Spirit
(*e.g.* Joel ii. 28, 29). It is plain from the early chapters of
Acts that this expectation took a pre-eminent place in
primitive Christian thought. We are unable to determine
to what extent it was due to the teaching of Jesus. The
evidence of the Synoptic Gospels does not suggest that
Jesus emphasised the idea of the Spirit. In one or two
places the term appears to have been substituted in the
tradition for a more general expression. The statements of
the Fourth Gospel presuppose Paul as well as the very
unique interpretation of Jesus which is there embodied.
In any case, the extraordinary ferment of spiritual power
and enthusiasm which prevailed among the Christians of
the early Apostolic Age was associated with that outpouring
of the Spirit which was believed to usher in the Messianic
Era. We must consider in the next chapter in what
measure Paul was affected by the conception current in the
Church.

The most important feature of his own conception of the
Spirit is its relation to Christ. The risen Lord who appeared
to him was essentially ' Spirit.' The result of this revelation was for him, above all else, a new consciousness of
spiritual power—power able to achieve undreamed-of
moral effects. In the primitive community the fresh
quickening of spiritual life was vaguely associated with
the Spirit. In Paul's case the idea was far more concrete
and personal. The Spirit as experienced by him was the
Spirit of Christ. This was central for Paul's Christianity.
' If any one have not the Spirit of Christ, he does not belong
to him.' [1] Yet we must not narrow his conception, for in
the preceding clause of the passage quoted he has spoken
of the ' Spirit of God ' as ' dwelling in you.' A few sentences
later he describes the new life of the Christians as due to
' the Spirit of him that raised Jesus from the dead.' [2]
Nor is this all. Interchangeable with the idea of the

[1] Rom. viii. 9b.   [2] Rom. viii. 11.

Spirit of Christ or the Spirit dwelling in the believer is that of the believer as being ' in Christ ' or ' in the Spirit.' [1]

The usages we have examined prepare us for Paul's remarkable identification of Christ with the Spirit : ' Now the Lord is the Spirit.' [2] Yet the clause which follows puts us on our guard against a too literal interpretation, for it runs : ' and where the Spirit of the Lord is, there is liberty.' Paul, in other words, leaves a fluctuating margin between his conception of Christ and the Spirit. He was convinced that in the crisis on the road to Damascus he had come into touch with a living Person, but that Person belonged to the sphere of the Spirit. His essential being was Divine Spirit. The result of Paul's contact was experience of transforming power. When he thinks especially of this power, he speaks of the Spirit. When he dwells on the source of his new energy, he speaks of Christ. But always that fellowship with Christ which presupposes a living faith is the condition of the Spirit's indwelling. The Spirit is, indeed, the Divine response to the faith of the Christian.

We do not stay to deal with Bousset's theory that it is not the Christ who appeared to Paul at his conversion whom he identifies with the Spirit, but the ' Lord ' (Κύριος), worshipped in the services of the Christian community.[3] If there is anything which distinguishes Paul's conception it is its *personal* character. The Divine power which has laid hold of him and now operates through him is no vague world-soul, but is definitely individualised. Of course, in dealing with so impalpable a reality as spirit, his language is bound to fluctuate. Thus, when he attempts to determine the relation of the Divine energy to the human personality which it quickens, it is necessarily impossible to divide the ground between the Divine and the human. But in the great majority of instances in which he uses ' spirit ' (πνεῦμα), he thinks of the Spirit of God (or of Christ) as dwelling in the Christian, or of the

---

[1] *E.g.* 2 Cor. v. 17 ; Rom. viii. 9.
[2] 2 Cor. iii. 17. [3] *Op. cit.,* p. 145.

inner life of the Christian as recreated by the Spirit. It
is true that there are about a dozen cases in which Paul
applies this term to the inner life apart from the influence
of the Divine Spirit. In this usage he follows that of the
Old Testament. For in some post-exilic passages ' spirit ' is
used as a synonym for ' soul.' [1] But that does not alter
the fact that when Paul speaks of the Spirit, he has in
view either the energy of God (or of Christ), acting upon
human nature, or human nature as renewed by such Divine
action.

The extraordinary significance for Paul of his contact
with Christ as spirit lies in the conviction that he was now
moving among the forces of the coming age, the age of
final redemption. His hope of the consummation of God's
saving purpose, his assurance that God would complete
what he had begun, was powerfully confirmed by this
experience of vital power. The great promises of the
Messianic epoch were actually beginning to take shape.
The Spirit was God's pledge of coming blessedness.[2] It
was the first-fruits of the splendid harvest which awaited
believers.[3] By its agency the love of God was shed abroad
in men's hearts, as Paul's own experience could testify.
Its presence, as known and felt, was the evidence that its
possessors were ' children ' of God.[4] For the Spirit disclosed to the receptive nature a new view of God. It
taught men to cry ' Abba, Father.' [5] In this experience
Paul found a wonderful corroboration of his conviction of
Christ as working through the Spirit. For it was the
Spirit of God's Son which had been sent forth into their
hearts.[6]

In a later section we must investigate the relation of
the Spirit to the moral life of the Christian. Meanwhile
it ought to be noted that Paul's personal experience
exercised an epoch-making influence upon the conception
of the Spirit in the early Church. We can easily gather,
not only from Acts, but from Paul's own Epistles, that

---

[1] See p. 37, *supra*.
[2] 2 Cor. i. 22.
[3] Rom. viii. 23.
[4] Rom. viii. 16.
[5] Rom. viii. 15.
[6] Gal. iv. 6.

the consciousness of the Spirit was associated with abnormal manifestations, such as 'speaking with tongues,' 'prophesying,' etc. There was grave danger lest the spiritual enthusiasm of the Christian community should evaporate in mere fitful and unprofitable emotion. Paul recognised the peril. With a firm grasp of the true value of equipment with the Spirit, he saw the necessity of self-control and discipline in giving play to this wonderful energy. From him the immature communities learnt once for all that the genuine action of the Spirit is not spasmodic or eccentric : that it is a power for worthy living. For those who assimilated the apostle's teaching, the Spirit became the normal principle of Christian life and conduct.

(f) The New Attitude to God

A recent investigator of Paulinism has justly said that for Paul God was first and chiefly the Father of Jesus Christ. The statement reveals at a glance the revolution accomplished in his religious thought and experience. The significance of that revolution may be expressed by a suggestive modern phrase, 'the Christlikeness of God.' From the day of his conversion onwards, Paul interpreted the nature and purpose of God not from the traditional beliefs of Judaism, but exclusively in the light of the revelation of Christ to his soul. His contact with Christ was not an accident, nor was it the fulfilment of a dominating resolution. It was Divine from beginning to end. God was behind it : God was in the heart of it. It was intended to alter the entire basis of his religious life.

The first thing which impressed him was that he had been made the object of an amazing and wholly undeserved compassion. As he hurried on in a career whose *raison d'être* turned out to be a senseless defiance of the Divine purpose, the unspeakable mercy of God had singled him out, had checked his folly, and illumined his soul with a heavenly light. This unmerited Divine tenderness is always before his mind, and becomes one of his watch-

words in the term ' grace,' a term which gets its colour from
the crisis of his conversion. It is not mere pity : that
seems too casual an idea to the apostle. Grace is something
positive, basal, essential to the very character of God.
It is Christ who has shown what it means. Often, indeed,
the grace of God implies primarily for Paul the gift of His
Son Jesus Christ, and since this supreme gift, in certain most
important aspects, cannot be separated from that of the
Spirit, grace frequently suggests that special working of
the Divine energy. But, in the first instance, Paul from
the nature of the case was profoundly influenced by the
concrete form, if we may so say, in which the grace of
God was expressed. Christ was the Revealer of this content of the Divine nature. As the result of the revelation,
Paul never ceases to wonder at the incomparable Divine
generosity. Thus the very circumstances of his conversion
brought into bold relief the fatherly character of God.

Now we need not suppose that Paul realised within a few
days all that was involved in this transformation of his religious life. And yet the completeness of the transformation
must have led a mind like his almost at once to seek for
an adjustment between the new experiences which flooded
his soul. Hence, the conception of Jesus, incarnate and
crucified, as God's unspeakable gift for the sake of sinners,
must have soon taken a regulative place in his efforts to
understand his wonderful new attitude to God. The very
revelation of Christ to him as the Chosen of God, with all
the light he could shed upon it from what he had already
learnt of Christ's life and activity and gospel, would in itself
almost immediately lay the foundation of his new relationship to God. Almost immediately he would become aware
that the old suspicion and fear of God as task-master and
judge had vanished, and an amazing vision of His heart,
which seemed too good to be true, had begun to flash upon
his soul. And then as he meditated upon the cross and all
that led up to it, he reached the profound conclusion that
' God was in Christ reconciling the world unto himself.' [1]

[1] 2 Cor. v. 19.

The fact that the issue of the crisis was a sense of obligation to proclaim the message of Jesus to the heathen is itself a comment on the meaning of the experience for Paul. It was a surprise to discover the God whom Jesus revealed. For instead of being struck down with terror by the entrance into his life of a power which he felt to be distinct from himself, his soul was filled with love and joy and hope.   He had found that it was the good pleasure of God to act on different lines from those which he had all along taken for granted.   He had striven to establish a good record in the eyes of the All-holy, striven with painful eagerness although with no permanent satisfaction.   And now, in the life which burst upon him, he realised that he had misunderstood the God he was yearning to please.   God's favour was not to be purchased by straining efforts.   Christ, crucified and risen, crucified for sheer love to men, risen because that love was Divine love, the very index of the heart of God— the Christ who had become manifest to him, was the demonstration that God's joy was to give rather than to receive. And the giving was infinitely lavish.   All that he had learnt of Christ convinced him that God did not wait for men to approach Him, but that He anticipated them in the wonder of His grace.   This had been Paul's own experience. God had followed him with the subtle influences of His mercy, had in Christ laid hold of him and mastered him. All that was necessary on his part was to surrender to that loving grasp.   To the trusting soul which took God as He revealed Himself, laying aside its prejudices however deep-rooted and long-standing, to the surrendered life God made over the wealth of His priceless gifts.   This fundamental aspect of the new attitude to God is what Paul calls Faith. It lies at the heart of his conversion.   In that hour he showed himself willing to be taken captive by the Divine hand.   His receptivity to the influences which radiated from the risen Lord became for him, as he was well aware, the channel of new life.

In the history of Old Testament religion, faith had meant the belief that God would fulfil His promises to His people.

That, of course, was an important factor in religious life, and had achieved valuable results. Later, and especially in Hellenistic Judaism, it denoted firm conviction as to the actual existence of invisible things, above all of God Himself. Both these meanings are to be found in the Pauline Epistles, but they are completely overshadowed by the profound expansion of significance which the idea of faith undergoes in Paul's hands. For him it is primarily the complete response of the soul to the good news of God embodied in Christ. That no doubt includes the great acts in which Christ has accomplished the Father's purpose, His incarnation, His redeeming death, His resurrection and exaltation as Saviour. But even in these instances it does not merely signify assent to the truth that such events have happened. It involves sympathy with their redemptive value and acceptance of the purpose of God as disclosed by them. But for Paul it chiefly describes a relation between one person and another, the grateful and reverent submission of the entire inner nature to the Divine heart whose love appeals to men in Jesus Christ. This relation constitutes the basis of all those descriptions of the dealings of God with the soul which lead to the new attitude on which Paul has so joyously entered. We are sometimes repelled by the technical ring of such terms as justification, adoption, righteousness. When we try to analyse their precise meaning, we discover certain formal elements in them, due primarily to Paul's environment. But, as a matter of fact, they are all attempts from differing angles of vision to set forth the wonderful approach to God of which Paul has become conscious. He knows himself to be on a wholly new footing with the Almighty. Probably the description of widest range which he can give of it is Sonship. He does not use this word. He calls the new status Adoption. The atmosphere of the term comes from his own experience. Men who have wandered far from God, and have been guilty of all manner of sin and disobedience, have utterly forfeited their right to any place in His family, that family for which they were destined in creation. But God, in that infinite grace of His which has become manifest in Jesus Christ, deliberately invites them to become His children. He adopts them, makes them His children out of sheer goodness, deals with them as children, lavishes on them all the love that a father can bestow. This is not theory. Paul is sure that it has happened in his own experience. That unspeakable Divine love of which Christ is the pledge has made him heartily ashamed of his sin. He has given himself to a new bondage, the bondage of Jesus Christ, and that means peace with God. The old uncertainty and fear have become impossible. He has grasped the full significance of the father's answer in the Parable of the Lost Son : ' Son, thou art always with me, and all that I have is thine.' That is the focus of the message of Jesus Christ. It is also the clue to Paul's new attitude towards God.

Quite plainly such a standpoint involves the doom of Legalism. There is no idea of bargain in such a relationship. There is no suggestion of a *quid pro quo*. Paul has simply taken the gift held out to him in Jesus Christ, the gift of salvation. Hence the thought of earning some reward from God loses all relevance. There is no comparison between man's obedience and God's unspeakable gift. Thus the apostle can say from the depth of his heart : ' Christ is the end of the law to every one who believes.'

By this new attitude to God we are warned against the notion that the centre of gravity in Paul's religion was eschatology. We must give all due emphasis to the stress he lays on the consummation of the Kingdom of God. We must estimate at its full value the importance he attached to that life in a perfected spiritual organism which was to begin with the Second Advent. We must recognise the place he assigned to a final verdict of God at the Judgment, the last word on the destiny of individuals. We must endeavour to appreciate his yearning to get rid of the hampering influence of existence in the flesh. But while, in one or two instances, Paul's sensitive conscience seems to tremble before the final issues of life, the very core of his religious position is the certainty that he has already been received into the realm of God's grace. He is already an heir of God. He possesses the Spirit, which is the pledge and foretaste of the heritage of blessedness awaiting him. And, after all, this is the most important fact of his religion. He can say with unwavering conviction : ' We know that all things work together for good to them that love God, who are the called according to his purpose. . . . We are more than conquerors through him that loved us.' [1]

[1] Rom. viii. 28, 37.

CHAPTER V

ST. PAUL AND THE CHRISTIAN TRADITION

(a) *The Historical Jesus*

IN the famous passage in which he speaks of his conversion Paul firmly emphasises the independence of his Gospel and his apostolic vocation. The shaping of his Christian convictions he ascribes directly to the influence of the risen Christ with whom he had been brought in contact.[1] It is impossible to regard any vital element in his Christian consciousness as coming to him at second-hand. And we have tried to show in the preceding section that his experience on the Damascus road was decisive for the regulative features of his new position. But we must not exaggerate Paul's assertions in Gal. i. For these are made in a controversy which is for the apostle a matter of life or death. So he does not pause to qualify them.

It has already been pointed out that Paul the persecutor and champion of the Pharisaic ideal must have formed certain definite impressions of the sect he was seeking to extirpate, and that he cannot have ignored the significance of Jesus. The extent of his knowledge must remain a matter of conjecture, but the fact that he identified the living Person who appeared to him with Jesus of Nazareth is sufficient proof of the influence exerted on his mind by the information he had received regarding the alleged Messiah. But it is of much greater moment to remember that immediately after the supreme crisis Paul associated himself with the Christian community. There is no reason to doubt the report in Acts that he became intimate in

[1] Gal. i. 1, 11, 12.

Damascus with a Christian disciple named Ananias,[1] and he must speedily have got into touch with the other believers in Christ who were to be found in that region. His own evidence that he was a marked man in Damascus [2] corroborates the vague information of Acts as to his bold proclamation of the Gospel,[3] and warns us against taking too literally the bare statements of Galatians referred to above. Even from Gal. ii. 1 it is obvious that Paul had been for a considerable time a fellow-worker with Barnabas, and the passage in Acts which mentions their early intimacy [4] has often been insufficiently appreciated. Paul himself describes a journey to Jerusalem from Damascus, which he dates apparently three years after his conversion, ' to interview Peter.' [5] An unprejudiced reader can have little doubt that this visit is identical with the sojourn at Jerusalem narrated in Acts ix. 28, 29 : only that Luke wishes to put as favourable a construction as possible on the relations of the new convert to the Christians of the Mother-Church, and leaves the impression that the visit was considerably longer than Paul's own statement permits us to believe, and of a much more public character. Paul singles out Peter and James as the apostles whom he met. In view of later events that is suggestive. At every stage in his career, Paul was in immediate contact with those who had known Jesus and their friends or converts. Hence it was inevitable that from the outset of his Christian course he should be familiar with all that was essential in the tradition of the Church.

This being so, his fundamental positions as a Christian would be profoundly affected by the information which came to him regarding the life and teaching of the Lord, and the attitude towards that life and teaching which he found in the primitive community. Various misconceptions have arisen at this point. It is true that soon after Paul's mission-work among Gentiles began to assume large proportions, he was brought into sharp conflict with the

---

[1] Acts ix. 10 ff.
[3] Acts ix. 22-25.
[2] 2 Cor. xi. 32 f.
[4] ix. 27.
[5] Gal. i. 18.

older sections of the Church as to the obligation on Gentile converts to keep the Mosaic Law. From the emotion revealed by the broken sentences which open Gal. ii., it is clear that he was anxious, at least for a time, about the decision of the Jerusalem apostles. And even after they had shown their genuine Christian insight by refusing to lay down a rigid rule of compliance, and by giving Paul a free hand for his own special sphere, representatives of the Mother-Church continued to dog his steps and to urge on his converts that he was preaching a mutilated Gospel. But this special aspect of the situation in no way justifies the idea that Paul occupied a different Christian position from that of the primitive Church. As we have seen, there is no suggestion that they were at variance on the supreme question of Christology.[1] Jülicher has cogently pointed out the all-important matters of agreement between Paul and so unassailable a witness to the standpoint of primitive Christianity as the Gospel of Matthew.[2] They were at one as to Christ's resurrection and exaltation, His universal Lordship, His relation as Son to the Father. Both alike acknowledged His Messianic dignity and His sinlessness. Indeed Paul himself makes direct reference to his indebtedness to those who were in Christ before him, when he declares to the Corinthians : ' I handed on to you first of all that which I myself received, that Christ died for our sins according to the Scriptures, and that he was buried, and that he was raised on the third day according to the Scriptures, and that he appeared to Cephas, then to the twelve.' [3]

But further, the notion of Paul's isolated position is deduced from his alleged indifference to the earthly career of Jesus. The paucity of references to Jesus' teaching and activity is insisted on as a proof that Paul was not interested in the historical person : that his attention was absorbed by the exalted Lord. Now it is plain that he could never completely adopt the attitude of those who

---

[1] See, e.g., Wernle, Einführung, p. 177.
[2] Paulus u. Jesus, p. 30.
[3] 1 Cor. xv. 3-5.

had companied with Jesus. He did not feel the necessity of such a course, for he was deeply conscious of his own special vocation, and believed that, in the Divine wisdom and grace, he had been prepared for his task by the most fitting type of discipline. Moreover, the nature of his individuality did not lend itself to be the external reflection even of so solitary and incomparable an ideal as that embodied in the life of Jesus. What he assimilated of His precepts and example would inevitably be woven into the very texture of his Christian character and be manifested through the mirror of his marked personality.

But apart from such psychological considerations, the aim of Paul's correspondence must be kept in view if we are to avoid hasty inferences regarding the place which it gives to the life and teaching of Jesus. These letters were never intended to be missionary addresses. In every instance the apostle writes to men and women who were already believers in Christ, and who had received at least some training within the Christian community. His purpose almost invariably is to warn against perils to which he knows his readers are exposed, to encourage in circumstances of trial and temptation, or to give practical guidance on problems of Church life which had been referred to him by the community in question. It is surely obvious that he will take for granted a more or less accurate acquaintance on their part with the salient features of Jesus' character and history. No more reckless assertion could be made than that His life on earth was for Paul an unimportant episode. As Johannes Weiss suggestively puts it, 'the fundamental presupposition of Paul's Gospel is that Christ accomplished his work of redemption in the flesh.' [1] It is scarcely necessary to quote passages. In Paul's view the cross is the crowning-point of that humiliation which was involved in the earthly life of Jesus.[2] An outstanding element in his description of the Son of God is 'that he was born of David's seed by natural descent.' When he explains the redemption which brings

[1] *Das Urchristentum*, p. 167.   [2] Phil. ii. 7, 8.

sonship, he emphasises the fact that the Redeemer was
born of a woman, born under the Law.[1] At a later point
we shall have occasion to examine the material in some
detail.   Meanwhile a further misconception which bears
on our present subject must not be overlooked. It has
been frequently asserted in recent theological literature
that between Paul and Jesus there is a chasm which cannot
be bridged. Jesus is solely concerned with the claims
of the moral imperative which He identifies with the will
of the Father in heaven. Paul assigns central importance
to a scheme of redemptive facts or events which must
be accepted with a view to salvation.

From the course of the preceding discussion it is sufficiently clear that this is an altogether misleading description of Paul's position. But it does take account of a
truth which is vital for any comparison between Paul and
Jesus. The comparison, to put it in a sentence, cannot be
made on equal terms. We are ignoring the real character
of the situation when we say : ' Such and such was the
teaching of Jesus : but this is the teaching of Paul.' We
forget that the supreme factor in Paul's religious experience
was the Person of Jesus Himself in every stage through
which He passed from His entrance into the world to His
final exaltation. Therefore it is irrelevant to compare
their points of view. Jesus, as all His followers and Paul
himself were convinced, stood in a relation to God which
no one else could share. His contact with His Father knew
no barrier. Paul as a Christian found God in Jesus Christ.
He was never conscious that the medium distorted his
vision. Its inestimable worth was bound up with the love
of Him who humbled Himself and became obedient even
unto death. We must carefully examine his view of the
mediation. But let us remember that apart from it
Paul would not have come to understand God at all.

Accordingly it would be erroneous to estimate Paul's
relation to the historical Jesus from a comparison of the
form of their teaching. But it is not difficult to show that

[1] Gal. iv. 4.

at every turn Paul, like the primitive Church, presupposes the life and doctrine and influence of Jesus. How, it may be asked, would such a background be likely to appear in occasional writings like the Pauline Epistles ? We should expect no more than incidental references. And the more spontaneously these appear, the more evidently do they presuppose a close and accurate acquaintance of Paul with the tradition of Jesus. The readiness with which he can use his material appears throughout his writings. When the Corinthians, in their perplexity about the resurrection, put definite questions to him on the matter, he takes his stand on the resurrection of Christ Himself, and, without constraint, enumerates various appearances of His to individual disciples and to groups of believers.[1] In dealing with abuses connected with the observance of the Lord's Supper at Corinth, of which news had reached him, he gives an account of Jesus' farewell meal with His disciples, so vivid and so graphic as to show his thorough acquaintance with the details.[2] In reply to the difficulties raised about marriage by persons of ascetic tendencies in the Corinthian Church, he directly appeals to the Master's teaching : ' For married people these are my instructions (and they are the Lord's, not mine). A wife is not to separate from her husband—if she has separated, she must either remain single or be reconciled to him—and a husband must not put away his wife.' And then he proceeds : ' To other people I would say (not the Lord) : if any brother has a wife who is not a believer, and if she consents to live with him, he must not put her away ; and if any wife has a husband who is not a believer, and if he consents to live with her, she must not put her husband away.' [3] This instance is extraordinarily instructive for our purpose. Where the disciples have preserved a ruling of Jesus on any point of perplexity, that ruling is necessarily decisive. In the present instance Paul can cite the opinion of Jesus on divorce, which has been handed down to us in the Synoptic

---

[1] 1 Cor. xv. 3-8.   [2] 1 Cor. xi. 23 ff.
[3] 1 Cor. vii. 10-13 (M.).

tradition.[1] But the question of mixed marriages, which was bound to create difficulties in a heathen-Christian community like that at Corinth, had never been before Jesus. So the apostle deals with it on his own responsibility, taking care to make plain that he has not the Master's authority for his advice. The passage clearly indicates Paul's attitude towards and dependence on the teaching of Jesus. A further interesting example occurs in a section of 1 Corinthians in which the apostle, who has been urging the stronger-minded Christians to respect the scruples of the weak and to deny themselves, seeks to show that he himself has never asserted his ' rights ' in his dealings with the Corinthian community. One example of his self-renunciation is afforded by his refusal to accept support from them. ' Do you not know that as men who perform temple-rites get their food from the temple, and as attendants at the altar get their share of the sacrifices, so the Lord's instructions were that those who proclaim the gospel are to get their living by the gospel ? ' [2] Here, as a matter of course, he points out Jesus' counsel on the subject, which he accepts, and expects his readers to accept, as authoritative. It will be observed that all the illustrations we have given are taken from the First Epistle to the Corinthians. The fact is suggestive, for this happens to be the only letter in which a number of practical questions affecting the life and organisation of the Church were dealt with by Paul at the request of his converts. If more of such inquiries had been preserved in documents (for the situation must have been common), it is almost certain that we should have found numerous additional references to definite instructions of Jesus.

We do not propose to collect evidence for Paul's knowledge of details in the career of Jesus. A meagre amount is available in the existing sources, and if any samples of the apostle's instruction of converts had been handed

---

[1] Mark x. 1-12, with parallels. It is, of course, impossible to say whether Paul was here dependent on written documents or oral tradition.
[2] 1 Cor. ix. 13, 14 (M.).

down, more would undoubtedly have been forthcoming.
But in this connection it may be frankly admitted that in
Paul's mind all else in Jesus' earthly experience was overshadowed by His entrance into humanity, His self-sacrificing death on the cross, and His resurrection to glory and
triumph. Whatever emphasis he may have laid on the
proof of Jesus' love and compassion afforded by deeds of
which he was informed, nothing could be compared with
the knowledge that ' while we were yet sinners, Christ
died for the ungodly.' However often he may have alluded
to the Divine power energising in Jesus, its supreme expression was His victory over death and the grave.

But before we examine more carefully the influence of
Jesus' teaching, with which he became acquainted in the
Christian community, upon the religious thought of Paul,
it is worth while to note the impression left on his mind
by what he learnt of the Master's character. Here again,
as might be expected, we have to do with incidental
allusions and not with elaborate references. But the very
fact that they are introduced so artlessly reveals Paul's
intimacy with the historical tradition. When pleading for
a fair judgment of his own conduct, which had been
maligned by opponents within the Christian Church, he
appeals to the Corinthians ' by the gentleness and reason-
ableness of Christ.' [1] In writing to his much-loved converts at Philippi, he calls God to witness that he yearns
for them all ' with the affection of Christ Jesus himself.' [2]
When exhorting the strong to bear the burdens of the weak,
he reminds them that ' Christ never pleased himself, but,
as it is written, the reproaches of those who denounced
thee fell upon me,' the Old Testament quotation showing
that he had in mind the scorn and abuse which the
Master had to bear in accomplishing His mission.[3] It is
quite probable that when, in setting before the Corinthian
Christians the duty of a liberal contribution to the collection organised for the poorer brethren in Jerusalem,
he speaks of ' the grace of the Lord Jesus Christ, who,

[1] 2 Cor. x. 1.   [2] Phil. i. 8 (M.).   [3] Rom. xv. 3.

though he was rich, yet for your sakes became poor,' [1]
he is thinking of Jesus' actual poverty in His earthly existence. Of special interest are the indications that Paul
portrayed the character of Jesus to his converts as the
ideal for imitation. In the passages in question he often
associates himself with his Lord, as supplying the standard
of ethical life. This is simply an example of his pastoral
skill and insight. For it is the unanimous testimony of
missionaries that their own lives have to serve in the
first instance as a pattern for immature heathen converts.
In his earliest letters he gives thanks that his readers
' began to copy us and the Lord.' [2] In 1 Corinthians,
which we have so often cited, he entreats them : ' Copy me,
as I copied Christ.' [3] And when he warns Christians in
Asia against yielding to pagan vices, he declares : ' That
is not how you have understood the meaning of Christ, for
it is Christ whom you have been taught, it is in Christ that
you have been instructed, the real Christ who is in Jesus.' [4]
References of such a kind plainly imply that the man who
made them not only had an intimate knowledge of the
character and conduct of the historical Jesus, but laid the
profoundest emphasis upon them in the discharge of his
work as a missionary.

But we must further observe that the fundamental note
of Jesus' teaching, the revelation of the Fatherhood of God,
dominates Paul's religious conceptions from beginning to
end. This can be made clear in a variety of directions.
We may be surprised that the apostle has not given a
larger place to the idea of the Kingdom of God, on which
Jesus laid so much emphasis. There are, of course, various
instances of its occurrence in his Epistles, and these reveal
the same shades of meaning as those which appear in the
Synoptic Gospels. In some passages, as, e.g., 1 Thess. ii. 12,
1 Cor. xv. 24, etc., the term ' kingdom ' is essentially
eschatological. Others, as, e.g., 1 Cor. iv. 20, Col. i. 13, as
plainly presuppose that the Kingdom has already been

[1] 2 Cor. viii. 9.　　　　　　[2] 1 Thess. i. 6.
[3] 1 Cor. xi. 1 (M.).　　　　　[4] Eph. iv. 20, 21 (M.).

inaugurated, and exists as a power in the world. But the very fact that the Kingdom-idea has fallen into the background in Paul's mind only shows the more conclusively that he has penetrated behind the form to the inner substance of Jesus' thought. For we are not unduly pressing the data when we assert that for Paul the conception of the Family of God, as established and knit together in Christ, takes the place of the Kingdom.[1] To make good this position, evidence might be adduced from the whole range of Paul's writings. A few typical instances will suffice.

No statement more powerfully sums up Paul's notion of the Christian life than that which forms the climax of one of his greatest arguments in Galatians : ' You are all sons of God through faith in Christ Jesus.' [2] The rich significance of these words is disclosed in a later sentence of the paragraph : ' When the fulness of the time came, God sent forth his Son, born of a woman, born under the law, to redeem those under the law, that we might receive our adoption. Now because you are sons, God sent forth the Spirit of his Son into our hearts, crying, Abba, Father. So that you are no longer a slave but a son, and if a son then also an heir through God.' [3] Practically everything of moment in Paul's experience of religion is here expressed —the Incarnation, the Redemption in Christ, the gift of the Spirit, the crucial relation to God of sonship, the right to the completed inheritance. And it is plain that the terms in which he formulates his experience go back to the teaching of Jesus. It was He who, out of the depth of His own unique consciousness, disclosed the high truth that men are called to be sons of God, not in abstract name, but in the reality of a personal relationship. His consciousness of Sonship, although solitary, sets the norm for those whom He is not ashamed to call His brethren. Thus, His redemption of men from their false relation to God, the relation of

---

[1] We do not here refer to the parallel conception of the Body of Christ, which will be examined in the next chapter.
[2] Gal. iii. 26.   [3] Gal. iv. 4-7.

guilty fear, and the bestowal of that Spirit which is His own life-principle, introduce them into what Paul calls ' the liberty of the glory of the children of God.' In Christ Jesus they are constituted God's sons.

The intimate affinity of Paul with Jesus is equally manifest in what he teaches concerning the Family-spirit. When Jesus was asked, ' Which is the supreme of all the commandments ? ' He replied : ' The chief is : Hear, O Israel, the Lord our God is one Lord, and thou shalt love the Lord thy God with all thy heart and all thy soul and all thy mind and all thy might : the second is this : Thou shalt love thy neighbour as thyself.' [1] It is needless to recall Paul's wonderful eulogy of love in 1 Cor. xiii., a passage in which the matchless grace of the thought is almost equalled by the rhythmical beauty of the language. His estimate, as there unfolded, may well have been derived, as some eminent scholars have suggested, from the life and character of Jesus Himself. However this may be, Paul makes plain by the language which he employs that he stands in the direct succession of Jesus. In Rom. xiii. 8 ff., when formulating various Christian duties, he makes this most suggestive statement : ' Be in debt to no man apart from the debt of love one to another. He who loves his fellow-man has fulfilled the law. Thou shalt not commit adultery, Thou shalt not kill, Thou shalt not steal, Thou shalt not covet—these and any other commands are summed up in the single word, Thou shalt love thy neighbour as thyself. Love never wrongs a neighbour : therefore love is the fulfilling of the law.' [2] That this is no isolated reference becomes plain from Gal. v. 14 : ' The whole law is fulfilled in one command, namely, Thou shalt love thy neighbour as thyself.' The keynote of Paul's ethical thought, which cannot be dissociated from the outcome of his religious faith, he has caught once for all from the teaching of Jesus.

[1] Mark xii. 29-31.　　　　　[2] Chiefly M.

(b) *Eschatological Conceptions*

A careful reader of the Pauline Epistles must be impressed by the prominence given by the apostle to the element of Hope. We have already exemplified this in the section on the *Messiah* in the preceding chapter. The very existence of a Messianic ideal involved such a feature. And it belonged, of course, to the essence of Paul's pre-Christian consciousness. Now we have seen how completely his conception of Messiah was altered by his experience of the risen Jesus. In the strict sense, the ardent expectation of those who waited for the Kingdom of God was already in process of being realised. Phenomena were visible which testified to the power of the unseen world. Unique gifts and graces in the Christian community were the evidence of a new order. Fellowship with the living Christ lifted the soul out of the present. Even now Christians were in possession of redemption.[1] This redemption was different from the earlier hope of national deliverance. It was embodied in the forgiveness of sins, and had no political bearings at all. In one aspect of it, nothing more satisfying could be conceived. Yet, as has been noted, Paul was keenly alive to the hampering conditions inseparable from bodily life and the evils imposed by the existing constitution of the world. Redemption will only be complete when the present organism of flesh and blood shall be exchanged for the spiritual organism, which will be a perfectly adequate expression of the renewed life of the Christian : when this age, which is cursed with futility and death, shall give place to that which is to come, the epoch of ' glory,' in which men shall be transformed into the very image of God. It is evident that Paul has developed these ideas from a deep-rooted personal instinct. But he has also preserved a large amount of the eschatological material of Judaism. Here again we may explain the fact by saying that he remained true to his Jewish inheritance. But how are we to reconcile that with his altered con-

[1] Col. i. 14.

ception of Messiah ? How are we to account for the extraordinary prominence he assigns to the Parousia, the Second
Advent of Christ, with all its eschatological accompaniments ? Has he here elaborated on apocalyptic lines the
contents of his Damascus experience ? Or is he attempting
to combine two incongruous ideas, the traditional machinery
of Jewish eschatology with the spiritualised Messianic doctrine involved in his own Christian view of Messiah ?

The clue to his procedure is at least partly to be found
in the attitude of the early Church. The New Testament
writings, almost without exception, reveal an eager longing
for the consummation of God's redeeming purpose, which
will coincide with the return of Christ. It is plain, therefore, that primitive Christianity was possessed by an
overpowering eschatological enthusiasm. The Apocalypse,
which is a typical product of its age, closes with the
words : ' He who bears this testimony says, Even so : I
am coming very soon. Amen, Lord Jesus, come ! ' (M.).
The ejaculation corresponds to the final salutation of so
completely different a document as Paul's first letter to
the Corinthians : ' If any one has no love for the Lord,
God's curse be upon him. Maran atha ! ' (' Lord come ! ')
In what is probably the latest book of the New Testament,
the writer is chiefly concerned with meeting the scoffing
reproach hurled at Christians : ' Where is his promised
advent ? Since the day our fathers fell asleep, things
remain exactly as they were from the beginning of
creation.' [1] The return of Christ introduces the resurrection and the judgment. Sometimes the final consummation is preceded by a limited rule of Christ on earth,
during which all opposing forces are subdued.

The Synoptic Gospels indicate that we must allow for
something more than the traditions of Jewish Messianism
in attempting to account for this constant strain in the
religion of the primitive Church. It is extremely difficult
to determine with any accuracy the eschatological teaching
of Jesus. A comparison of parallel passages shows the

[1] 2 Pet. iii. 4 (M.).

effect of varying traditions.   Not only so.   In an atmosphere of such eager expectation of the Parousia as that
in which the report of Jesus' words was handed down,
His sayings were exposed to modifications likely to stamp
them with eschatological features.[1]   But after due allowance has been made for such influences, there remains a
residuum of evidence which cannot be explained away.
Here we can only touch the subject.   Various utterances
of Jesus appear to imply that He expected the Kingdom
of God to be consummated within a comparatively short
period.   More than once He associates this consummation
with His own return in glory.   When, however, we consider
that the Gospel which He brought laid supreme emphasis
on the immediate recognition of the love of the Father and
its present enjoyment by His children, it is obvious that
questions of chronology cannot be of primary importance
for Jesus' conception of the Kingdom.   So that His predic-
tion of its immediacy as an eschatological magnitude may
simply express the prophetic certainty that the cause of
God *must* be victorious.   Whatever be the precise explanation of this aspect of His teaching, it was natural that its
literal form should above all else appeal to men and women
who had been taught to look forward to a definite moment
in history at which God should intervene, either directly,
or through His Vicegerent, the Messiah.   Paul found this
expectation dominant in the Christian community when he
entered it.   He was profoundly impressed by it, as we can
gather from such passages as 1 Thess. iv. 13—v. 11 ; 1 Cor.
xv. 20-28 ; Rom. xiii. 11-13.   He can describe the change
through which his heathen converts have passed as a turning to God from idols, ' to serve a living and true God, and
to wait for the coming of his Son from heaven—the Son
whom he raised from the dead, Jesus who rescued us from
the wrath to come.' [2]   And he uses the expectation in his
letters as a powerful motive to self-discipline and watchful-

[1] See on the whole subject the admirable discussion in Moffatt's *Theology
of the Gospels*, pp. 41-84.
[2] 1 Thess. i. 9, 10 (chiefly M.).

ness of life. It is of interest to note that in his eschatological teaching he constantly reflects not only the thought but also the language of Jesus.

(c) The Era of the Spirit

No conception, as we have discovered, was more central for Paul than that of the Spirit. This we endeavoured to trace, primarily, to his conversion-experience. The supreme crisis of his life was always identified by the apostle with a new consciousness of spiritual power. That power he could only ascribe to the risen Lord who had revealed Himself. Thenceforward, possession of this high endowment was regarded by Paul as the main criterion of the Christian life. A remarkable example of his position is found in 1 Cor. xii. 3, where, in distinguishing between genuine and spurious spiritual manifestations, he declares : ' No man can say, Jesus is Lord, except by the Holy Spirit.' He admits, as this passage shows, the existence of spiritual phenomena which are worthless and perilous. These were visible in heathen communities, and, so far as their external form was concerned, might easily be confounded with those of the Christian society. The crucial difference lay in the fact that the Holy Spirit was directly associated with Christ. He is described as ' the Spirit of God's Son,' or ' the Spirit of Christ.' ' Where the Spirit of the Lord is,' Paul asserts, ' there is freedom.' [1] Obviously then, in his judgment, the Spirit is above all else the witness to the power and presence of the living Christ and all that that involves.

We cannot tell how early in his Christian career Paul came to formulate his conception of the Spirit along the lines which are discernible in the Epistles. But we know that when he entered the Christian Church he was confronted with experiences similar to his own, which were grouped together under the category of the Spirit.

The opening chapters of Acts are of priceless value as

[1] 2 Cor. iii. 17.

revealing the tone and feeling of early Christianity. ' Day after day,' we are told, ' they resorted with one accord to the temple and broke bread together in their own homes : they ate with a glad and simple heart, praising God and looked on with favour by all the people.' [1] The truthfulness of the picture is corroborated throughout the New Testament. Alike in Paul and other writers we overhear the same note of exhilaration and joy.[2] More than once the temper of these primitive believers is described by the term παρρησία, glad, courageous self-expression. This excites the amazement of the Jewish authorities in the case of Peter and John.[3] The writer of Acts definitely associates it with the Spirit : ' When they had prayed, the place where they were met was shaken, and they were all filled with the Holy Spirit, and began to speak the word of God with glad fearlessness.' [4] The connection of this attitude with the Spirit belongs, no doubt, to the primitive thought of the Church. For the early traditions, incorporated in Acts, are saturated with the conception of the Spirit. The chief emphasis, indeed, is laid upon abnormal phenomena. Again and again in Acts, speaking with ' tongues ' is singled out as typical of the Spirit's operation in the life of believers.[5] Paul's discussion of spiritual gifts, in reply to the question addressed to him on that subject by the Christians at Corinth, shows the firmly established place this endowment held in the esteem of the community.[6] Most scholars are now disposed to identify this ' glossolalia ' with a phenomenon which belongs to all outbursts of spiritual enthusiasm. In such times of nervous tension, the emotional life bursts through its ordinary barriers, and men and women break forth into ejaculations of praise and prayer, often quite unintelligible to their neighbours, but serving as an outlet for their pent-up feeling. Paul clearly indicates the restraints which ought to be placed upon such manifestations. And, as we have seen, his profound

---

[1] Acts ii. 46 (M.). Cf. iv. 33, v. 41.
[2] Cf. Phil. iv. 4 ; 1 Pet. ii. 9 ; Jas. i. 2.
[3] Acts iv. 13.   [4] Acts iv. 31.
[5] Acts ii. 4, x. 46, xix. 6.   [6] 1 Cor. xiv.

influence probably did more than anything else to keep them under control, and to turn this exuberance of emotional vitality into the channels of moral action. But already in the early Church the more wholesome conception of the significance of the Spirit had begun to assert itself. Indeed from the beginning fearless proclamation of the Gospel was traced to the power of the Spirit, just as definitely as gifts of healing or interpretations of truth or glossolalia.[1] But naturally what was extraordinary attracted special attention. Behind all lay the conviction that the Messianic Age had begun to dawn.

Now already in the Old Testament the new era, so ardently longed for, was connected with a unique outpouring of Divine influences. In Isa. xi. 2, it is said of the Messianic King that ' the spirit of the Lord shall rest upon him, the spirit of wisdom and understanding, the spirit of counsel and might, the spirit of knowledge and of the fear of the Lord.' Jeremiah speaks of the wonderful days to come in which God will put His law in the inward parts of His people, and write it in their hearts.[2] Ezekiel has the same idea of the ' new spirit ' which is God's Spirit.[3] First Enoch describes the Messiah very much in terms of Isa. xi. 2,[4] and later, the Psalms of Solomon speak of the wisdom, righteousness, and might of God's Anointed as wrought by the Spirit.[5] In Isa. xxxii. 15 the epoch of bliss is ushered in by the outpouring of the Spirit from on high.

The early Christians, quoting the apocalyptic words of Joel,[6] are convinced that all these forecasts have found their realisation through the exalted Jesus. The pronouncement of Peter in Acts ii. 32 f. gives the clue to the general belief : ' This Jesus God raised up, as we can all bear witness. Exalted then by God's right hand, and receiving from the Father the long-promised holy Spirit, he has poured on us what you now see and hear.' [7] This indissoluble association of the Spirit with Jesus had already

---

[1] See Acts iv. 31 as above.
[2] Jer. xxxi. 33.
[3] Ezek. xxxvi. 26, 27.
[4] 1 Enoch xlix. 3.
[5] Pss. of Sol. xviii. 8.
[6] Joel ii. 28 ff. Cf. Acts ii. 16 ff.
[7] Chiefly M.

H

before Paul's time ensured that the conception should not degenerate into a mere external superstition.

Enough probably has been said to indicate that Paul must have been under real obligations to the Christian community which he entered, in formulating both for his own mind and for his audiences in the mission-field a fruitful conception of the Spirit.[1] Yet it is none the less clear that he worked out to its proper consummation the idea, which was apt to be lost in the midst of startling phenomena, that the Spirit, as the gift and pledge of Christ, was not an endowment for special occasions or special activities, but rather the life-principle of every trustful and loyal disciple.

(d) The Death of Christ

From the very dawn of his Christian career Paul was obliged to reflect upon the significance of the death of Jesus, the Messiah. In the next chapter we must carefully examine his interpretation of the facts. But, with a view to that investigation, it is of moment to ask : From what point of view was this crucial event regarded in the circle of primitive believers ? The pre-eminent position given to the story of the Passion in the Synoptic tradition bears witness to the absorbing interest which it created in the early Church. And in their work among their own fellow-countrymen the first preachers of the Gospel must necessarily have endeavoured to explain the meaning of the cross to those who considered it as discrediting the claims of Jesus.

When we turn to the early chapters of Acts, we find some illumination as to the direction which was being taken by Christian thought on the subject. It accords with what

[1] We have not discussed the question of Jesus' teaching on the Spirit. The data in the Synoptics are quite inadequate for the purpose. Those in the Fourth Gospel are an interpretation which presupposes Paulinism. And yet the place given by the writer to the conception of the Spirit is more intelligible if some traditions of Jesus' teaching on the subject were current in the Church. Cf. Luke xxiv. 48, 49 ; Acts i. 4 f.

we might expect in the opening stages of reflection. The simplest point of view is that which regards the death of Jesus as a crime committed by the Jews, in ignorance of its full and awful import. ' I know, brethren,' says Peter, ' that you acted in ignorance, as did also your rulers.' [1] Stephen compares the murder of ' the Righteous One ' with the persecution and slaying of the prophets in earlier generations.[2] But from the beginning their action is regarded as no mere accident, due to an outburst of human malice. It belongs to a deliberate and predetermined purpose of God. The Jews were only instruments to carry out His will, ' to do what thy hand and thy counsel had decreed to happen.' [3] Indeed, even when blaming their ignorance, Peter describes it as the means which God took to carry out that which He had announced long before by the mouth of the prophets.[4] The Second Psalm is quoted as declaring that ' the kings of the earth rose up and the rulers gathered together against the Lord and against his Christ.' [5]

Again and again in the earlier section of Acts the forgiveness of sins is more or less vaguely associated with the person of Jesus as crucified. Thus, immediately after he has pointed to the fulfilment of prophecy in the suffering of Christ, Peter urges upon his hearers repentance ' with a view to the blotting out of your sins.' [6] Having described Christ as ' the stone rejected by you builders ' (Psa. cxviii. 22), he asserts that ' in no other is there salvation.' [7] No better example of the position could be given than Acts v. 30, 31 (M.) : ' The God of our fathers raised Jesus whom you murdered by hanging him on a gibbet. God lifted him up to his right hand as our pioneer and saviour, in order to grant repentance and remission of sins to Israel.' In all these passages—and they are only a selection—there is no attempt to explain the relation of forgiveness to the death of Jesus. Yet the words in our last quotation which

---

[1] Acts iii. 17.
[2] Acts vii. 52.
[3] Acts iv. 27, 28 ; ii. 23.
[4] Acts iii. 18.
[5] Acts iv. 26.
[6] Acts iii. 19.
[7] Acts iv. 12.

speak of ' hanging him on a gibbet,' and which are themselves cited from Deut. xxi. 22, undoubtedly suggest a particular drift of reflection. And it may be noted that the reference is found not only here, but also in Acts x. 39, Gal. iii. 13, and (probably) 1 Pet. ii. 24. The original passage describes the man who is ' hanged on a gibbet ' as ' accursed by God.' What can be the meaning of a curse lying upon One who was perfectly righteous ? We have seen that the idea of a suffering Messiah was read into the prophets by the early Christians. The suffering, the curse, must somehow be related to human sin. Now already in Judaism there were traces of the belief that the merit of an innocent man could atone for a guilty.[1] This position at least was reached in the primitive Church, for Paul can say : ' First and foremost, I passed on to you what I had myself received, namely that Christ died for our sins, as the Scriptures had said.' [2] It is instructive to notice that on this crucial matter Paul appeals not to any saying of the Master but to the Old Testament as interpreted in the Church. If we ask what Scriptures were so expounded, Isaiah liii. will inevitably suggest itself. As soon as the earliest Christians began to explore the Old Testament for light on the stumbling-block of the cross, they were bound to be impressed by the extraordinary delineation of the Servant of Jahweh in that chapter. There they read of one who was ' despised and rejected of men,' who ' was wounded for our transgressions and bruised for our iniquities,' who ' was brought as a lamb to the slaughter, and as a sheep before her shearers is dumb, so he openeth not his mouth.' But of peculiar significance would be the declaration of ver. 10 : ' If he should make his soul an offering for sin, he should see his seed, he should prolong his days, and the pleasure of the Lord should prosper in his hand.' The idea of the sin-offering would illuminate the mystery of Deut. xxi. 22 f. The cross would receive a profound meaning in the light of the prophetic word : ' The Lord laid on him the iniquity of us

[1] 4 Maccab. xvii. 22.   [2] 1 Cor. xv. 3 (M.).

all' (Isa. liii. 6). It might be precarious to infer a definite doctrine of the death of Christ in the early Church from the fragmentary data at our disposal. The evidence suggests that it was interpreted now from one standpoint, now from another. But enough material has survived to reveal the germ of Paul's conception of Christ as the propitiation and sin-bearer. Indeed, a careful examination of Isa. liii. in the LXX discloses at various points the essential background of Paul's doctrinal construction. The Servant 'bears our sins' (τὰς ἁμαρτίας ἡμῶν φέρει). He 'shall have many for his inheritance and shall share the spoil of the strong, because his life (ψυχή) was delivered up (παρεδόθη) [1] unto death, and he was reckoned among the transgressors (ἀνόμοις) and he bore (ἀνήνεγκεν) the sins of many, and was delivered up because of their transgressions.'

We have observed that in recording the traditions which he had received in the Church regarding the death of Christ, Paul appeals to the authority of the Old Testament. Yet the Church had preserved sayings of the Lord which could at least find some place in the scheme of thought under review. In an incidental statement of the purpose of His mission, Jesus declared that He had come 'not to be served (διακονηθῆναι) but to serve, and to give his life (ψυχήν) a ransom (λύτρον) for many.' [2] It is difficult not to discern here the influence upon His religious thought of the Servant-passages. The same thing is true of His remarkable utterance at the Last Supper : 'This is my blood of the covenant (or, 'the new covenant in my blood,' so Luke and Paul) poured out for many.' [3] For in Isa. xlix. 8, 9 the Servant is described as 'given for a covenant of the people . . . that thou mayest say to the prisoners, Go forth : to them that are in darkness, Show yourselves.' [4] These, and other passages which might be quoted from the

---

[1] Used by Paul in his central statements regarding the death of Christ : *e.g.* Rom. iv. 25, viii. 32 ; Gal. ii. 20 ; Eph. v. 2, 25.

[2] Mark x. 45 and parallels.

[3] Mark xiv. 24.

[4] The best MSS. of the LXX have the 'covenant' in verse 6 as well.

Gospels, indicate that Jesus' thoughts on the profoundest aspects of His own mission were moving among Old Testament forecasts and symbols, and there can be no doubt that the wonderful figure of the 'Servant' exercised a unique influence upon His Messianic consciousness.[1]

[1] See a series of articles by the present writer on 'The Self-consciousness of Jesus and the Servant of the Lord,' in the *Expository Times* for 1908.

CHAPTER VI

THE FUNDAMENTAL POSITIONS OF PAULINISM

(a) *In Christ*

IN the preceding chapters an attempt has been made on the basis of the data furnished by the Epistles to set forth, first, the features characteristic of Paul's pre-Christian religious experience, secondly, those conceptions which were brought into the forefront by the transformation of that experience due to his conversion, and finally, the influences already dominant in the early Church which seem to have affected the apostle's religious thought. All these elements must have had normative value in the shaping of his fundamental positions. No man can shake off his past like a worn-out garment. His ancestral heritage of ideas will assert itself, even when in principle he has discarded it. The symbolism in which the mind takes refuge has a strange fashion of surviving, after the things signified have been seen in a new light. It is needless, in view of Chapter IV., to lay further emphasis on Paul's spiritual crisis. In each section of our present discussion its central significance becomes more and more clear. But we must not minimise the fact that Paul entered a society in which a theology had begun to take shape. When we recognise that that society was guided by original disciples of Jesus, it is plain that he could not afford to ignore interpretations of facts and experiences which were regarded by the large majority of Christians as authoritative. Keeping all these factors before us in their right proportions, we ought to be able to outline the fundamental positions of Paulinism.

In taking as our starting-point Paul's famous description of his Christian status, we would endeavour to adhere to the *genetic* method which was vindicated in the opening chapter. We are least likely to err if we begin with that stratum in his religion in which Paul himself always finds his surest standing-ground, the immediate and unassailable reality of his personal relation to Christ. What, then, is the content of the phrase, ' in Christ,' which Paul loves to use when he desires to represent the profoundest aspect of his religious life ? We must not lay too much stress on the form of the expression, and yet we must not attempt to explain it away. The impression made upon Paul by the revelation of the living Lord was an impression of boundless love and grace. It is probable that in his pre-Christian days he had heard of Jesus' self-sacrificing devotion to the needy and the outcasts. But his personal experience was decisive. And when he found the clue to Christ's character and mission in the voluntary humiliation of the cross, the sense of a love inestimable by human standards overpowered him. He was swept away in its current. This infinite love claimed him. And he yielded himself up to Christ as His willing slave. Henceforward his connection with Christ was the primary element in his religious life : ' What things were gain to me, these I have counted loss for Christ : indeed I count anything as loss compared to the supreme value of knowing Christ Jesus my Lord. For his sake I have lost everything (I count it all the veriest refuse) in order to gain Christ.' [1] The consequence of ' gaining ' or ' knowing ' Christ he describes as being ' in Christ.' As the result of a searching investigation of the phrase, Deissmann [2] reaches the following conclusion : ' The formula ἐν Χριστῷ constructed . . . by Paul characterises the relation of the Christian to Jesus Christ as an existence in the pneumatic Christ to be conceived locally. This thought, for which there is no analogy in any relation of man to man, we may clarify by means of the

---

[1] Phil. iii. 7-8 (chiefly M.).
[2] *Die neutestamentliche Formel ' in Christo Jesu,'* pp. 97, 98.

analogy of the notion underlying the phrases ἐν πνεύματι and ἐν τῷ Θεῷ, the notion of dwelling in a Pneuma-element which may be compared to the air. The question whether we have to take the local idea, which is the basis of the formula, in its proper sense or merely as a rhetorical metaphor, cannot be decided with certainty, yet the former alternative has a higher degree of probability. In any case, whether it is to be understood literally or metaphorically, the formula is the characteristic expression for the profoundest fellowship conceivable between the Christian and the living Christ.'

The statement is illuminating, even although we may not assent to all its positions. It is true that we cannot rule out the possibility that Paul conceived ' spirit ' in a semi-physical sense, although there are no clear indications of this in the Epistles. And we must certainly correlate the formula ' in Christ ' with that which may be substituted for it, ' in the Spirit.' But it would be hazardous to press the ' local ' significance of the formula, as Deissmann is inclined to do. Indeed it seems highly probable that the usage is metaphorical, when we recollect that Paul describes the same personal relationship by saying : ' Christ lives in me.' [1] Here the element which might be compared to the air would be Paul's human nature, which is obviously out of the question. If it be observed that these interchange-able phrases primarily denote the interaction of two wills, the will of Christ which dominates and inspires the inmost life of the Christian, and the will of the Christian which submits to and glories in that sovereignty, suggestions of ' locality ' seem irrelevant. Nor is a literal interpreta-tion necessary. Paul's Epistles abound in examples of metaphors equally daring.

But we must not go to the other extreme, and thin down the apostle's conception. If any conviction was central for his religious life, it was that of communion with Christ. His most famous description of the experience occurs in the passage to which reference has been made

[1] Gal. ii. 20.

above : ' I have been crucified with Christ, so it is no longer
I that live, but Christ lives in me : and the life which I now
live in the flesh, I live by faith, faith in the Son of God who
loved me and gave himself for me.' [1] The same intimacy
of relationship is expressed, almost incidentally, in 1 Cor.
vi. 17 : ' He who joins himself to the Lord is one spirit
[with him].' In Rom. vi. 5 he asserts that ' if we have
grown into him [Christ] by a death like his, we shall grow
into him by a resurrection like his.' [2] How much does
this involve ? Does it mean that the fundamental element
in Paul was a mystic absorption in Christ ? It has become
fashionable to emphasise the mysticism of Paul. And if
by ' mysticism ' we mean that contact between the human
and the Divine which forms the core of the deepest religious
experience, but which can only be felt as an immediate
intuition of the highest reality and cannot be described
in the language of psychology, the emphasis is thoroughly
justified.[3] Over and over again Paul bears witness to this
unfathomable intimacy between himself and the exalted
Christ and all that it means for his personal life, although
he nowhere attempts to analyse its significance. Thus,
in Phil. iv. 13 he makes the triumphant confession : ' I
can do all things in him that strengthens me.' And the
same type of experience lies behind the uplifting assurance
that came to him from Christ : ' My grace is sufficient for
you, for my power is perfected in weakness.' [4] Even more.
We may frankly admit that some of those visions to which
he refers might be called mystical in a strict sense, notably
his ' rapture ' to the third heaven, narrated with such
emotion in 2 Cor. xii. But, as J. Weiss pointedly remarks,
the fact that he mentions them in detail shows that they
cannot have been frequent occurrences.[5] Indeed there is
no trace of the characteristically mystical idea of *absorption*
in God or in Christ. Even in the famous passage quoted
above, in which his language suggests that his own individu-

---

[1] Gal. ii. 20.   [2] M.
[3] ' Up to a certain point all Christians are mystics ' (Bigg, *Epp. of
St. Peter and St. Jude*, p. viii).
[4] 2 Cor. xii. 9.   *Das Urchristentum*, p. 397.

ality has been replaced by that of Christ, he guards against any interpretation which might be termed mystical in the technical sense by proceeding to describe his life as strictly personal, a life of faith in the Son of God.

Here we touch the very foundation of Paul's religious experience. The appeal of the love and grace of Christ, of which he became conscious at his conversion, penetrated to his inmost being. It set in motion all the activities of his soul. And this response, which carried his whole nature with it, he calls Faith. We have already seen how much faith includes for Paul : how it takes into account the historical basis of the Gospel in the incarnation, death, and resurrection of Jesus : how it interprets these in the light of the revelation made to him as an individual : how it is woven of love and adoration and trust and obedience. The relationship of faith does not imply for Paul the dissolving of the separate personalities involved, and the blending of them in one. Although he can speak of being ' in Christ,' yet he looks forward to being ' with Christ.' [1] Faith remains throughout the link which binds the 'bond-servant' (δοῦλος) to his ' Lord ' (Κύριος). The union is one of dependence, not absorption. But that does not derogate from its reality and power. Rather does it prevent the relation from becoming mere contemplative ecstasy. It is the channel by which Divine resources are imparted. And the supreme Divine gift which is bestowed on faith is that of the Spirit.[2]

But in this connection the Spirit is scarcely distinguishable from Christ Himself. Paul's statement in Rom. viii. 9, 10 reveals his point of view : ' You are not in the flesh but in the Spirit if the Spirit of God dwells in you. Now if any one have not the Spirit of Christ, he does not belong to him. But if Christ be in you, the body indeed is dead because of sin, but the Spirit is life because of righteousness.' Here Christ and the Spirit are virtually synonymous. Probably we should be most true to Paul's standpoint in saying that he regards Christ as operating in the inner life

[1] Phil. i. 23.　　　　　　　　　[2] *E.g.* Gal. iii. 2.

of the Christian through the Spirit.[1]   From this activity
of the exalted Lord are derived all the highest blessings
of the Christian life.   These we must examine in a later
paragraph.   Meanwhile it ought to be noted that this
supremely intimate relation of union with Christ constitutes for Paul the pre-supposition of everything that
counts in salvation.   Without anticipating our subsequent
discussion of such central Pauline ideas as justification,
death to sin, and the final redemption, we must briefly
notice the bearing upon them of the present conception.
While in his more theoretical and controversial statements
Paul follows an ' order of salvation ' which implies successive
stages, as a matter of practical experience their common
basis is found in union with Christ.   That is the apostle's
religious starting-point.   His doctrinal constructions are
interpretations of it.   When he speaks of God justifying a
man because of his faith, receiving him into a new relation,
the relation of a child to his Father, his language seems at
times unduly to objectify the process, to keep it apart
from the experience of the individual.   But for Paul the
very existence of faith means that the subject of it is ' in
Christ.'   Hence, all God's dealings with the individual
stand on that footing.   To quote the apostle himself,
God's grace is ' bestowed on us in the Beloved.' [2]   That
is to say, God comes into touch with men in virtue of their
relation to Christ.   So too with the nature of the new life.
Paul has formulated, as we shall discover in the next
section, something of a theory regarding the ' death ' of

---

[1] J. Weiss (*op. cit.*, p. 355, note 3) suggestively illustrates Paul's usage
from Philo's doctrine of the ' powers ' of God which penetrate into the
world and man.   He quotes from Zeller's exposition (*Phil. d. Griechen*
iii. 2, p. 365) : ' In his doctrine of the Powers, two ideas cross, the religious
conception of personal mediating beings, and the philosophical of imper-
sonal : he unites both, without observing their contradiction : indeed
he cannot possibly observe it, because otherwise the rôle of mediators,
the double nature of the Divine Powers, would at once be lost, by means
of which on the one hand they must be identical with God, so that it
might be possible for a finite being by means of them to partake of
Deity, while on the other they must be separate from Him, in order that
Deity, in spite of this participation, should remain apart from any contact
with the world.'

[2] Eph. i. 6 (M.).

the believer to sin. That theory is implicated in his conceptions of the Flesh and the Law. But when you get
behind his logic, you reach the crucial fact that the man
who is in intimate connection with Christ, from the nature
of the case feels the utter incongruity of sin, and must
break with it if that connection is to endure. In union
with Christ he takes Christ's attitude towards sin and
Christ's attitude towards holiness. Contact with Christ
can mean nothing else than new life. 'If any man be in
Christ, he is a new creature : the old things have passed
away : new things have come into being.' [1] Plainly, this
relation to Christ is also the guarantee of a completed
salvation. To have a part in it is to share in His whole
experience : to die with Him, to rise with Him, to be
changed into His likeness as exalted, that condition which
Paul calls 'glory.' 'You died, and your life has been hid
with Christ in God : when Christ, our life, shall be revealed,
then you also shall be revealed with him in glory.' [2] The
pledge of final redemption, that redemption of the whole
personality on which Paul laid so much emphasis, is often
identified with the gift of the Spirit.[3] But this only confirms the fact already indicated, that Paul regards this
vital union of the believer with Christ as mediated by the
Spirit, through whom God meets faith.

(b) The Crucified Redeemer

It may be truly said that when Paul speaks of the death
of Christ, the resurrection stands in the background of his
mind. He invariably interprets the cross in the light of
the resurrection. This follows the order of his religious
experience. It was the risen Christ he came to know in the
spiritual crisis of his career. And this knowledge, which is
far deeper and larger than a mere intellectual process,
remains the foundation of his victorious Christian life. It
is the condition of that central relationship which is

---

[1] 2 Cor. v. 17.   [2] Col. iii. 3, 4.
[3] *E.g.* 2 Cor. v. 5, i. 22 ; Eph. i. 13, 14.

expressed by the phrase, 'union with Christ.' But the
living Lord to whom he clings with all the might of his
unfaltering faith has passed through death, the degrading
death of the cross. There can be little doubt that Paul
recalls a personal impression when he describes Christ
crucified as a 'cause of stumbling' (σκάνδαλον) to the
Jews.[1] Even when the accounts of Jesus which reached
him in his persecuting zeal disclosed features so rare as to
prompt to caution in his project, the conception of a
crucified Messiah closed his mind, and hardened his resolve
to extirpate such blasphemy. And now he had discovered
in this degraded impostor 'life-giving Spirit.' The Christ
whom he knew as the source of inward power, the Christ
who had convinced him of the boundless love of God, had
met and conquered death. His crowning vision of Christ
was a vision of love. Love was the clue to His words and
deeds. Such was the tradition of those who had companied
with Him. But Paul had no need of evidence at second-
hand. The love of Christ had been demonstrated to him
immediately. Tradition merely confirmed his experience.
Must not Christ's death also be illumined by love ? Must
it not serve some generous purpose ? When questions
like these emerged, it is plain that the death of Christ
would become the subject of Paul's profoundest reflection.

He was compelled to start with certain assumptions,
assumptions about which he never argued. Christ was the
sinless Son of God. Paul shared that position with the
whole early Church. Yet Christ had suffered death. Now,
for Paul as a Jewish thinker death was the penalty of sin.
'The wages of sin,' he declares, 'is death': [2] 'through
sin came death.'[3] Here he stood in line with the great
prophetic tradition : 'the soul that sinneth it shall die.'[4]
The tradition was handed on in the Rabbinic schools.
'Satan and Yezer (the Evil Impulse) and the Angel of
Death,' said R. Simon b. Lakish, 'are one.'[5] 'See, my

---

[1] 1 Cor. i. 23 ; cf. Gal. v. 11.
[2] Rom. vi. 23.   [3] Rom. v. 12.   [4] Ezek. xviii. 4.
[5] *Baba Bathra*, 16a (qu. by Schechter, *Some Aspects of Rabbinic Theology*,
p. 244).

children,' said R. Chaninah b. Dosa to his disciples, ' it is sin that kills.' [1] There is little doubt that when Paul speaks of death, he regards it synthetically, not distinguishing, as we are wont to do, between its physical and spiritual aspects, but viewing the experience in its entirety as involving primarily separation from God. That Jesus Christ, being what He was, should die, was to his mind a perplexing problem. But the perplexity was intensified as he reflected on the nature of Christ's death. It was death by crucifixion. The degradation of such a doom was universally acknowledged. ' May the very name of a cross be far removed not only from the bodies of Roman citizens, but even from their thoughts, their sight, their hearing.' [2] In the Pentateuch it was singled out for special execration : ' Cursed by God is every one who is hanged on a tree.' [3] Paul leaves out the words ' by God ' when he associates the passage with the death of Christ, but his quotation of it in Gal. iii. 13 shows its importance for his thought. This particular death lies under the curse of the Law. And Paul cannot tear his mind away from the significance of such a ban. ' He humbled himself, becoming obedient as far as death, and that the death of the cross.' [4] What could this unspeakable shame mean for the Messiah of God, the ' Lord of glory ' ? Christ could not lie under any Divine curse. The thought was blasphemy. And yet, as Paul was convinced, Christ had given Himself willingly to the cross.

We have already tried to estimate the interpretations of the death of Christ which Paul must have found in the Christian community when he entered it. Although the data are meagre, it is plain that two main traditions were being emphasised. On the one hand, the crucifixion was no mere accident, but an integral part of the Divine purpose. On the other, it was felt that the whole experience was illuminated by the mysterious hints and suggestions

---

[1] *Berachoth*, 33a (qu. by Schechter, *op. cit.*, p. 247).
[2] Cic. *pro C. Rabirio*, v. 10.
[3] Deut. xxi. 23 (LXX).
[4] Phil. ii. 8.

of such Old Testament passages as Isaiah liii. There, unquestionably, the ' Servant of Jahweh ' was represented as bearing the burden of sins not His own, as giving Himself for a sin-offering.   Hence the idea of propitiation, which in post-exilic Judaism received an extraordinary prominence in the sacrificial system, was sure to attach itself to reflection on the death of Christ.   It is also noteworthy that in 4 Maccabees (xvii. 22, vi. 29), a Jewish document which probably belongs to the first half of the first century A.D., the conception that righteous men atone for sinners is clearly set forth.   We have seen that the language which Paul often uses in connection with the death of Christ reflects the terminology of Isaiah liii.   And the fact that Jesus' own mind, when He spoke of the significance of His mission, reveals the influence of these Old Testament ideas, must have powerfully affected the drift of Paul's thought.

It is probably accurate to say that Paul has no fully elaborated theory of the significance of the death of Christ, but we can discern the outlines of certain attempted constructions.   These have their starting-point in principles belonging to the religious heritage of his race, modified by his personal experience and interpreted in the light of his communion with the risen Lord.   We might expect that one who had found his sorest bondage in the tyranny of the Law and who regarded its claims, which he could not satisfy, as aggravating sin and provoking resentment against God, would bring the death of Christ into some connection with his deliverance.   This he does from two divergent but related standpoints.   First of all, he regards men as confronted by the Law as an imperious, almost personified power, which issues its commands and punishes disobedience.   Now men were unable to render a complete obedience, they were unable to achieve righteousness.   But for the Law it was all or nothing.   Those who failed came under its curse.[1]   Here is one ray of light for him on the mystery of the cross.   Here is an explanation of the curse which Christ voluntarily bore.   ' Christ

[1] Gal. iii. 10.

redeemed us from the curse of the law, having become accursed on our behalf.' [1] He had never been guilty of disobedience. But in accordance with the will of the Father He suffered for men the penalty of the broken Law : it exhausted its claim in the vicarious Redeemer. For it was a recognised principle that ' he who has died is absolved from sin.' [2] Those, therefore, who are united to Him by faith are for ever released from its obligations. They have no longer to torment themselves with a fruitless struggle. Christ is ' the end of the law with a view to righteousness to every believer.' [3] ' Him who knew not sin he (God) made sin on our behalf (i.e. dealt with as a sinner : appointed for him the cross) that we might become the righteousness of God in him.' [4] They are accepted in Christ.[5] In Him a right relation to God becomes once for all possible.

More or less closely linked with this is another interpretation on which he lays emphasis. In Rom. viii. 3 he refers the ineffectiveness of the Law in procuring righteousness to the resistance of the flesh. The ' flesh,' as we have seen, is Paul's description of human nature as it is known in actual experience, i.e. as defiled by sin. Sin, like the Law, is represented almost as a personal Power. It wars against the higher aspirations of the soul and prevents obedience to the righteous will of God. Therefore, if sin is to be vanquished, the flesh must somehow be robbed of its vitality. Now Christ, in becoming incarnate, entered into the common life of humanity, conceived by Paul as the living organism of ' sinful flesh,' [6] in order to redeem it. His death was a judgment upon the flesh, i.e. upon sinful human nature with which He had identified Himself, and which He represented as the Second Adam.[7] Those who become one with Him through faith are included in that judgment. But in the death which was sin's condemnation He passed out of all relation to sin.[8] The resurrection was the triumphant proof that He had got

[1] Gal. iii. 13.
[2] Rom. vi. 7.
[3] Rom. x. 4.
[4] 2 Cor. v. 21.
[5] Eph. i. 6.
[6] Rom. viii. 3.
[7] 1 Cor. xv. 22, 45 ; Rom. v. 12-19.
[8] Rom. vi. 10.

beyond the reach of its dominion. So all who have been
united with Him are sharers in His crucifixion and His
resurrection.[1] Their old nature was crucified along with
Him. They now live in Him to God.[2] This new life into
which they have passed is the life of the Spirit.[3]

These closely related interpretations of the death of
Christ are perhaps the nearest approach on Paul's part to
a theoretical construction. It is easy to see how the ideas
of atonement and sacrifice may be found in them, although
they are not definitely expressed. In the first instance,
Christ is represented as giving Himself up willingly to
endure that which men merited because of their disobedience. He atones for their sins. 'As through the
disobedience of the one man [Adam] the many were
constituted sinners, so also through the obedience of the
one the many shall be constituted righteous.'[4] Through
Him they receive reconciliation with God. In the second
there are similar implications. Christ's voluntary death
means the doom of sin, that sin which hindered men from
entering upon the right relation to God. So He removes
all barriers and enables them to come into fellowship with
the Father through Himself. It is obvious, however, that
there is no attempt to equate the sacrifice with any special
rite of Jewish ceremonial. Even when in 1 Cor. v. 7 (M.)
he says, 'Christ, our paschal lamb, was sacrificed,' the
context shows that he is only using a metaphor. A similar
general statement in Rom. iii. 24 f. suggests that we are
not to ask in detail what constitutes the propitiation:
'Justified for nothing by his grace through the redemption
which is in Christ Jesus, whom God set forth in propitiatory
power[6] by his blood (i.e. by his death) to be received by
faith.'[7] The clause which follows, 'in order to demonstrate
his righteousness at the present time, that he might be
righteous himself, and accept as righteous him who believes
in Jesus,' simply points out that the cross makes plain that

[1] Rom. vi. 6 ; Gal. ii. 19.   [2] Rom. vi. 11.
[3] Rom. viii. 10.   [4] Rom. v. 19.   [5] 2 Cor. v. 18.
[6] So Denney.   [7] Rom. iii. 24, 25.

God cannot trifle with sin, for there Christ submits to its doom, and that all who, in union with Him, assent to this judgment of God upon sin, are accepted in His sight as righteous. Paul makes no attempt to explain the precise bearing of the propitiation on God.

Plainly, his treatment of the theme is many-sided. He seems to be feeling out for analogies (necessarily imperfect) by which he can express the discovery which has flashed upon his inmost soul, that the Divine heart suffers in and with and for the sin of the world. As Wernle has well said,[1] ' Paul interpreted the atoning death from above, instead of from beneath.' In his view, God is the inspiring Power in it from beginning to end. Nothing is so true to his profoundest conception as the statement that ' God was in Christ reconciling the world unto himself.' [2] For Paul's deepest experience there was no sense of a transaction between the Father and the Son. The Divine attitude of grace towards the sinful is paramount.

It may be well at this point to illustrate in a few sentences the richness and breadth of Paul's interpretation of the death of Christ, gathering up part of the material which has already been used. (a) Often he simply emphasises the fact of Christ's love in dying : e.g. Gal. ii. 20, ' The Son of God, who loved me and gave himself for me ' ; 2 Cor. v. 14, ' The love of Christ constrains us who have reached this conviction, one died for all.' (b) He also regards the cross as an overpowering exhibition of the love of God : e.g. Rom. v. 8, ' God proves his own love towards us, because while we were still sinners, Christ died for us ' ; viii. 32, ' He who spared not his own Son, but gave him up for us all, shall he not with him give us all else besides ? ' (c) The death of Christ is the great instrument of God's own reconciliation between men and Himself : e.g. Rom. v. 10, ' If, when we were enemies, we were reconciled to God by the death of his Son ' ; 2 Cor. v. 19 (quoted above). (d) On the cross Christ made atonement for sin : e.g. Rom. v. 6, ' While we were still weak, Christ died in due

[1] *Anfänge*, p. 146.　　　　[2] 2 Cor. v. 19.

time for the ungodly ' ;   Rom. iii. 24-26 (quoted above).
(e) Christ's death is a redemption from evil : e.g. Gal. iii. 13,
' Christ redeemed us from the curse of the law, having
become accursed for us ' ; Eph. i. 7, ' In whom we have
redemption through his blood, the forgiveness of our sins.'
(f) Christ's death makes possible the destruction of the
principle of sin in human nature : e.g. Rom. vi. 6, ' Knowing this that our old man was crucified with him, that the
body of sin might be destroyed, so that we should no longer
be in bondage to sin ' ; Rom. viii. 3, ' God, sending his
own Son in the likeness of sinful death and for sin, condemned sin in the flesh.'   (g) Christ's death is a willing
sacrifice on His part : e.g. Eph. v. 2, ' As Christ also loved
us, and gave himself for us an offering and a sacrifice
to God ' ; 1 Cor. v. 7, ' Christ, our paschal lamb, was
sacrificed.'

This classification is by no means exhaustive, yet it is
sufficient to reveal the depths and heights which Paul had
discovered in the Cross of Christ. It suggests that the
apostle could never be content to confine the interpretation
of so unfathomable an aspect of the self-manifestation of
God to men within the frame-work of any single formula.
Indeed, his discussion of what he calls the ' folly ' of the
cross (1 Cor. i. 18–ii. 5) as contrasted with the more intellectual or rationalising presentation of the Gospel which
found favour at Corinth, and which he designates ' wisdom,'
implies that he trusted to the direct appeal of Christ
crucified to the restless, sin-burdened conscience.

In any case, the ultimate clue to the meaning of the
cross for Paul's mind is to be found in his own experience.
When he exclaims, ' I have been crucified with Christ,'
or when he declares, ' We were buried with him through our
baptism into his death, that as Christ was raised from the
dead through the glory of the Father, so we also should
walk in newness of life,' [1] we do not require to look for an
explanation of his figures in the mystery-cults of Attis or
Osiris. He is using the great events of the Passion to set

[1] Rom. vi. 4.

forth the transformation of his own life which has been brought about through his union with Christ by faith. As Christ, in dying, realised to the full the Divine judgment on sin and never flinched from His loyalty to righteousness, so the Christian, identifying himself with Christ's attitude to sin, through the power of Christ in his soul vanquishes the evil bias of his nature. As Christ could not be holden of death, but, in virtue of the Spirit of holiness which was His life-principle, rose to glory, so the Christian, clinging to the risen Lord, is raised into the new atmosphere of glad obedience to the Divine will.[1] Accordingly, Paul's large conception of the death of Christ is an endeavour, by means of inherited as well as freshly minted ideas, to expound the significance of his contact with a gracious, forgiving God in Jesus Christ. However theoretical certain elements in it may appear, the heart of it is a profound and soul-satisfying vision of God. And so the word of the cross becomes on his lips a call to repentance, faith, love, and obedience.

(c) The New Relation to God—its Beginning, Development, and Issues

For Paul, religion denoted fundamentally the right attitude to God. In his pre-Christian days he had taken for granted that the will of God for men was embodied in the legal code of Judaism. Hence men's sole obligation was to obey. But as they found that to be impossible, their religious outlook was hopeless. There was nothing more to be done. The supreme wonder of Paul's conversion-crisis was that there God took the initiative. That was his unassailable conviction. The God who met him in

---

[1] Paul regards the ritual of Baptism as an impressive picture of the Christian's crucial experience. As, in Christ's name, he is plunged into the baptismal water, he passes out of contact with his old environment, he dies to his past. As he emerges out of the water, he enters into a new environment, which is the realm of the Spirit, or 'the kingdom of the Son of God's love' (Col. i. 13). To associate magical notions with Paul's view of Baptism is to misconceive the whole manner of his approach to Christ. We shall discuss the topic in a later section.

Jesus Christ transferred him into a realm of forgiveness and peace and hope. Of course he was conscious of this gracious transformation long before he attempted to analyse its significance. In any case it must be noted that the various descriptions he gives of it are regulated by the circumstances in which they are given and the purposes for which they are intended. We do not for a moment minimise the central importance which he assigns to the conception of Justification by Faith. But in this case, too, environment counts. It is not accidental that Justification is most prominent in those Epistles which directly reflect the burning controversy with Judaism regarding the validity of the Law into which Paul had to plunge for the defence of his missionary Gospel. And the very emergence of this controversy intensified the emphasis which he laid on the idea.

J. Weiss may be right in asserting that the most comprehensive description of salvation in Paul is Reconciliation.[1] Both here and in Justification the crucial feature consists, as we have suggested above, in the initiative of God. That is a practical certainty for Paul, whatever be the terms in which he formulates it. And he exults in it as the antithesis of his old Pharisaic belief. Let us observe what this means. For Pharisaic Judaism the centre of gravity lay in the doctrine of Retribution at God's great day of reckoning. The history of apocalyptic thought shows how, along with the growth of individualism in religion, a growth plainly visible in Ezekiel, who has not unfairly been called 'the father of apocalyptic,' the idea of retribution became more and more prominent, until at length it might be regarded, in Bousset's phrase, as 'the shibboleth of the pious.'[2] Now originally this conception marked a deeper understanding of the moral order. It was a reaction against the simple and superficial view current in Israel, that righteousness of conduct was rewarded by material prosperity, while ungodliness was visited with outward affliction and loss. But when

---

[1] *Op. cit.*, p. 384.   [2] *Die Religion d. Judentums*,[2] p. 222.

in a time of sore calamity men could only appeal to the
justice of God, the doctrine was apt to overshadow other
elements in the Divine action which could not be ignored
with impunity. For sensitive consciences the conception
had a double edge. Soon it began to react on the idea of
God with serious consequences. Judgment became the
supreme function of the Almighty. And when the standard
of judgment was an elaborate code of precepts, it was no
wonder that those who faced the facts shuddered with
foreboding at the thought of the final verdict.

For Paul, Reconciliation took the place of Retribution.
On the basis of unassailable personal experience, he can
describe his Gospel as ' the ministry of reconciliation.' [1]
He can say of himself : ' I am an ambassador on Christ's
behalf, God appealing by me, as it were, I entreat you, on
Christ's behalf, to be reconciled to God.' [2] Through his
contact with the risen Christ, his whole conception of the
Divine attitude to men has been revolutionised. God's
disposition towards them is not cold, not even impartial.
He yearns for men's love. Christ's sacrifice, which is God's
sacrifice, is the convincing demonstration of it. So Paul's
Gospel, which is really the formulation of his own discovery
of God in Christ, pleads with men to accept the gift which
He offers in His Son, to allow the Father to restore
His erring children to His fellowship. The initial step
in this wonderful redeeming process Paul calls ' being
justified.' Its most startling expression is found in the
phrase : ' He that justifies the ungodly.' [3]

It need scarcely be said that the idea of Justification has
its background in the Old Testament. Typical instances
are Isa. v. 23 : ' Woe unto them . . . which justify the
wicked for a bribe ' ; [4] and Exod. xxiii. 7 : ' I will not
justify the wicked.' [5] These passages reveal the forensic
meaning of the term, ' to give a decision in favour of.'

---

[1] 2 Cor. v. 18.   [2] 2 Cor. v. 20.   [3] Rom. iv. 5.
[4] In the LXX (which Paul seems always to use): οὐαὶ . . . οἱ δικαι-
οῦντες τὸν ἀσεβῆ ἕνεκεν δώρων.
[5] The LXX here varies from the Massoretic text : οὐ δικαιώσεις τὸν
ἀσεβῆ ἕνεκεν δώρων. F omits ἕνεκεν δώρων.

That of course implies : ' to pronounce them not guilty.'
When the final verdict of God upon individual lives was
placed in the forefront of Jewish religious thought, the
supreme problem for anxious souls came to be : ' Shall I
be acquitted or condemned, declared righteous ($\delta\iota\kappa\alpha\iota\omega\theta\hat{\eta}\nu\alpha\iota$)
or ungodly, in the great day of reckoning ? ' The question
had been a burning one for Paul, as for all earnest Pharisees.
And now the man who had despaired of obtaining a favourable verdict on the ground of achieving obedience to the
law, who had concluded that sin was too strong for him,
joyfully recognises that a new order has been unveiled.
To quote his own words : ' Now we have a righteousness
of God disclosed apart from law altogether : it is attested
by the law and the prophets, but it is a righteousness of
God which comes by believing in Jesus Christ. And it is
meant for all who have faith. No distinctions are drawn.
All have sinned, all come short of the glory of God, but
they are justified for nothing by his grace through the
ransom provided by Christ Jesus.' [1] In this connection the
new attitude or relation to God is called ' righteousness.'
That was the attainment aimed at in legal obedience.
Now it comes or is brought about, not by laborious efforts,
but by believing in Jesus Christ. It is the gift of God to
faith. We have seen what faith means for Paul : not the
assent to certain truths, although that is included : not
even primarily the belief that God is and that He is the
rewarder of those that diligently seek Him,[2] although that
is for him a presupposition : but the trustful surrender of
his whole being to Christ, as crucified and risen, and the
complete identification of himself with Christ's attitude to
God and to sin. Hence God's gracious judgment on a life
grounded, as Paul represents it to be, on faith, is not
arbitrary or unreal. It presupposes a very definite relation
to Christ. And when the apostle speaks of ' justifying the
ungodly,' he means that the sinner has, in dependence on
Christ, turned his face in a new direction, and that God in

---

[1] Rom. iii. 21-24 (M.).   [2] Heb. xi. 6.

His mercy deals with him as with one who has made a fresh start. Paul is too practical not to recognise that the progress of the new life may in many cases be slow. That accounts for his frequent exhortations to members of the Christian community to be on their guard against evil, *e.g.* Rom. vi. 13 : ' You must not let sin have your members for the service of vice, you must dedicate yourselves to God as men who have been brought from death to life.' [1] But he has such complete confidence in the faithfulness of God, whose purpose of love lies behind every changed career, that he cannot believe that a life in which the Divine Spirit has begun to work will ever be lost.[2]

Justification, which can scarcely be distinguished from forgiveness, except that it emphasises the *positive* element in God's act of grace, places men on a new footing in relation to God. Peace and joy take possession of their souls. The love of God is shed abroad within them by the Holy Spirit.[3] This relationship, from which fear and shrinking are banished, Paul calls Adoption. The term sounds technical, but when its significance is examined we discover the very heart of Paul's religion. It is needless to look for its origin in the usage of mystery-cults. It is, as we have already seen, a transcript of his own experience. There is only a formal distinction between it and the ' birth from above ' of the Fourth Gospel. In the one case, emphasis is laid on admission into the family of God, in the other on the operation of the life of God. In both instances the result is the relation of a son or child to the Father. Here, obviously, Paul comes into direct line with the central teaching of Jesus. For Jesus the child is the emblem of simplicity and artlessness. He loves and reverences and depends upon his Father. He trusts Him completely, and is sure that He will always do the best for him. These human ties are but dim reflections of those which link the soul to God. But Jesus' use of them indicates that in the child relationship He discerns the most life-like picture of

---

[1] M.
[2] *E.g.* Phil. i. 6.
[3] Rom. v. 1, 5.

that fellowship with God which is the true end for human personality.

We have noticed in an earlier section how close is the affinity between Paul's position and that of Jesus in His classical exposition of Sonship, the Parable of the Lost Son. The profound utterance of the father may be recalled : ' Child, thou art always with me, and all that I have is thine.' [1] It might almost be felt that Paul's mind had been dwelling on these words, when he exclaims : ' All things are yours.' [2] Here is revealed an element which brings a sense of exultation to the spirit of the apostle, what he elsewhere calls ' the glorious liberty of the children of God.' This was the direct antithesis of his former religious condition. For that he could find no name but ' slavery.' It was all compact of fear and uncertainty and distrust and foreboding. In Christ he is master of circumstances— the world, life, death, things present and things to come. For now he is an heir of God.[3] This victorious condition Paul always associates with the gift of the Spirit. It gives their content to the prayers of the Christian. Sonship and freedom constitute the atmosphere which the Spirit creates. ' The sons of God are those who are guided by the Spirit of God. You have received no slavish spirit that would make you relapse into fear : you have received the spirit of sonship. And when we cry, Abba, Father, it is this Spirit testifying along with our own spirit that we are children of God.' [4]

The keynote of this life of sonship is heard in the term ' glorying ' which Paul delights to use.[5] Its occurrence in Rom. ii. 17, 23 suggests that in the vocabulary of Judaism it expressed the satisfaction of the man who had made good his claim upon God by fulfilling his legal obligations.[6] If that be so, its significance is all the richer in its new application. For Paul it has been stripped of every hint

[1] Luke xv. 31.   [2] 1 Cor. iii. 22.
[3] Rom. viii. 17.
[4] Rom. viii. 14-16 (M.) ; cf. Gal. iv. 6.
[5] καυχᾶσθαι: e.g. Rom. v. 2, 3, 11 ; Phil. iii. 3.
[6] See J. Weiss on 1 Cor. i. 29.

of self-confidence. Rather does it now connote the most complete self-abnegation : ' God forbid that I should glory except in the cross of our Lord Jesus Christ, by which the world has been crucified to me and I to the world.' [1] Everything that counts, everything that has enduring worth, is bound up with Christ. He is the sole standard of values. He kindles the heart with an exultation which the sharpest tribulations are powerless to quench.[2]

Now this exultant mood of Paul's is constantly related to the future. Typical of his attitude is Rom. v. 2 : ' We exult in hope of the glory of God.' And so we are reminded that for him both Justification and Adoption are in a very real sense daring anticipations of God's final purpose. An illustration of his complete view of Justification is to be found in Gal. v. 5 : ' We by the Spirit, as the result of faith, eagerly expect the righteousness we hope for.' The statement is extraordinarily comprehensive. Christians possess the gift of the Spirit, which is the Divine response to faith. But this possession is not an end in itself. It is the basis of a splendid hope, that hope whose content is righteousness. And righteousness here means the perfected relationship to God which can never be annulled. That relationship is made final at the consummation of the Kingdom when Christ shall appear. Adoption is viewed by Paul in the same perspective. It is of course a reality here and now. But it has by no means reached its final stage. This comes out clearly in Rom. viii. 23 : ' Even we ourselves who have the Spirit as a foretaste of the future, even we sigh to ourselves as we wait for the redemption of the body that means our full sonship.' [3]

Paul seldom refers to the stages by which believers are prepared for the consummation. Occasionally he reveals a sense of incompleteness which spurs him on to higher endeavour : ' Not that I have already attained this or am already perfect . . . my one thought is . . . to press on to the goal for the prize of God's high call in Christ

[1] Gal. vi. 14. [2] Rom. v. 3. [3] M.

Jesus.' [1]   Once or twice he speaks of the actual process :
' Though my outward man decay, my inner man is renewed
day by day ' ; [2] and more concretely : ' We all with unveiled face (as contrasted with the veiled face of Moses
in Old Testament story), reflecting the glory of the Lord,
are being transformed into the same likeness from one
glory to another—for this comes of the Lord the Spirit.' [3]
When it is remembered that glory in Paul's usage means
the revealed nature of God, the Divine life as manifested,
we can realise the grandeur of his conception of the
existence which awaits the redeemed soul.

We have seen how inevitable it was that Paul, steeped
as he must have been in the eschatological tradition of
Judaism, and participating in those ardent expectations of
the coming æon which the early Church associated with
the teaching of Jesus, should keep his gaze fixed on the
Parousia of Christ which is to usher in the final Messianic
salvation.   In his earliest letter, he describes the Christian
life of his converts at Thessalonica as ' serving a living and
true God and waiting for the coming of his Son from
heaven.' [4]   In one written nearer the middle of his career
he speaks of ' these days of waiting till our Lord Jesus
Christ is revealed.' [5]   And in that which marks the close
of his activity he characterises his readers and himself
as those who ' eagerly wait for the Saviour from heaven,
the Lord Jesus Christ, who will transform the body of our
humiliation (i.e. the earthly life) into the likeness of the
body of his glory.' [6]   It is, however, scarcely possible to
trace in his writings any consistent scheme of eschatology.
Thus, for example, he never discusses such questions as
the fate of those who reject the Gospel of Christ,[7] or a
possible intermediate state.   And although the idea of
the final Judgment appears frequently, it is difficult to
determine his view of its precise relation to the other events
of the End.   Besides the Parousia, to which reference has

[1] Phil. iii. 12-14 (M.).   [2] 2 Cor. iv. 16.
[3] 2 Cor. iii. 18 (partly M.).   [4] 1 Thess. 1. 10.
[5] 1 Cor. i. 7 (M.).   [6] Phil. iii. 20.
[7] These he designates ' the perishing ' : e.g. 2 Cor. iv. 3 ; 1 Cor. i. 18.

been made, Paul lays special emphasis on the resurrection, and this becomes more prominent as his expectation of surviving until the Parousia grows more uncertain. Naturally the picture which he has formed owes much to his conception of the resurrection of Christ. It will mean a transformation of being with a view to entrance into a new order, as it meant for Christ.[1] Such a transformation he also anticipates for those who are still alive when Christ returns.[2] He gives various hints of the process for which he so eagerly longs. It is an exchanging of that earthly body of flesh which he feels so burdensome and which ' cannot inherit the kingdom of God,' [3] for a spiritual ' organism,' prepared by the Divine power, and destined to be a fit instrument for the perfected spirit.[4] He can describe it as ' the image of the heavenly,' which is equivalent to the likeness of the exalted Christ. This he names in the passage already quoted from Philippians, ' the body (or organism) of his glory.' That is to say, believers are to share in the exalted life of the Lord Himself.

Thus we are brought back to the significance for Paul of the Parousia. Now in so far as he is true to the eschatological tradition of Judaism, this represents to him the complete triumph of God, the consummation of the Divine kingdom. And occasionally that aspect is placed in the forefront.[5] But in contrast with the usual tendency of Jewish apocalyptic he is as a rule far more concerned with the destiny of individual believers than with the realised victory of God as such. In the great epoch of Christ's appearing, death is to be swallowed up by life,[6] and this will be the victory of those who are united to him. Hence the condition of blessedness which the Parousia inaugurates is specially designated ' life ' or ' eternal life.' [7] It is the disclosure of a high potentiality already present. ' You died,' he says, ' and your life has been hid with

[1] Phil. iii. 20.   [2] 1 Cor. xv. 51-53.
[3] 2 Cor. v. 1, 2, 4 ; 1 Cor. xv. 50.
[4] 2 Cor. v. 1 ; 1 Cor. xv. 44-46.
[5] See especially 1 Cor. xv. 24-28.
[6] 1 Cor. xv. 54, 55.   [7] Occasionally ' salvation.'

of legalism. No one had been better acquainted than
Paul with the tormenting challenge of innumerable
ordinances. His pre-Christian view of obligation had never
got beyond these. But now, in Christ, all separate maxims
—and the apostle has still to urge these on his converts—
are absorbed in the high ideal which Jesus has promulgated.
The new spirit is the decisive factor. That spirit is to
determine the kind of activity for which every separate
situation calls. The more completely the Christian
suffers the Divine power to possess him, the more certainly
will he be delivered from morbid scruples regarding each
separate moral decision he has to make. His enlightened
judgment will enable him to strike the balance between
freedom and self-limitation. Paul's discussion of this process in Rom. xiv.[1] is a classical example of spiritual and
ethical tact. And no better instance of his normative
position could be found than Gal. v. 14 : ' The whole law
is fulfilled in one sentence, Thou shalt love thy neighbour
as thyself.' It is surely not a mere coincidence that this was
the obligation which Jesus placed next to that of complete
devotion to God.

This recognition of Paul's supreme motive at once
suggests that, like all healthy moral energy, his ethic will
be largely social. And the range of the term ' social '
will be regulated by his circumstances and environment.
Not that this latter influence must be exaggerated. For
when Paul urges the members of the Christian community
at Rome, ' Bless those that persecute you, bless and do not
curse them,' [2] it is plain that he looks far beyond the circle
of his brethren in Christ. And when he follows up such
injunctions by bidding them to ' be in debt to no man
except to love one another,' [3] we cannot doubt that his
conception of ' neighbourship ' was derived from that of his
Master and equally wide in its scope.[4] But due importance
ought to be assigned to the situation in which he found
himself. As an ardent missionary, he was absorbed in the

---

[1] Cf. 1 Cor. viii. and ix.   [2] Rom. xii. 14.
[3] Rom. xiii. 8.   [4] Luke x. 30-37.

work of spreading the Gospel over the Græco-Roman world. No part of his labour was more pressing than that of guiding his converts into a life worthy of the name they bore. Hence there is nothing abstract or theoretical in his moral teaching. It reaches down to the most elementary duties, the avoidance of theft, drunkenness, lying : and it ascends to the moral heights from which Jesus had beckoned, self-denial, love of enemies, forgiveness. Above all, the Christian community affords the best training in ethical discipline. Plainly the types of moral action with which Paul deals will depend upon the actual problems that confront the immature Christian communities. A primary question will be that of their relation to their pagan environment. Paul handles it with masterly sagacity. It came before him definitely in a request for advice from Corinth regarding sacrificial meat. Some members of the Church, taking full advantage of the Christian position that an idol is ' nothing,' [1] are able to treat the situation with indifference. It matters nothing to them that the meat they eat has been consecrated in a temple. ' The earth is the Lord's, and the fulness thereof.' For others the old associations are decisive. It is a violation of conscience to partake of such food.[2] Which attitude is to be regulative ? ' All things are allowed,' says the apostle, ' but not all things are expedient. All things are allowed, but not all things edify.' [3] Hence, ' it is a good thing neither to eat flesh nor to drink wine, nor anything that your brother feels to be a stumbling-block.' For Paul the criterion of love among the brethren is normative.[4]

A further point of discussion was the relation of the sexes. Naturally Paul used no uncertain language regarding all breaches of personal purity, a subject on which gross laxness prevailed in heathen society. Nor does he shrink from taking the highest ground : ' Do you not know that your bodies are members (literally, limbs) of Christ ?

[1] 1 Cor. viii. 4.   [2] 1 Cor. viii. 7.
[3] 1 Cor. x. 23.   [4] Rom. xiv. 21.

Shall I then take the members of Christ and make them the members of a harlot ? God forbid.' [1] It is from the same lofty platform that he estimates the position of woman. In this matter he has been seriously misunderstood. His injunction that women should keep silence in the public services of the Church [2] has been seized upon as an indication of his contempt for the sex. In reality the advice is given lest Christian women should incur the suspicion of a forwardness which offended the sensibility of the ancient world.[3] Paul's position is clearly discernible in Gal. iii. 28 : ' There is no longer Jew or Greek, there is no longer slave or freeman, there is no longer male or female : you are all one in Christ Jesus.' This passage also goes to the root of the apostle's attitude towards slavery. But there happens to be extant an application to a particular case of the principle here laid down. Onesimus, the slave of Philemon, a Christian belonging to the community at Colossae, had run away from his master. He drifted to Rome, and there under Paul's influence became a convert to Christianity.[4] The apostle had the delicate duty of sending him back to his master : and in the singularly beautiful note which he gives him to hand to Philemon he reveals his own standpoint. ' Perhaps this was why you and he were parted for a while, that you might get him back for good, no longer a mere slave, but something more than a slave, a beloved brother : especially dear to me, but how much more to you as a man and as a Christian.'[5] If a slave can be treated as ' a beloved brother,' his social position has lost its bitterness. If Paul's principle of the oneness of Christians in Christ be adopted, slavery as an institution is doomed. He made, indeed, no attempt to interfere in any formal way with the existing social order. He goes so far as to advise slaves not to be troubled by their condition. ' Of course, if you do find it possible to get

---

[1] 1 Cor. vi. 15.   [2] 1 Cor. xiv. 34.
[3] Some scholars regard verses 33b-35 as a later interpolation. Verses 34-35 are placed by most Western authorities after verse 40. Certainly the words seem to contradict 1 Cor. xi. 5. See J. Weiss *ad. loc.*
[4] Philem. 10.   [5] Philem. 15, 16 (M.).

free, you had better avail yourself of the opportunity. But a slave who is called to be in the Lord is a freedman of the Lord.'[1]   As the context of this passage shows, the consideration which weighs with him is the imminence of the Parousia.[2]

When Paul deals with the relation of the Christian to the State, it is from the standpoint of the practical missionary. He lived in the epoch of the *Pax Romana*. Nowhere was the boon of a carefully organised yet non-despotic government more highly prized than in the Provinces which were the scene of Paul's evangelistic work. It is not, therefore, surprising that he preserves an attitude of respect towards the Imperial rule. Here, as in his whole estimate of society, he is guided by the principle which he lays down in Rom. xii. 18 : ' If it be possible, so far as that rests with you, live peaceably with all men.' But he directly enjoins submission to the State, on the ground that it has been divinely ordained to rule righteously and put down evil.[3] Christians are to discharge their duties to the State as genuinely moral obligations. '

It has often been observed that at various points of his ethical outlook Paul reveals affinities with the popularised philosophy of his time. But from beginning to end it is plain how that outlook was determined by religious motives.

(e) The Body and the Members of Christ

We have found that Paul's ethical teaching is predominantly social. From the nature of the case the society which chiefly absorbs his attention is the Church, the community of Christians. His conception of the Church is most clearly realised by means of his favourite metaphor, the Body of Christ.[4] The previous course of discussion has shown that for Paul the fundamental aspect

---

[1] 1 Cor. vii. 21, 22 (M.).   [2] *Ibid.*, verses 26, 29, 31.
[3] Rom. xiii. 1-7.   [4] See especially 1 Cor. xii. ; Eph. iv. 1-16.

of Christianity is the union of the believer to Christ. That union is constituted by the Spirit, who mediates the life of Christ in response to the faith of the individual. An obvious inference from this process is the communion of Christians in Christ through the same Spirit. The one Spirit, as the real life-principle of the society, suggests the correlative idea of the one Body, the living organism which gives expression to the life of the Spirit. This is ideally the embodiment of the mind and will of Christ. Hence the Christian community is designated by Paul the Body of Christ, and those who belong to it His members. A typical expression of his view is found in Rom. xii. 4, 5: 'As we have many members in one body, and all the members have not the same function, so we, though many, are one body in Christ, and severally members one of another.' [1]

Let us examine the essential features of Paul's idea of the Church, as set forth in this most suggestive figure.

(1) There is a singular lack of reference in the Epistles to *external organisation*. This certainly does not mean that Paul was negligent of order in the life of the Christian society. We have direct evidence of the emphasis which he laid upon it.[2] But his was the period of charismatic functions in the Church.[3] It is highly significant that when he ranks the offices in the Church, he places first apostles, secondly prophets, thirdly teachers.[4] Probably none of these represent permanent officials. They are all persons endowed with a special 'gift' ($\chi\acute{a}\rho\iota\sigma\mu a$), which they readily place at the service of the Christian society. They are to be found where their work is most required. It may be that the terms 'helps' and 'administrations,' which occur later in the same context, stand for the more concrete 'deacons' (literally, 'servants': cf. Mark x. 45, which perhaps helped to establish the usage) and 'overseers' ($\acute{e}\pi\acute{\iota}\sigma\kappa o\pi o\iota$), titles only found in Philippians,[5] which is probably the latest of Paul's Epistles. The

---

[1] Cf. 1 Cor. xii. 12.
[2] E.g. 1 Cor. xiv. 40.
[3] E.g. 1 Cor. xii. 4-11.
[4] 1 Cor. xii. 28.
[5] Phil. i. 1.

existing data suggest that during the period of Paul's activity the organisation of the Church was in a flexible condition. What primarily concerns the apostle is the spiritual vigour of the Body.

(2) The health of the Body depends on the *unity* of the Spirit which pervades it. Paul constantly dwells on this idea ; *e.g.* Eph. iv. 3-6 : ' Endeavouring to keep the unity of the Spirit in the bond of peace. There is one body, and one spirit, as you were called in one hope of your calling ; one Lord, one faith, one baptism, one God and Father of all, who is above all, and through all, and in all.' The important point to be noted in all his utterances on this theme is the *inwardness* of the conception. It seems highly probable, as has been hinted, that there was as yet no such thing as uniformity of organisation. Paul's general view of the situation, in so far as it can be reconstructed from the available evidence, would lead us to suppose that he was prepared for large divergence in the methods of Christian service. For he delights to dwell on the manifoldness of the gifts bestowed by the Spirit for the upbuilding of the Christian society. But he constantly keeps in the forefront the obligation to unity of mind and heart in the separate Christian communities. ' I beseech you, brethren,' he writes to the Corinthians,[1] ' by the name of the Lord Jesus Christ that you all speak the same thing, and that there be no divisions among you ; but that you be perfectly knit together in the same mind and the same judgment.' This is simply the application to a particular case of his great general principle : ' God has tempered the body together, with a special dignity for the inferior parts, so that there may be no disunion in the body, but that the various members should have a common concern for one another.' [2] That is to say, the supreme object of membership in the Body of Christ is mutual service and helpfulness.

(3) But Paul's conception of the Body of Christ implies **that** the Church is the special representative of her living

[1] 1 Cor. i. 10.   [2] 1 Cor. xii. 24, 25 (M.).

Lord upon earth. Christ is frequently described as the ' Head ' of the Body,[1] and of course that is always presupposed. The head requires the body. The brain controls the limbs. The will demands an instrument to carry out its purposes. Here is outlined the daring idea that the Church is the direct manifestation of the life of Christ to humanity, the supreme witness to the Divine intention for the universe. On the other hand, contact with the Head ensures that the Body shall attain its full development, growing up completely into Him.[2]

A special aspect of the Divine purpose for mankind, which lies close to the apostle's heart, is that on which he may be said to have staked all his activity—the fellowship of Gentiles with Jews in the common salvation of Jesus Christ. The proclamation of this great discovery he regards as his peculiar function : ' The Divine secret was disclosed to me by a revelation . . . namely, that in Christ Jesus the Gentiles are co-heirs, companions, and co-partners in the promise.' [3]   In this union of those who had been aliens with the members of the historic community of Israel ' in one body through the cross,' Paul recognises the disclosure of ' the full sweep of the Divine wisdom.' [4]

The unity of the members of the Body of Christ in Him their Head receives solemn expression in the sacraments of Baptism and the Lord's Supper. It is absurd to say that ' Paul created the sacramental conception.' [5] He found these rites in the Christian community when he entered it. And there is no evidence to show that he enhanced their importance. It is significant that in so careful and systematic a delineation of his religious beliefs as the Epistle to the Romans there is no reference to the Lord's Supper.[6]

---

[1] *E.g.* Col. i. 18, ii. 19 ; Eph. i. 22.
[2] Col. ii. 19 ; Eph. iv. 12-16.
[3] Eph. iii. 3, 6 (M.) ; similarly Col. i. 25-27.
[4] Eph. iii. 10 (M.).
[5] So Wernle, *Anfänge*, p. 166.
[6] There is no force in the position taken by Professor Lake in his *Earlier Epistles of St. Paul*, p. 384, and elsewhere, that Paul did not need to refer to beliefs which were ' common ground to him and all other Christians.' As a matter of fact he does invariably recur to such beliefs, as, *e.g.*, that in the Holy Spirit.

CH. VI.] FUNDAMENTAL POSITIONS OF PAULINISM 151

And in 1 Cor. i. 17 he distinctly subordinates Baptism to
the preaching of the Gospel. Still, like his fellow-Christians
throughout the Church, he regarded these rites as of real
value for the quickening of faith. No statement in the
Epistles suggests that he looked on Baptism as the originat-
ing cause of faith. Indeed the baptismal formula, 'into
the name of Christ,' takes for granted that the candidate
had come already into a definite relation with Christ—
that he had formed a definite estimate of the ' name ' by
which he was called.[1] Even the utterance of Gal. iii. 27 :
' All of you who had yourselves baptized into Christ have
put on Christ,' in no way conflicts with the clear teaching
of the entire Epistle that faith is primary. For the whole
context shows that in this passage faith is the presupposition
of Baptism.[2] Baptism marks the definite entrance of the
convert into the Christian community. As such it was
an event of epoch-making importance in his history. It
was of course a symbol, and as such Paul uses it to set
forth his profound conception of dying and being buried
with Christ in relation to the old sinful life, and rising with
him to the new life of righteousness.[3] But Baptism is more
than a symbol. As in this impressive rite the convert
takes the decisive step of turning his back on his old
spiritual environment, and making himself over to the
lordship and obedience of Christ, his faith is powerfully
intensified : he receives a fresh inspiration : the solemn
ritual becomes to him a real pledge of the unfailing grace of
God.

It is not otherwise with the Lord's Supper. Paul nowhere
implies that fellowship with Christ is inaugurated by the
Eucharist. He deliberately states his view of its significance in 1 Cor. xi. 26 : ' As often as you eat this bread and
drink this cup, you represent ($\kappa\alpha\tau\alpha\gamma\gamma\epsilon\lambda\lambda\epsilon\tau\epsilon$) the Lord's
death till he come.' To quote a statement which the

[1] See Sokolowski, *Geist u. Leben bei Paulus,* p. 270.
[2] See verses 23, 24, 25, 26 ; so also in Col. ii. 12.
[3] Rom. vi. 3, 4. It is worth noting that in the most remarkable description of this experience (Gal. ii. 19, 20) there is no mention of Baptism.
It is, therefore, quite irrelevant to say that for Paul the experience is
conditioned by Baptism.

present writer has made elsewhere,[1] 'the bread and wine represent not the flesh and blood of Christ as such, but His human person as slain on the cross. Therefore communion with the body and blood of Christ means communion with the Lord as crucified, and all that this involves. Hence we never find the apostle speaking of " eating the flesh " or " drinking the blood " of Christ. He is careful to associate the solemn actions only with the bread and the cup. It is thus apparent that the Lord's Supper sets forth visibly, for Paul, the supreme spiritual experience which he has described in Gal. ii. 19 : " I have been crucified with Christ." And as the apostle can never dissociate the Crucifixion from the Resurrection, the appropriation of the benefits of the death of Christ which is quickened by the sacred celebration will carry with it a like appropriation of the resources of the risen Lord.' Here, as in Baptism, to the believing consciousness the symbol becomes a sacrament, a convincing pledge of the mercy of God in Christ the crucified. But Paul does not, any more than in Baptism, ascribe to the actions a magical effect. The spiritual benefit is the Divine response which is never denied to adoring faith. It may be noted, finally, that the common meal is the most impressive exhibition of the unity of the Body of Christ. Paul is keenly alive to this when he declares : ' Many as we are, we are one bread, one body, since we all partake of the one bread.' [2]

(f) The Cosmic Relations of Christ

Starting from his own experience, Paul was convinced that the most momentous event in the history of the individual was his redemption from sin and from the sway of that hierarchy of evil forces to which he regarded the present world-order as subject. Only by this means could humanity attain the destiny appointed for it in the wisdom and loving-kindness of God. Now the sole medium of the

[1] St. Paul and the Mystery-Religions, p. 270.   [2] 1 Cor. x. 17 (M.).

redemptive process is Christ. He is the Last Adam, the Second Man,[1] who, as life-giving Spirit, counteracts the principle of sin and death which had attained universal sway through the transgression of the First.[2] As such, He becomes the Founder of a new humanity.[3] Hence His incarnation, death, and resurrection are not mere incidents of a personal history. Their bearing is universal. For the establishing of right relations between the God who is over all and the creatures whom He has made for likeness to Himself is central in the world of being, which Paul of course conceives as a moral and spiritual order.

It is an easy and natural step from this position to find in Christ the focus of the cosmic system, the constitutive principle of universal life. Paul's statements are remarkable. Already in 1 Cor. viii. 6 (M.) he speaks of ' one God, the Father, from whom all comes, and for whom we exist, and one Lord, Jesus Christ, by whom all exists and by whom we exist.' But the formulation of the idea is most clearly seen in the Captivity-Epistles, written from his Roman prison towards the close of his career. By this time his great controversies with Judaizers on behalf of the liberty of the Gospel have lost their intensity. Circumstances have thwarted the extension of his own missionary labours. And although he is still in constant communication with all parts of his mission-field, he has some leisure to reflect on the unfathomable significance of that Lord who is the end and aim of his activity, ' in whom are hid all the treasures of wisdom and knowledge.' It is true that in the Epistle to the Colossians, in which especially these meditations find expression, he was confronting a definite situation in the Churches of the Lycus-valley, a challenge by the adherents of an obscure theosophy to the supremacy of Christ. But the whole tone of Colossians and Ephesians, not to speak of the unique passage on the incarnation in so thoroughly practical a letter as Philippians, indicates clearly enough the regions in which his thought was moving.

---

[1] 1 Cor. xv. 45, 47.   [2] Rom. v. 12.   [3] 1 Cor. xv. 22.

The most important statement for our purpose is Col.
i. 15-20, and it is worth noting that Paul links it on to a
reminder of the redemption which his readers have attained
though God's ' beloved Son,' because that is the real basis
in his experience of the cosmic functions of Christ on which
he proceeds to enlarge. ' He is the likeness of the unseen
God,' says the apostle, ' born first before all the creation
—for it was by (better, ' in ') him that all things were
created both in heaven and on earth, both the seen and the
unseen, including thrones, angelic lords, celestial powers
and rulers ; all things have been created by him and for
him ; he is prior to all, and all coheres in him.' Then after
emphasising Christ's headship of His Body, the Church, in
virtue of the pre-eminence He has reached as ' the first
to be born from the dead,' Paul continues : ' It was in him
that the Divine Fulness willed to settle without limit, and
by him it willed to reconcile in his own person all on earth
and in heaven alike, in a peace made by the blood of his
cross.' [1] Thus the paragraph ends as it began in the
atmosphere of redemption.

It is perhaps true to say that the far-reaching inferences
which Paul has here made are already involved in his
conception of Christ as the Son of God. But even if this
be so, it does not alter the conclusion at which we have
already hinted, that in Christ crucified, the Redeemer of
men from an evil order of things and its conqueror,[2]
Paul is assured that he has come into touch with Ultimate
Reality. Hence he feels justified in elaborating the implications which such a Reality involves : pre-existence,
mediation of the Divine activity in creation, the sustaining
principle of the universe, the goal of all being. All these
things are implied in the passage quoted above. But the
fact that, after using an aorist tense to state the creation
of all things by Christ, ' he lapses into perfects and presents,
is a suggestive hint that he contemplates ' Christ's pre-
existence, ' through the medium, so to speak, of the

[1] (M.).   Cf. Eph. i. 10, 22, 23.
[2] Col. ii. 15.

exalted life . . . His function as Creator is proleptically conditioned by his achievement as Saviour.'[1]

The description of Christ's cosmic significance reveals intimate affinities with tendencies of thought current in contemporary Hellenistic speculation. Even the language Paul uses in defining the relations of the created universe to Christ, more especially the prepositional phrases, ' by him,' ' through him,' ' for him,' ' in him,' find remarkable parallels alike in the literature of Stoicism, and (through Stoic influence) in the regular vocabulary of the popularised philosophy of the day.[2] It is natural, as an induction from the facts, to conclude that the apostle has here an apologetic aim in view : that of set purpose he desires to exhibit Christ as satisfying the presuppositions of a type of philosophy of religion which had become influential throughout the Roman Empire. For on every side speculation was busy with the conception of mediating influences between God and the world. The prominence of the Logos-hypostasis in the Stoics and in Philo, who mirrors the movements of his time, indicates the drift of Hellenistic metaphysics. And Paul's statement that ' all coheres in ' Christ reminds us of the common Stoic position that life and order in the universe depend on the world-soul, which is the constitutive principle in the system of created things. This world-soul received the names of Logos and Pneuma in Stoicism. The very term Paul employs in Col. i. 17 for ' coheres ' ($\sigma \upsilon \nu \acute{\epsilon} \sigma \tau \eta \kappa \epsilon \nu$) appears in precisely the same connection in contemporary literature : e.g. in the anonymous Περὶ Κόσμου, ·6 (which has many traces of Stoic influence) : ' All things are of God ($\acute{\epsilon} \kappa\ \Theta \epsilon o \hat{\upsilon}$), and through God ($\delta \iota \grave{\alpha}\ \Theta \epsilon o \hat{\upsilon}$) cohere ($\sigma \upsilon \nu \acute{\epsilon} \sigma \tau \eta \kappa \epsilon \nu$) for us.'[3]

Of course the special occasion which prompted this remarkable formulation of Paul's inferences as to the cosmic functions of Christ was, as has been noted, the emergence in the Churches of the Lycus-valley of a hybrid

[1] H. R. Mackintosh, *The Person of Jesus Christ*, p. 70.
[2] See E. Norden, *Agnostos Theos*, pp. 240-250.
[3] Quoted by Norden, *op. cit.*, p. 250. Other instances in J. Weiss, *Das Urchristentum*, p. 370, *n.* 1.

blend of doctrines in which the worship of angels, ecstatic
visions, and ascetic ordinances held an important place.
In Paul's eyes the peculiar peril was the attempt to reach
God by another path than Christ. The propagandists
were evidently emphasising the existence of a chain of
mediating beings linking the material to the spiritual.
Through purifying mystery-ritual the soul could come into
touch with these, and thus attain the Divine. Paul
attacks the error by exalting Christ as the sole channel of
life and power between God and the universe, and in the
process discloses the large horizons of his thought regarding
the ontological significance of Him whom he had come to
know as Redeemer and Lord.

It is by no means improbable that here Paul, as at other
points, touched Hellenistic speculations through a Jewish
medium. In the Wisdom-literature of Judaism the conception of Wisdom had received a remarkable personification, as, e.g., in Prov. viii. 22, 23, 29, 30 : 'The Lord
possessed me in the beginning of his way before his works
of old. I was set up from everlasting . . . When he
appointed the foundations of the earth, then I was by him
as a master-worker '; and Wisd. of Sol. ix. 2 : ' By
means of thy wisdom thou didst create man.' It is
difficult to draw any sharp distinction between this
personification and the Spirit of God. ' She is a breath of
the power of God,' says the author of Wisd. of Sol. (vii.
25 ff.), ' and a clear effluence of the glory of the Almighty
. . . She is an effulgence (ἀπαύγασμα) from everlasting
light, and an unspotted mirror of the working of God, and
an image (εἰκών) of his goodness. And she, being one,
hath power to do all things, and remaining in herself
reneweth all things : and from generation to generation
passing into holy souls she maketh men friends of God
and prophets.' Paul would be familiar with this realm of
thought, for it was influential in the Rabbinic schools.
It is noteworthy that he designates Christ the ' image '
(εἰκών) of God, using the very term applied to Wisdom
in the passage just cited. Philo gives the same description

of the Logos, an hypostasis with which Paul was probably
acquainted. But Paul had also identified the exalted
Lord with the Spirit.[1] Hence, when he endeavours to set
forth the universal bearing of Christ, who had been for
him not a metaphysical abstraction but a living, redeeming personality, it was natural that he should express his
ideas by means of thought-forms and a terminology which
had already provided a meeting-point for Hellenistic and
Jewish speculation. It may be observed incidentally that
it was easy for a thinker of that age to pass from personified
concepts to personality.

The evidence of 1 Cor. viii. 6 suggests that, apart from
the definite situation presupposed in Colossians, Paul's
mind was occupied with the ultimate consequences of his
profound conception of Christ. There are no clear data
to establish the position, often hastily affirmed by some
modern scholars, that these consequences were involved
in the apocalyptic idea of Messiah. We are on far surer
ground in regarding them as inferences from what he had
discovered Christ to be in his own experience and in that
of the Church, inferences which he clothed in language
which would appeal to his readers, both Jewish and
Gentile. Only it seems hazardous to attempt a detailed
analysis of his statements. J. Weiss, *e.g.*, commenting on
the phrase ' in him were created all things ' (Col. i. 16),
asserts that these words must be taken in their most literal
sense. ' With his creation all was created : he contains
the All in himself . . . This can only be understood if
Christ is here identified with the Logos. In Philo the
Logos as compendium of all God's creative " ideas " contains the whole world " in idea," the " kosmos noetos."
It is doubtful . . . whether Paul had recourse to this
conception . . . Presumably he conceived of the process
more materially : the pre-mundane Son of God, as " life-
creating Spirit " contained the energies and elements of
all being *realiter* in himself : thus he was in a certain sense
the world itself.' [2] We may admit the close kinship be-

---

[1] *E.g.* 2 Cor. iii. 17 ; cf. 1 Cor. xv. 45.   [2] *Christus*, pp. 46, 47.

tween Paul's idea of the pre-incarnate Christ and the contemporary notion of the Logos. But it is altogether arbitrary to read into the apostle's statements meta-physical conceptions for which there is no evidence in his writings. His thought was, in all likelihood, no more metaphysical than that of the Wisdom-literature of his nation, his affinities with which we have noted above.[1]

We must be content with the same vagueness in esti-mating Paul's description of the final goal for the universe, the ' summing-up of all things in Christ, the things in heaven and the things on earth ' (Eph. i. 10). To force on the words an abstract, pantheistic construction would be to fall into contradiction with various statements of the apostle as to the real individuality of believers in the future glorified existence.

It has already been observed that for Paul the birth, death, and resurrection of Christ are more than events in a personal history. They belong to God's redemptive purpose. They are normative for the development of the world-order, and yet the apostle is so completely dominated by the impression of the historical Person which has been wrought in him through his experience of the living Lord and the tradition current in the community, that only once does he treat of the pre-mundane existence of Christ, which he is compelled to postulate in view of the central religious significance he has discovered in Him. The passage occurs incidentally in an exhortation to lowliness, and its primary purpose is to emphasise the humility of Christ. It con-tains much that is undefined, and it scarcely lends itself to dogmatic construction, but it none the less indicates that Paul's mind had dwelt earnestly on what may be called the presuppositions of the Incarnation. ' Though he was divine by nature,' he writes to the Philippians, ' he did not snatch at equality with God, but emptied himself by taking the nature of a servant : born in human

---

[1] Windisch greatly exaggerates the influence of the Jewish conception of the Divine Wisdom on Paul's Christology in his essay in *Neutestament-liche Studien für G. Heinrici*, pp. 220-234.

guise and appearing in human form, he humbly stooped in his obedience even to die, and to die upon the cross. Therefore God highly exalted him, and gave him the name which is above every name, that in the name of Jesus every knee should bow . . . and every tongue confess that Jesus Christ is Lord, to the glory of God the Father.' [1] Here we have Paul's clearest utterance as to the pre-existence of Christ, a pre-existence which he regards as in some sense individual. The most difficult phrase in the paragraph is that which speaks of an ' equality with God ' at which Christ did not snatch. Plainly the apostle views the pre-incarnate attitude of Christ from the standpoint of his post-resurrection existence. He had come into contact with him as the glorified *Lord* to whom was due the universal worship of men. His possession of this name (Κύριος), as we have seen, placed Him side by side with God in the eyes of humanity. That is what Paul means by ' equality.' But He had reached that glory by a path of lowly obedience which led through the scorn and rejection of His earthly life, and the shame and agony of the cross. This was the cost of redemption, although Paul does not here explicitly refer to that. The incarnation was a great act of self-renunciation for the sake of mankind, a great act of obedience in which the Son made Himself one with His Father's will that He might bring sinful men to God. Possibly the noteworthy expression, ' did not snatch at equality with God,' contains a reminiscence of the First Adam, who, in disobedience to the Almighty, yielded to the temptation to ' be as God ' (Gen. iii. 5). It is remarkable that even here Paul does not dwell on the metaphysical implications of his statement. He hastens to the act of humble self-denial, revealing the true focus of his interest. We are not, therefore, justified in attempting to analyse what he means here by the Divine Nature (μορφή) of the pre-incarnate Christ. Nor is it legitimate to use the passage as evidence for the conception of Christ as the ' Heavenly Man,' which some scholars have attributed to

[1] Phil. ii. 6 ff. (partly M.).

the apostle. There is no trace of such a conception here,
nor, in our judgment, anywhere in his writings.[1] Paul leaves
in obscurity that of which the pre-existent One ' emptied '
Himself.[2] He is content to view the incarnation,[3] even
when placed in its cosmic setting, as a wonderful disclosure
of the grace of Christ,[4] that grace which lies behind the
salvation He has accomplished for humanity. And thus
once more an utterance which touches realms of speculation in which human thought grows dizzy is found to
have its real basis in the conviction that self-sacrifice
belongs to the very nature of God.

[1] See an article by the present writer in *Expositor*, 1914, pp. 97-110.
[2] J. Weiss quite arbitrarily says, of ' the body of his glory ' (Phil. iii. 21).
[3] He never uses any term like this.
[4] Cf. 2 Cor. viii. 9.

PART II

PHASES OF EARLY CHRISTIAN THOUGHT IN THE MAIN INDEPENDENT OF PAULINISM

CHAPTER I

THE FIRST EPISTLE OF PETER

(a) The Situation

IN the Introduction a brief sketch has been given of the historical background of the Epistle, so far as it can be reconstructed from the very fragmentary data which are available. One or two features of the evidence ought to be emphasised. (1) The most striking fact as regards the external attestation of the document is the place of authority assigned to it by Polycarp,[1] who writes shortly after the first decade of the second century.[2] In making his quotations from the Epistle, he does not mention Peter's name, but his pupil Irenæus regularly assigns it to the apostle. (2) On the other hand, most modern scholars agree that, in view of its more or less correct Greek style, the actual composition of the Epistle cannot be the work of Peter. The problem is elucidated by the words of chap. v. 12 (M.) : ' By the hand of (διά) Silvanus, a faithful brother (in my opinion), I have written you these few lines of encouragement.' A remarkable parallel is found in the description given by Dionysius of Corinth (*Euseb. H. E.*, iv. 23, 11) of Clement's Epistle to the Corinthians, in which the same preposition (διά) emphasises Clement's function as mouthpiece of the Roman Church. Silvanus, already a person of authority in the Christian community and one of Paul's trusted fellow-missionaries (1 Thess. i. 1,

---

[1] See Chase, *H. D. B.*, iii. p. 781.
[2] See Lightfoot, *Apostolic Fathers*, Part II., vol. i. p. 428.

2 Thess. i. 1, 2 Cor. i. 19, Acts xv. 32, 40, etc.), is more than
the bearer of this Epistle. He has had the responsibility
of shaping the apostle's exhortation, and it may well be
that some of the marked affinities with Paul are due to
the fact that Silvanus, as coadjutor of the great Gentile missionary, 'acquired a sympathy or familiarity with
his characteristic modes of thought and expression.' [1]
(3) The language of chap. iv. 3 is sufficient proof that the
Epistle is addressed to Christians who had been converted
from Paganism. Since, however, by the second half of
the first century the Christian community regarded itself
as the true heir of the chosen people, the distinction
between its Jewish and Gentile elements had ceased to be
of primary importance. It has been suggested that the
order in which the various provinces are mentioned,
'Pontus, Galatia, Cappadocia, Asia, and Bithynia,'
'reflects the road followed by the bearer of the letter.' [2]
No reason can be given for the selection of these particular
localities, but Peter's name and authority would be
familiar to them all. (4) It is almost impossible to doubt
that 'Babylon,' which is obviously the place of writing
(v. 13), is a cryptic name for Rome as the symbol of
arrogance, secular power, and ungodliness. It is used
frequently in this sense in the Apocalypse (e.g. xiv. 8,
xviii. 2, 10, 21).[3] A tradition of the Church which goes as
far back as Papias gives this interpretation,[4] and there is
no valid testimony which associates the apostle with the
real Babylon. Now, as early as A.D. 96, we have the
witness of Clement (ad Cor. v. 1-4) as to Peter's martyrdom,
and the context of the statement certainly seems to imply
that he suffered at Rome.[5] A combination of the facts
would suggest that when the Epistle was written the
Christian community of the metropolis had already

[1] Moffatt, *Introduction*, p. 332. See also Zahn, *Einleitung*, ii. pp. 10, 11.
[2] Moffatt, *op. cit.*, p. 327.
[3] Hart (*E. G. T.*, v. p. 19) points out that the Jewish author of Book V.
of the *Sibylline Oracles* (dated by Geffcken shortly after 70 A.D.) uses
Babylon for Rome.
[4] See Zahn, *op. cit.*, ii. pp. 19, 20.
[5] See Zahn, *op. cit.*, i. pp. 445-448 ; ii. 22-27.

experienced the skilfully planned outbreak of Nero's rage and cruelty, an outbreak which finally led to more or less organised persecution of the Church.

The actual character of the *persecutions* referred to in the Epistle is the most important question of all for the reconstruction of its environment. Rash inferences have been drawn by many scholars from the somewhat incidental and unstudied allusions found in the document. When these are examined without prejudice, they are seen to reflect a situation which must have been common, as soon as the Christian movement became a force to be reckoned with. The chief strain in the exhortations of the Epistle, which bear upon the sufferings of its readers, is the appeal to live down the slanders of ignorant pagan critics by their blameless conduct.[1] We know from the literature of the early Church that insinuations were made against the Christians as to shameful orgies and unnatural crimes. This was the penalty of their quiet gatherings for worship and their fraternal love. Nero had taken advantage of the situation to make the Christians at Rome the scapegoats of his own crime. But, further, it is interesting to observe that just as Paul, after urging his readers at Rome to overcome evil with good, proceeds to enjoin submission to existing authority,[2] so Peter in a precisely similar context exhorts Christian slaves to obey their masters, even when they make unreasonable demands and treat them cruelly. Here we get a hint of special hardships which have to be borne for Christ's sake by men and women who were at the mercy of those who had the power over them of life and death. The innumerable occasions on which heathen rites mingled with the details of family life would afford opportunities for such harsh tyranny.

Various scholars have held that iv. 15 (' Let no man suffer as a murderer or a thief or an evil-doer or an officious meddler,[3] but if as a Christian, let him not be

---

[1] *E.g.* ii. 12, 15 ; iii. 16.   [2] Rom. xii. 19—xiii. 5.
[3] It is probably best to explain the *hapax legomenon*, ἀλλοτριοεπίσκοπος, as Zeller does, from contemporary philosophical usage, which shows that the charge of meddlesomeness was brought against ardent Cynic propa-

ashamed, but let him glorify God because of this name ')
presupposes the process mentioned by Pliny in his famous
letter to Trajan, in which the Christians were condemned,
not because of any alleged crime, but ' on account of the
Name alone ' (*propter nomen ipsum*).   That would of
course point to a period of organised persecution by the
Imperial authorities, such as appeared in the reigns of
Domitian and Trajan.   But, as Bigg aptly observes, this
Epistle shows that they *were* regarded as evil-doers.[1]   And,
in any case, the statement of iv. 14, ' If you are re-
proached in the name of Christ, you are blessed,' words
which are probably an echo of Matt. v. 11, suggests something much less formal than a legal indictment for bearing
the name ' Christian.'   Followers of Christ would inevitably
look upon the sufferings involved in their loyalty to their
Lord as endured for His name.   This interpretation tallies
with what we have seen to be the general character of the
allusions throughout the Epistle.[2]   Nor is it at all under-
mined either by iv. 12 (' Do not be surprised at the ordeal
which has come to test you '), or by v. 8 (' Your enemy
the devil prowls like a roaring lion looking out for some one
to devour ').[3]   In every region where Christianity got a
foothold, there would necessarily come a time when the
attention of their neighbours would be directed to the
members of the new sect.   This time had arrived in the
Asiatic provinces for which the Epistle is intended.   If it
was written after Nero's savage attack upon the Christians
at Rome, we might naturally suppose that the eddies of
that disturbance had spread to the more distant parts
of the Empire.   Perhaps this very fact is indicated by v. 9 :
' Knowing how to pay the same tax of suffering as your
brethren throughout the world ' (M.).   The reference to the
machinations of the devil is not more emphatic than Paul's

gandists. ' A Christian might give great offence by ill-timed protests
against common social customs, such as the use of garlands, or of meat
offered to idols at dinner parties ' (Bigg, *ad loc.*).
   [1] *Commentary on St. Peter and St. Jude*, p. 30.
   [2] For a discussion of details, marked by great historical insight, see
Bigg, *op. cit.*, pp. 24-33.   [3] M.

warning in Eph. vi. 11 ff., that Christians are confronted by Satanic wiles, and have to struggle not against mere human adversaries but against spiritual forces of evil in the heavenly sphere.

It seems appropriate, therefore, to assign the Epistle to a date not long after Nero's persecution, anywhere between 64 and 66 or 67 A.D.[1]

(b) Essentially Practical Character of the Theology

The clue to the contents of the Epistle is given in v. 12, which describes the purpose of the writer as being to testify ' that this is what the true grace of God means ' (M.). When the Epistle is examined in the light of that statement, we find that ' the true grace of God ' embraces the splendid hope which has been disclosed in the resurrection of Christ, and all the kindness which God the Father has shown to men. But this Divine grace, in the generosity of its scope, is emphasised for a definite reason. The communities addressed are called to pass through severe trials. These are a sharp test of faith and conduct. There is the danger of feeling disappointed at such an issue of their new career. Might they not have expected peace rather than conflict ? Is it worth while to continue in so difficult a course ? Such disillusionment will be reinforced by the temptation to compromise with the lower moral standard which confronts them on every side. It will be natural to fall back into heathen ways and so escape suffering. But the Lord whose name they bear, for whom they have to face shame and pain, was Himself a sufferer, and He had done no wrong. It was through suffering that He achieved the redemption of man, and He bore all with lowliness and calmness. They are called to share in His experiences, to follow in His steps. And they are not left to meet their trials alone. They belong to God. They invoke Him as Father. They have been born again of immortal seed. God's power is at their disposal : the Spirit of Him who has

[1] For an excellent discussion of the date, see Moffatt, op. cit., pp. 338-342.

called them to His eternal glory in Christ Jesus. Only, they have a great moral duty both to God and to men. They must live worthily of the Holy One who has redeemed them at such a cost. They must spend their days as pilgrims, in the midst of an impure environment, so controlling all evil lusts and tempers that their pagan neighbours will be impressed by their conduct, and led to glorify God because of them. This will remove all valid causes of slander and maltreatment. If they have to suffer, it will be suffering for righteousness' sake, as Christ's was. And at the end the unfading crown of glory awaits them.

Obviously, the Epistle, from its *raison d'être*, is essentially practical. The arrangement of thought is homiletical and not logical.[1] It is the pastoral address of an earnest and affectionate Christian missionary to communities of whose circumstances he is aware. If it be said that Hope is the central idea of the Letter, we must note that its prominence is due to the depressed conditions of the readers. It is quite illegitimate on this account to call Peter the Apostle of Hope. When occasion demands, Paul gives it equal importance. Here it has no theological, but entirely a religious significance. It is when the author speaks of the Christian life that he shows originality.[2] Those ideas which may be justly described as theological are introduced not for their own sake, but in order to confirm and enhance the practical considerations which the apostle uses to cheer and encourage his readers. Hence we must be on our guard throughout against reading into his reflective utterances more than he intended them to contain.

(c) *Affinities with Paul*

The most delicate problem raised by an investigation of the thought of our Epistle is that of its relation to the religious standpoint of Paul. Sweeping statements have been made for which there is no justification. ' Is not

---

[1] See Gunkel, *Die Schriften d. N. T.*, ii. p. 530.
[2] See W. Bauer, *Die katholischen Briefe*, p. 31.

everything,' asks Wernle, ' in 1 Peter from the first line to
the last Pauline language and Pauline thought ? ' [1] The
fallacy which lies behind such a view is the assumption
that there was no attempt to shape religious ideas in the
early Church except that made by Paul.   It may be granted
that his was by far the most powerful intellect brought
to bear upon the data of Christian experience, and that
probably no other leader in the Apostolic Age had the same
natural bias to systematise the material which lay before
him.   But we have already adduced evidence to show
that when Paul entered the Christian community he found
reflection busy with the work of interpreting such facts as
the death and resurrection of Jesus Christ, the gift of the
Spirit, and the Second Advent.   And there can be little
doubt, as we have seen, that he largely accepted the fundamental positions which had already been taken up.[2]   As it
happens, we have important testimony that Peter was in
agreement with his brother apostle on the basal value of
faith.   Paul can appeal to him on this common ground :
' Knowing that a man cannot be justified by the works of
the law, but only through faith in Christ Jesus, we also
(*i.e.* we Jews) put our trust in Christ Jesus.' [3]   Accordingly,
it is quite illegitimate to say that the central place given
to faith or to the atoning death and resurrection of Christ
in this Epistle is due to the influence of Paul.   He unquestionably elaborated ideas which he found only in
germ, and in various instances moulded them into forms
which dominated later generations, but often the less
articulate conceptions of the earlier epoch were more
easily assimilated.   Hence much of the fundamental
agreement between this Epistle and the essentials of
Paulinism must be referred to the common heritage of
the apostolic Church.   That rich store of ideas we shall
examine in the following section.   There we shall find the
paramount influence of the Old Testament, and especially
of the prophets, on Peter's religious thought, as well as

---

[1] *Einführung,* p. 137.   So also Holtzmann, *op. cit.*, ii. p. 350 f.
[2] See esp. 1 Cor. xv. 3 ff.   [3] Gal. ii. 16.

many reminiscences of the teaching of Jesus. Throughout
we are conscious of a simple, earnest, affectionate nature,
whose keen sympathies make him receptive rather than
originative : who would therefore readily respond to the
impress of a stronger mind, and yet by the force of his
spirituality impart something of his own tone to the convictions on which he places value.

A comparison of 1 Peter with the Pauline Epistles
undoubtedly suggests that the author was acquainted with
some of them, notably that to the Romans. Thus, in
iii. 9, Peter urges his readers not to return evil for evil
(μὴ ἀποδίδοντες κακὸν ἀντὶ κακοῦ), using the very phrase
which Paul has in Rom. xii. 17. What is specially
significant is that in both contexts it is introduced between
admonitions to lowliness and advice to preserve peace
with all men. His knowledge of Rom. xii. is further
attested by his use within the same paragraph (ii. 2, ii. 5)
of the same rare adjective (λογικός) for ' spiritual ' as Paul
employs (xii. 1), and the same conception of Christians as
offering spiritual sacrifices well-pleasing to God (xii. 1).
Equally remarkable is the employment by Peter (ii. 6, 8)
of the same quotations from Isa. xxviii. 16, viii. 14 as appear
in Rom. ix. 33, and, a few sentences later (ii. 10), of the
same passage from Hosea (ii. 23) as Paul cites in Rom. ix. 25.
There are some interesting parallel expressions in Rom. xiii.
1-7 and 1 Pet. ii. 13-17, but here Peter's thought follows
quite independent lines. We must confess that we find it
as difficult as Dr. Bigg does to discover those subtle affinities
between 1 Peter and Ephesians which appeal so strongly
to Hort and others.[1] There are a few vague parallels, but
no close inter-relation of ideas is at all prominent.

It is of course impossible to get beyond conjecture in
accounting for Peter's knowledge of the Epistle to the
Romans or any other of Paul's Letters. But the fact that
he wrote from Rome reminds us of his intimate connection
with that particular Christian community, which must have

[1] See Hort, *The First Epistle of St. Peter*, p. 5, and Zahn's list of alleged
parallels, *op. cit.*, ii. p. 36.

reckoned Paul's Epistle among its most treasured posses-
sions. If, as has been suggested, Silvanus, a friend and
fellow-labourer of Paul, was directly concerned in the
shaping of Peter's Epistle, it is not surprising that echoes
of the great missionary's words, as well as of his thoughts,
should here and there be overheard.

When we examine the normative ideas of the Epistle
in the light of the fundamental positions accepted throughout the Church, we are not impressed by their alleged
reproduction of Paulinism. It is not surprising, *e.g.*,
to find a function of the highest import assigned to faith
in this Epistle. But its colour is different from that of
Paul's watchword. In Paul, as we have observed, faith
is the supreme channel of spiritual life and power. It is
the nexus of the most intimate fellowship between the soul
and Christ. For Peter, as for all Christians of the Apostolic
Age, salvation is impossible without faith. But the special
nuance of his conception may be discerned in i. 20, 21,
where he speaks of Christ as revealed ' at the end of the
ages on your account, who, through him, believe in God
that raised him from the dead and gave him glory, so that
your faith and hope is in God.' [1] This attitude reminds us
rather of the Synoptics than of Paul. In view of it, we
can understand why Paul's central idea of justification
does not occur in 1 Peter. Nor is it legitimate to quote
the important passage on Christ's atoning death (ii. 21-24)
as a proof of the Paulinism of the author. The profound
delineation of the Servant of the Lord in Isa. liii. has a
much more inward relation to it, and we know how much
emphasis was laid on that delineation in the early Church,
in its endeavours to interpret the scandal of the cross.
At the same time we are reminded every here and there
that Paul's powerful exposition of the Gospel has left its
permanent mark on the general Christian position. In the
passage just referred to, the writer states as the purpose of

[1] This rendering seems preferable to that favoured by Moffatt and
others : ' so that your faith is also hope in God.' See Hort's strong
arguments *ad loc.*

Christ's atoning death, ' that we having died (ἀπογενόμενοι) [1] to sins, might live unto righteousness.' This is an echo of Rom. vi. 2, 11, 18. Yet no stress is laid on Paul's crucial idea of dying and rising with Christ. And, what is equally noteworthy, Peter speaks of a death to ' sins,' individual acts of transgression, while Paul invariably represents the experience as a death to ' sin,' sin being conceived as a terrible semi-personified Power to which men are in slavery. A similar example of Pauline influence may be traced in iii. 18, where it is said of Christ that he was ' put to death in the flesh, but made alive in the spirit.' Here is Paul's favourite antithesis of flesh and spirit, which appears again in iv. 6.[2] But that Peter has in no sense adopted Paul's psychology is obvious from his regular use of ψυχή, ' soul ' (i. 9, 22 ; ii. 11, 25) to denote the inner life on its religious side. In this connection it may be noted that he has no trace of that eschatology, built up on the conception of πνεῦμα, ' spirit,' which is so normative for Paul's religious thought.

(d) The Atmosphere of the Common Church-consciousness

Dr. Moffatt's description of the author of 1 Peter as ' a primitive Christian who had breathed the Messianic atmosphere of the better Judaism,' [3] gives the exact clue to the general standpoint of our Epistle. For it reveals far closer affinities with the current Christian thought of the early apostolic Church than with that world of ideas which sprang from the creative genius of Paul. Its religion has its root in the Christian Messianism which dominated the Palestinian community of believers from the outset. Even those conceptions which may be regarded as more or less

---

[1] Bigg's hesitation as to whether ἀπογίνεσθαι could ever have been used as a direct antithesis to ζῆν is invalidated by the evidence from pre-Christian papyri in Moulton and Milligan's *Vocabulary, sub voce.*

[2] See also iv. 1 f. : ' Since, therefore, Christ has suffered in the flesh, equip yourselves with the same purpose (ἔννοια in LXX usually translates מְזִמָּה), for he who has suffered in the flesh has got rid of sin,' which is unmistakably connected with Rom. vi. 7 : ' He who is dead is absolved from the claims of sin.'   [3] *Op. cit.*, p. 331.

peculiar to the Epistle have an intimate connection with the ' better Judaism ' from which the earliest disciples of Jesus were drawn.

The conviction that Jesus was the Messiah, confirmed and established as it was for them by His resurrection, carried with it the most far-reaching consequences. The brotherhood which bore His name stepped at once into the position of the ' true Israel,' the real ' people of God.' Probably nowhere else in the New Testament does the belief find such splendid expression as in chap. ii. 9, 10 (M.): ' You are *the elect race, the royal priesthood, the consecrated nation, the people who belong to him, that you may proclaim the wondrous deeds* of him who has called you from darkness to his wonderful light—you who once were *no people* and now are *God's people*, you who once *were unpitied* and now *are pitied*.' [1] This is their destiny as the people of the Messiah.

We do not dwell on the numerous passages which find Christ in the Old Testament, as we must examine certain special aspects of this idea in the next section. A very striking instance appears in the cento of verses from Isaiah and Psalms in ii. 3-8. But it may be noted in passing that the interpretation of Christ's death in the light of an Old Testament background reveals by its fragmentary character its proximity to the attempts made in the early apostolic community to shed light on the enigma of the cross. In harmony with this is the simple Christology which is presupposed in the Epistle, and which reminds us forcibly of Peter's addresses, as reported in the first half of the book of Acts.[2] Nothing explicit appears as to Christ's inner nature or His essential relation to God, questions which take so prominent a position in Paul's Imprisonment-Epistles, probably written shortly before this.

At no point is the dominant tone of the early Christian

---

[1] The italicised words are quotations from the Old Testament.
[2] For parallels, cf. i. 17 with Acts x. 34, xv. 9 ; i. 20 with Acts ii. 23 ; iii. 19, 20 with Acts ii. 25-28 ; iv. 16 with Acts v. 41.

society more manifest than in the emphasis laid by the
Epistle on the *hope* of the heavenly inheritance which
awaits believers.   Everything here is transformed Messianic
aspiration.   Hope had been for centuries the very nerve
of the Messianic idea.   And it had reached forward to a
heritage, often material enough in quality, but transcending
all previous experience.   But the Christian Messiah had
revolutionised the older expectation.   As risen and exalted
at God's right hand, He had become the pledge of immortal
life for His followers.   The heritage of God's people is no
longer a purified earth.   It is His ' eternal glory,' the perfected salvation,[1] which means complete assimilation to
the Divine likeness.   Perhaps Beyschlag is justified in
saying that in our Epistle the outlook of the Christian hope
towards the salvation yet to be revealed ' outweighs the
lofty feeling, so powerful in Paul, of already possessing
salvation.' [2]   At the same time we must not ignore the
fact, already emphasised, that owing to the situation of
the communities addressed the apostle was led to make use
of this conception as a motive to courage and endurance.

   That this stress on hope, however, is not merely the
result of the special circumstances appears from the
prominent place given to what the author is fond of
calling ' the revelation of Jesus Christ.'   The thought
belongs so essentially to his outlook that within this short
Epistle it appears again and again in various guises.[3]
Here we breathe the genuine atmosphere of the apostolic
Church.   Of course Paul has given full expression to the
expectation of the Parousia, but in the Imprisonment-
Epistles, which belong, roughly speaking, to the period to
which we have assigned 1 Peter, the vividness of the
expectation has been largely modified.   Indeed, Peter's
favourite idea of the ' revelation ' of Christ, which is
rare in Paul, finds its only direct parallels in 1 Corinthians
and 2 Thessalonians.[4]   Thus the Epistle is strictly true to

---

[1] v. 10; i. 9.   [2] *N. T. Theology*, i. p. 384.
[3] See i. 5, 7, 11, 13 ; ii. 12 ; iv. 7, 13, 17 ; v. 1, 4.
[4] 1 Cor. i. 7 ; 2 Thess. i. 7.

the ruling tradition of Palestinian Christianity, only
that the eschatological accompaniments of the Second
Advent are for the most part summed up in the rich
conception of ' glory,' which is by no means an exclusively Pauline idea.

In discussing Paul's indebtedness to the general Christian
standpoint found by him in the Church when he entered
it, we discovered the primary importance of the memory
of the historical Jesus. Our Epistle bears its testimony
no less clearly. A careful investigation of its text reveals
a remarkable number of reminiscences. These are all the
more convincing because they appear quite artlessly in
what is a practical exhortation.[1] But the impression of
Jesus' character as a man among men is best indicated in
chap. ii. 21 f., where Peter reminds his readers that Christ,
in the sufferings He bore on their account, has left them an
example that they should follow in His steps. The passage
which portrays that example is really a description of
Jesus' bearing during His trial.[2] Nothing could more
plainly show the indelible recollection of the Master
cherished by His disciples.

A reference may be made, in closing this section, to the
points of contact between our Epistle and *Hebrews*. There
is, indeed, nothing to suggest dependence on either side.
Moreover, each Epistle, notably Hebrews, presents a
series of marked idiosyncrasies. The parallels suggest
what, it is hoped, the present discussion has already made
plain, that both documents share in a common spiritual
atmosphere, that of the Christian community as a whole,
an atmosphere which cannot be dispelled by the individual
features which they possess. Such conceptions as faith
(with a different shade of meaning from that in Paul),
cleansing through the blood of Christ, inheriting the
promised blessing, antitypes of the Christian order as found
in the Old Testament, the finality of Christ's sacrifice,

---

[1] *E.g.* i. 13=Luke xii. 35; ii. 6 ff.=Matt. xxi. 42; ii. 12=Matt. v. 16;
ii. 21 f.=Matt. xvi. 21 f.; iii. 14=Matt. v. 10; iv. 7, 10=Mark xiii.
33, 34; v. 5, 6=Matt. xxiii. 12; v. 7=Matt. vi. 25 f.; v. 10=Luke xxii. 32.
[2] ii. 23. See Feine, *N. T. Theologie*, p. 572.

must all have been current in the apostolic Church.[1]   Their
appearance in common in two epistles, whose authors
are men of such different moulds, reminds us of the rich
heritage of religious thought which belonged to the early
Christian community, independently of Paul's epoch-
making constructions.

(e) Conceptions characteristic of the Epistle

1. Old Testament Prophecy

We have already noted the emphasis laid in this Epistle
on the connection between the old revelation and the new.
That was of course a position universally valid in the
early Church.   The use of the Old Testament as the Bible
of the Christian community had a large significance.   It
provided them with a vocabulary by which to express and
interpret their profoundest convictions, and, what was of
even greater importance, it supplied the background against
which they were able to understand the development of
God's redeeming purpose for humanity.

It was natural that the most spiritual minds should
find themselves specially at home in the prophetic writings
and recognise the kinship of these with the mind of Christ.
From beginning to end of this Epistle, Peter's memory
rings with echoes of the ancient preachers of righteousness.[2]
This feature he shared with his fellow-apostle Paul.   But
he proceeds to elaborate the relations between the prophets
and the era of salvation which had already dawned, in
very definite terms.   All Christian teachers were agreed
that the prophets had predicted the advent of the Divine
grace which was the actual experience of the apostolic
Church.   They were agreed that such passages as Isa. liii.

[1] Cf. i. 9=Heb. x. 39 ; i. 21=Heb. vi. 1, xi. 1 ; v. 9=Heb. xi. 33;
i. 2=Heb. xii. 24, x. 22 ; iii. 9=Heb. xii. 17 ; iii. 21=Heb. ix. 24 ;
iii. 18=Heb. ix. 26, 27, 28.
[2] The following collection of parallels is based on Moffatt's list (p. 332,
note) : i. 24 f.=Isa. xl. 6 f. ; ii. 6 f.=Isa. viii. 14, xxviii. 16 ; ii. 9 f.
=Isa. xliii. 20 f. ; ii. 22 f.=Isa. liii. 5, 9, 12 ; i. 11=Isa. liii. 7, 8 ; i. 18
=Isa. lii. 3 ; ii. 25=Isa. liii. 6 ; iii. 15=Isa. viii. 13 ; iv. 14=Isa. xi. 2.

pointed to the sufferings of the Messiah and the glory that should follow. Peter traces this superhuman knowledge to the inspiration of the Spirit of the Messiah within them (i. 11). His explanation is noteworthy. In Acts ii. 33 he is reported as ascribing to the risen Christ the gift of the Holy Spirit. But the Holy Spirit was acknowledged by all as the real source of prophecy, so that the same Christ stands behind the wonderful forecasts of the Old Testament, only that there He is the Pre-existent. There is therefore no line of demarcation between the spiritual insight of the old order and that of the new.[1] To show the high import attached by the prophets to the Messianic salvation, the apostle refers to their eagerness concerning the time and manner in which the Divine promise should be fulfilled. Probably he includes in his thought such apocalyptic speculations as that regarding the seventy weeks in Dan. ix. 24-27. That passage, in speaking of ' making an end of sin,' ' making reconciliation for iniquity,' ' bringing in everlasting righteousness,' as characteristic of the Messianic epoch, presupposes, it may be, the picture in Isa. liii., which had so profoundly impressed the mind of Peter. That his reflection was moving in the realm of apocalyptic is suggested by the further statement that the disclosure of the coming salvation was given them, not for their own age, but for that of the consummation. The idea is hinted at in Heb. xi. 40 (M.) : ' God had something better in store for us ; he would not have them perfected apart from us.' But it appears more clearly in Dan. xii. 9 : ' Go thy way, Daniel, for the words (*i.e.* the revelation made to him) are closed up and sealed till the time of the end.' This becomes a sort of principle in apocalyptic, *e.g.* 1 Enoch i. 2 : ' I understood what I saw, but not for this generation, but for the remote generations which are to come.' [2]

---

[1] Granbery quotes to the same effect *Ep. of Barnabas*, 5 : οἱ προφῆται, ἀπ' αὐτοῦ ἔχοντες τὴν χάριν, εἰς αὐτὸν ἐπροφήτευσαν (*Outlines of N. T. Christology*, p. 79).

[2] Quoted by Granbery, *op. cit.*, p. 80.

2. *The Death of Christ*

It is perhaps scarcely accurate to describe Peter's view of the death of Christ as a conception peculiar to his Epistle. Indeed he presents no rounded-off interpretation of the event any more than his brother-apostle Paul. But the combination of aspects in which he regards it, while revealing many affinities with Paulinism, is, in the New Testament, peculiar to himself. And it is specially instructive as an example of the manner in which ideas explanatory of so central a fact must often have been grouped in the apostolic Church.

His utterances on the death of Christ have been prompted by the practical necessities of the communities to which he writes. We must not therefore press them unduly, or credit the apostle with inferences from them which to us appear inevitable. On the other hand, the spontaneity and artlessness with which they occur suggest their dominance in Peter's thought, and the brevity of expression must not be allowed to conceal the wide reaches of reflection which lie behind it.

Before we attempt a connected survey of the various statements, it may be of value, first, to note their intensely practical bearing, and secondly, to give a brief analysis of their background. In i. 18, 19, the cost of redemption, ' the precious blood of Christ,' is made the ground of appeal for a serious and reverent life. In ii. 21-24, the patient suffering of Christ for righteousness' sake, in order to be the medium of healing to sin-sick souls, is exhibited as an example to Christian slaves, who have to endure punishment for doing right. Precisely the same ground is taken in iii. 18, where the apostle points to Him who died for sins, ' a righteous man for unrighteous, that he might bring us to God.' The typically Pauline conception that Christ's suffering in the flesh broke the power of sin, serves in iv. 1 f. as an incentive for His followers to live in complete loyalty to the will of God. The only other significant reference is that which, in the address of the Epistle (i. 2), describes the readers as 'chosen' by God, 'for obedience (*i.e.* to Him),[1] and for being sprinkled with the blood of Jesus Christ.' The association of the daily behaviour of his Gentile-Christian readers with so solemn a theme reminds us that the writer could take for granted their true appreciation of it.

When we examine the crucial passages in order to trace their background, we are at first confused by the variety of the conceptions represented. This variety accounts for the impression made upon some scholars that Peter's 'ideas about Christ's work of redemption are not unified and stable.'[2] They are not unified in the sense of forming a systematic doctrine, but there is no real discrepancy between them. As in the case of Paul, they disclose the many-sidedness of aspect which the death of Christ exhibited to the Christian consciousness of the Apostolic Age, and they exemplify the richness of the material supplied by the Old Testament to form the media of its interpretation. For it is in the Old Testament that his interpretations have their basis. Reference has been already made to the author's constant dependence on the prophets, more especially on Isaiah. His chief utterance on the meaning of the cross, ii. 21-25, is not only steeped in the thought but uses the actual language of Isa. liii. (esp. vv. 9, 12, 6), with a probable reminiscence of Deut. xxi. 23 in its mention of the 'tree.' The same passage seems to colour his ideas when he speaks of 'the righteous' dying for 'the unrighteous' (iii. 18). The metaphor is changed in i. 18 from 'the bearing of sins' to that of 'ransom.' Here, too, the language seems to echo Isa. lii. 3 (LXX).[3] Yet it may be legitimate to trace back his thought to the great deliverance of the chosen people which had been wrought by blood (Exod. xii. 13, etc.). Indeed this is made almost certain by his description of Christ as 'an unblemished and spotless lamb.' A lamb without

---

[1] Not to 'Jesus Christ,' as Dr. Moffatt translates. The significance of the text will appear immediately.

[2] *E.g.* Feine, *op. cit.*, p. 570.

[3] οὐ μετὰ ἀργυρίου λυτρωθήσεσθε.

M

blemish was appointed for the passover-sacrifice. No
doubt the comparison was frequent in the early Church,
for Paul also speaks of Christ as ' our paschal lamb ' which
' has been sacrificed.' [1]   With this he may quite well have
combined the recollection of the lamb in Isa. liii. 7, the
symbol of meek endurance, a symbol which was probably
suggested to the prophet by the sacrificial ritual.   There
remain the remarkable words in which the Christians to
whom the Epistle is sent are designated as ' chosen . . .
for obedience and for being sprinkled with the blood of
Jesus Christ ' (i. 2).   Plainly they presuppose Exod. xxiv.
7 f. : ' [Moses] took the book of the covenant ($\tau\hat{\eta}s$ $\delta\iota\alpha\theta\acute{\eta}\kappa\eta s$),
and read in the audience of the people : and they said,
All that the Lord hath spoken will we do, and *be obedient*.
And Moses *took the blood and sprinkled it on the people*,
and said, Behold *the blood of the covenant*, which the Lord
hath made with you upon all these conditions.'   This is
the passage which colours the thought of Jesus at the
institution of the Holy Supper, and its influence appears
repeatedly in the New Testament, notably in Heb. ix. 18-20.

These Old Testament references suggest the lines on
which Peter's view of Christ's death must be interpreted,
and they warn us against the error of drawing the sharp
distinctions between the component elements of that view,
into which some expositors have fallen.[2]   Three elements
are clearly discernible.   Christ is regarded as (1) ' bearing
the sins of men,' that is, taking upon Himself their consequences; (2) 'ransoming men from their sins'; (3) cleansing
or covering the sins of men that they might enter into
covenant with God.   In all three aspects Christ's voluntary
death is central.   In all three His action is concerned with
the removal of sin, as the supreme barrier between the
human soul and God.   In each case the idea of sacrifice
is implicit if not explicit.   No doubt the conception of
sacrifice carries with it the suggestion of atonement.   And

[1] 1 Cor. v. 7.   Cf. Heb. ix. 14 : δs . . . $\dot{\epsilon}\alpha\upsilon\tau\grave{o}\nu$ $\pi\rho\sigma\sigma\acute{\eta}\nu\epsilon\gamma\kappa\epsilon\nu$ $\check{\alpha}\mu\omega\mu\sigma\nu$ $\tau\hat{\omega}$
$\Theta\epsilon\hat{\omega}$.
[2] *E.g.* B. Weiss, *Der petrinische Lehrbegriff*, p. 264.

from these we cannot separate the thought of substitution, which is the very nerve of the two leading passages, ii. 24 and iii. 18. Probably the attempts made by the apostle to plumb the unfathomable depths of the Divine self-sacrifice represent quite faithfully the directions followed by the spiritual instinct of the early Church when confronted by the wonder of redemption. Even a hurried glance reveals the affinities with Paul. A more penetrating study, in the light of such cognate passages as Heb. ix. 18 ff., discloses the influence on Peter of the covenant-idea, that idea which the Master Himself had, in a moment of peculiar solemnity, used as the most fitting symbol in which to enshrine His act of redeeming love. We are inclined to think that this conception gained its prominence just because it had been, so to speak, consecrated by Jesus. It may be noted that the apostle does not discuss the question : How did the redeeming act of Christ mediate salvation to men ? But, as Dr. Denney aptly observes, ' to say substitution is to say something which involves an immeasurable obligation to Christ, and has therefore in it an incalculable motive power.' [1] Peter, however, lays marked emphasis on the purpose of redemption. In ii. 24 its result for those who welcome it is ' dying to sin and living to righteousness,' a moral transformation. In iii. 18 its aim is described as ' to bring us to God.' Here we again find ourselves in the realm of covenant-conceptions. In Hebrews, which is based on the covenant-idea, ' drawing near to God,' which is only a different way of stating the same fact of experience, is shown to be the supreme ideal of religion. There is therefore no real distinction between the two affirmations of our Epistle, for in Christianity religion and morality have been fused in an indissoluble unity.

3. *The Descent to Hades*

In speaking of Christ as having died, the righteous for the unrighteous, Peter adds the noteworthy statement that

[1] *Death of Christ*, p. 100.

although Christ was put to death as regards His flesh, He was made alive as regards His spirit, and to this he links the strange paragraph concerning Christ's preaching to the souls confined in Sheol.[1] These he describes as the contemporaries of Noah, who had on account of their disobedience been swept away by the Flood.[2] With this passage we must connect iv. 6, which speaks of the Gospel as having been preached to the dead as well as the living, in order that while they must be judged in human fashion as regards the flesh (*i.e.* their earthly life), they might ' nevertheless be enabled to live after the pattern of God ' [3] as regards the spirit. It is quite unnecessary to trace Peter's speculation to those heathen myths which tell of the visits of famous heroes to Hades.[4] It was probably due to two lines of reflection which would exercise many minds in the early Church. On the one hand, their thoughts must have turned to the multitude who had died in their sins, without having the opportunity of being brought face to face with the salvation offered by Christ. A specially notorious group of sinners were those belonging to the generation of the Flood.[5] On the other hand, the interval between Christ's death and resurrection would naturally suggest to Jews a sojourn in the world of the dead. The two ideas would easily be brought into connection. Here was an outlet for the compassion of the Saviour. He preached His Gospel to these captives in their prison-house. For Sheol was no longer regarded as the abode of pithless shades. It was partly a place of punishment, and partly an intermediate state. Possibly also such passages as Isa. lxi. 1 f., xlii. 7 lay in the background of the apostle's thought,[6] passages which, on the authority of Christ Himself, were applied to His function

---

[1] iii. 19, 20. It is difficult to take seriously Dr. Rendel Harris' emendation : ' in which also [ἐν ᾧ καὶ] Enoch [Ενώχ] went and preached,' where he assumes that the name has slipped out because an early scribe dropped some repeated letters. The emended passage interrupts the context, and would have to be regarded as an interpolation.

[2] Gen. vi. 12, 13.   [3] So Chase *H. D. B.*, iii. p. 793.

[4] So W. Bauer, *op. cit.*, p. 29.

[5] See Windisch's *excursus, Die katholischen Briefe* (Lietzmann's *Handbuch*), p. 69.   [6] So Chase, *op. cit.*, p. 795.

of liberating those in captivity.[1] That the idea embodied
in the paragraph had taken hold of Peter's mind is clear
from the wider statement of iv. 6, quoted above. There
the scope is enlarged to embrace more than the one generation, and the emphasis is laid, not on the Preacher, but on
the chance given to those whom the judgment of men had
already condemned, to enter on the higher divine life. The
theologumenon is a natural product of reflection. It was
probably widely current, as many traces of it are found in
second century literature, which do not seem to have any
immediate connection with 1 Peter.[2]

[1] *E.g.* Luke iv. 18-21.
[2] See especially the remarkable passage in *Odes of Solomon*, xlii. 19-26.

CHAPTER II

THE EPISTLE TO THE HEBREWS

A. Prolegomena

(a) Special Character of the Epistle

IF we are to grasp the significance of this important post-Pauline document, it will be necessary to give a very brief sketch of the situation which it presupposes.[1] The first impression which it makes is rather that of an elaborate discourse than of a letter. Each section of its careful argument culminates in a direct appeal to its readers,[2] and the author describes his communication to them as a ' word of exhortation ' (xiii. 22). There is something to be said for the hypothesis that actual homilies of the writer have been incorporated in it.[3] But numerous indications point to his intimate acquaintance with the community to which he writes, and suggest that some special circumstances in their history prompted the letter. Hence its impersonality lies only on the surface. From ii. 3 we can gather that the Gospel had been preached to the readers by personal followers of Jesus : from v. 12 that they had reached the stage when maturity might be expected. From his knowledge of them, the author is still able to be hopeful (vi. 9). He can point to an earlier time of struggle from which they had come forth as victors

---

[1] For an adequate discussion, see Professor Peake's *Critical Introduction to the N. T.*
[2] *E.g.* ii. 1-4, vi. 1-2, x. 19-25, etc.
[3] Clemen so explains chaps. iii.-iv., Bruce, chap. xi. The theory of F. Dibelius that Hebrews was an actual sermon, transformed into a letter by slight modifications and the addition of chap. xiii., is an exaggeration.

(x. 32, 33). They must brace themselves for a sharper conflict, remembering that discipline is salutary (xii. 4-11). The obscure allusions of chap. xiii. show that the writer was aware of dangerous symptoms of error which were appearing among them, and he urges them to recall the noble example set before them by leaders of their community now passed away.[1]

In the same context hints occur which throw some light on the nature of the Church addressed. It was plainly a community within a community, for the letter is not sent to the chief authority, and it presupposes a wider circle of Christians to be found in the same locality as the recipients. The latter observation is corroborated by a reference to their special gatherings for worship.[2] When it is borne in mind that most Christian communities in large cities must, owing to considerations of space, have been made up of various house-churches,[3] meeting in little groups, while under the supervision of a central authority, the background of the Epistle becomes sufficiently clear.[4] Further, the greeting sent by the writer from ' those belonging to Italy ' (xiii. 24) certainly suggests that the community is somewhere in Italy, and no centre is so likely as Rome. A keen controversy has in recent years been waged around the question : Were the readers Jewish or Gentile Christians ? The title of the Epistle, ' To the Hebrews,' which, of course, does not form part of the original document, but goes back to an early date, reveals the impression made by its contents. We cannot here enter into the details of the discussion. But one or two considerations may be adduced which seem to us decisive. The most important proof that the Epistle is written to *Jewish* Christians is supplied by the entire character of the author's apologetic. Every point he makes has a definite bearing on the Old Testament. It may, no doubt, be said that by this time the Old Testa-

---

[1] xiii. 4, 9 f. ; xiii. 7.
[2] xiii. 24, x. 25.   [3] Cf. Rom. xvi. 5 ; 1 Cor. xvi. 19.
[4] Professor Nairne's hypothesis of ' a group of scholarly men,' an ' exclusive circle of Hellenistic thinkers ' (*The Epistle of Priesthood*, p. 10), finds no adequate basis in the Epistle.

ment had become the Bible of Gentile Christians as well
as of Jewish. But for Gentile converts it had become
authoritative through the medium of the Christian Church.
Now, as Prof. Peake forcibly says, ' the writer never dreams
that his readers will reject an appeal to the Old Testament,
though he fears that they may reject Christ.' [1]   Indeed, his
whole argument presupposes a most minute knowledge of
and sympathy with the Jewish ritual, as embodied in the
Pentateuch, and the habit of using the Old Testament as
the criterion of religious obligations.   In any case, it would
be an extraordinary method of demonstrating the finality
of the Christian faith to *Gentile* converts, to prove in almost
wearisome detail that the *cultus* of Judaism has at every
point been superseded by Christianity.   It is scarcely too
much to say, with Reuss : [2]   ' For this writer there are no
Gentiles.'

The problem of authorship has never been solved.
The names of Barnabas, Apollos, Aquila (and Priscilla),
and others have been suggested.   Origen, the greatest
Biblical scholar of the early Church, frankly admits :   ' As
to who wrote the Epistle, God knows the truth.' [3]   The
question does not seriously affect the interpretation of its
theology.   The author was evidently a cultivated Jewish-
Christian of Hellenistic origin, educated, as we shall see,
in the Alexandrian school of Judaism, and possessing also
a rhetorical training.   He seems much less indebted to
Paul than to the common Christianity of the Church, and
he must have occupied an influential position as a Christian
teacher in the Diaspora.

It is difficult to fix the approximate date of the Epistle.
It was certainly used by Clement of Rome (last decade of
first century).   Some scholars have found in x. 32 ff. a
reference to the Neronic persecution.   But this is doubtful,
although by no means impossible.   One thing seems fairly
plain.   The Epistle was written at a time when the con-

---

[1] *Hebrews* (Century Bible), p. 16.
[2] Quoted by Dods, *E. G. T.*, iv. p. 231.
[3] In Euseb., *H. E.*, vi. 25.

troversy as to the Law was no longer a burning question as
between Jewish and Gentile Christians. That suggests a
date later than A.D. 64, and as the references to ritual by
no means necessarily presuppose that the Temple was
still standing, it may be placed as late as 81 or 85, in the
period when persecution arose under the rule of Domitian.

(b) The Perils of the Community

There is general agreement as to the spiritual condition
of this community, which has called forth the writer's
admonitions. Their grasp of the Christian hope was
slackening (iii. 6). Their faith was wavering (iii. 12, iv.
1, 11). They were in danger of falling away from Christ
in listlessness and apathy (vi. 6, 12). What they need is
to have ' an assured faith ' (x. 22), and to hold out patiently
even in the midst of trials (x. 35, 36). They must keep
their eyes fixed on Jesus, their great Leader in the life of
faith, ' who, for the joy set before him, endured the cross,
despising the shame ' (xii. 2). It is an awful thing to
' trample under foot the Son of God,' to ' count the blood
of the covenant a common thing,' to ' insult the spirit of
grace ' (x. 29). Hence, the whole exhortation may be
summed up in the words of iv. 14 : ' Let us hold fast our
(Christian) confession.'

If, as we have endeavoured to show, the readers were
converts from Judaism, it is easy to recognise the kind of
pressure which was loosening their hold of Christianity.
The Epistle itself contains definite references to trials
which had assailed them in the past, and fresh trials
belonging to the present.[1] And the same fact is indirectly
suggested by the constant stress which the author lays on
the sufferings and consequent sympathy of Jesus Christ,
their great High Priest.[2] It is just possible that State
persecutions formed part of their tribulation. But more
probably the hatred of their fellow-countrymen pursued

[1] E.g. x. 36; xii. 3-11.
[2] E.g. ii. 10, 11, 14, 17, 18 ; iv. 15, 16; v. 1, 2.

them both in public and private life, for we know how
bitter was the attitude of Jews to Jewish Christians
throughout the Roman Empire. But the tone of the
exhortations in the Epistle points to something deeper,
their own religious insecurity.

Their early enthusiasm had given place to spiritual
lethargy. The Parousia, to which they had looked forward,
was being delayed. Perhaps they began to miss in the
new faith the imposing system of rites and ceremonies in
which they had been brought up. Perhaps they were
confused as to the central doctrine of the apostolic Church,
the significance of the death of Christ.[1] In any case, as
Dods has well observed, even to the Christian Jew, in this
transition period, ' Christ must have created as many
problems as He solved.' [2]

But the appeals which have been cited suggest a more
definite peril than mere religious slackness. They are in
danger of giving up their Christian confession, and ' crucifying for themselves afresh the Son of God and putting him
to an open shame ' (vi. 6). How much does this mean ?
The Epistle itself sheds a certain light on the situation in
xiii. 13, where the readers are exhorted to go forth to
Jesus, ' who suffered outside the gates ' of Jerusalem as
a defiling criminal, leaving the camp and bearing His
reproach. The plain significance of this metaphorical
language is an appeal to them to break once for all with
Judaism.[3] Keeping this admonition in view, and observing
that the whole aim of the author's elaborate argument
is to show the superiority of Christianity to Judaism by
comparing the effectiveness of Christ's redemptive activity
with the failure of the most important rites of the Law to
bring men truly near to God, we are surely justified in
believing that the readers were being tempted to relapse

[1] See A. B. Davidson, *Hebrews*, p. 20.
[2] *Op. cit.*, p. 238.
[3] So the great majority of interpreters : see especially Zahn, *op. cit.*,
ii. p. 130. Even Holtzmann, who regards the Epistle as addressed to
Gentile Christians, frankly says : ' The passage [xiii. 13] is incontestable
evidence that we have here to do with a break with Judaism ' (*N. T.
Theol.*[2], ii. p. 324, *n.* 5).

into their old religion. Various expressions in the Epistle, it is true, such as ' departing from the living God ' (iii. 12), are quoted to show that the peril is apostasy from all religion. But, as Dods cogently remarks, ' The very point of the whole Epistle is that an abandonment of Christianity is an abandonment of God : that in it God has finally spoken.' [1] In the light of our hypothesis we can discern the full force of the author's language, when he warns them against ' crucifying the Son of God afresh, and putting him to an *open* shame.' This can only mean to identify themselves with the orthodox Jewish standpoint, which led to the crucifixion.[2] Our discussion of the theology of the Epistle will corroborate the above interpretation at numerous points.

(c) *Relation of the Author to Paulinism*

The purpose of the writer, as has been indicated, is to demonstrate to his readers that Christianity is the religion of ' the better hope by which we draw near to God ' (vii. 19). His method, which is determined by the fact that his readers are converts from Judaism and that they are being tempted to return to their former faith, chiefly consists in an elaborate comparison of the various arrangements provided by Old Testament religion for bringing men into that fellowship with God which is the true end of religion, with those made available through Christ. Before he enters on his main contrast, however, he shows the limitations which belonged to the origins of the Old Testament revelation.

In order to appreciate the standpoint from which he approaches his task and the perspective in which we must view his ideas, let us attempt to estimate, first, his relation to Paul, and, secondly, his affinities with Alexandrian Judaism.

---

[1] *Op. cit.*, p. 232.

[2] Dr. Moffatt, who argues against the hypothesis defended in the text, feels obliged to say : ' A Jewish danger may be admitted as a subordinate factor in the situation of the Christians to whom Hebrews is addressed ' (*op. cit.*, p. 450).

From the fourth century downwards, beginning with the Eastern Church, *Hebrews* was in general attributed to Paul. That was mainly the result of a hasty impression, which recognised the many features common to both, such as the emphasis laid on Christ's pre-existence, His redemptive death, and His heavenly exaltation : the conception of Jewish religion as having merely temporary validity : salvation as a fact of present experience and yet the object of ardent hopes : the prominent place assigned to faith. It is needless to point out that most of these ideas belonged to the regular content of the Church's belief, and could in no sense be regarded as the special property of Paul. Yet even in regard to them, more careful examination discloses the marked divergence of the respective authors' points of view.

We are doubtful whether at any point the formulation of religious thought in Hebrews can be attributed to the influence of Paul.[1] Traces, perhaps, might be detected in the idea of the provisional character of Judaism. But who would venture to deny that, in some form or other, this conception had taken hold of the mind of the Church towards the end of the first century ? Let us briefly test the relation of Hebrews to Paul at three crucial points, a process which will serve to illumine the general outlook of the author. And first, with reference to the Law, which for both writers usually means the normative religious system of the Old Testament. We have already observed that for Paul the Law denoted primarily a fixed scheme of commands and prohibitions. Its purpose was to produce righteousness, that is, a right relation to God. But that purpose was foiled by the opposition of human sin, and so, with its austere demand, the Law stood over against the sinner as a tyrannical task-master, intensifying his consciousness of sin but unable to remove its burden. Thus the Law actually turned out to be a barrier against fellow-

[1] Dr. H. MacNeill, in his admirable study, *The Christology of the Epistle to the Hebrews*, allows a quite subordinate influence to Paulinism : *e.g.* p. 143. It seems difficult to distinguish between this and the more or less general standpoint of the apostolic Church.

ship with God. With it Paul contrasts the Gospel as an
order of grace, which through Christ Jesus, who is to
believers the end of the Law, breaks down all barriers and
makes sinful men sure of the Divine love. Hebrews
approaches Jewish legalism along entirely different lines.
It views the old system from the standpoint of the covenant-
ritual, a ritual which has its centre in atoning sacrifices.
But these sacrifices, as merely animal, could not truly set
the conscience free from its burden of guilt, and thus
enable the worshippers fearlessly to draw near to God.
They were to be regarded as types or dim outlines of the
effective sacrifice to be offered at the end of the age by Christ.

In both writers, the bearing of the death of Christ upon
the salvation of men is central, and its final issue, which
Paul calls the ' justifying ' of believers, is virtually identical
with what our author describes as their ' perfecting.' But
the presuppositions of this redemptive process are altogether different. Paul, who usually sets forth his interpretation of the death of Christ by means of juridical
categories, speaks of ransom from the curse of the law,
condemnation of sin in the flesh, reconciliation to God
through the death of His Son. The idea of Christ as the
substitute for sinners is paramount. The conception of
sacrifice is of course present, but it forms only one element
in Paul's construction. The author of Hebrews starts
from another angle of vision. The ritual of the Day of
Atonement determines the direction of his thought.
Christ's death is the inaugural sacrifice of the New Covenant.
He is both victim and sacrificing priest. According to the
old ceremonial, only those purified by the blood of the
covenant-sacrifice had the right of access into the Divine
presence, an access symbolised by the entrance of the
high-priest, with the blood of the sacrifice, into the Holy
of Holies, where he made the annual offering of atonement
for the sins of the community. Christ has entered the
heavenly sanctuary once for all as the completely sufficient
offering. Those whose hearts, through His sacrifice, have
been ' cleansed from an evil conscience,' can draw near to

God with courage and confidence, assured that their fellowship with Him is being maintained. Hence, as Pfleiderer
points out, in Hebrews the ' subjective moral action ' of
Christ to some extent overshadows the ' objective fact ' of
atonement so prominent in Paul.[1]

Once more. For Paul, faith means that surrender of the
whole being to the once crucified and now risen Christ
which keeps us in union with Him and makes us sharers in
all His experiences. In Hebrews the profound conception of
union with Christ is lacking. Faith chiefly implies confidence in the reality of the heavenly world, and the assurance of that glorious heritage to which God has pledged
Himself. Since all these future blessings are guaranteed
in Christianity, faith is really synonymous with loyalty
to the Christian position.

(d) Relation to Alexandrian Judaism

The real background of the thought of our Epistle appears
in the peculiar phase of Judaism associated with Alexandria,
and embodied especially in the writings of Philo. Plato
(e.g. Timæus, 28 C, 29 B)[2] had spoken of the Creator of the
world as designing and carrying out His work according
to an unchangeable and eternal ' pattern ' (παράδειγμα).
Of this original the world is but a ' copy ' (εἰκών). This
conception laid hold of Philo's mind and became a fundamental element in his view of God and the world. It is
forcibly expressed in his treatise De Opificio Mundi (CW),
16 : ' God, in virtue of His divinity, knew beforehand that
a fair copy (μίμημα) could never come into being apart
from a fair pattern (παράδειγμα), and that none of the
objects perceivable by the senses could be flawless which
was not modelled after an archetype and a spiritual
idea (ἀρχέτυπον καὶ νοητὴν ἰδέαν), and thus when He prepared to create this visible world, He shaped beforehand
the ideal (νοητόν) world, in order to constitute the corporeal

[1] Paulinism (E. Tr.), ii. p. 64.
[2] Cf. Republic, 592 B : ἐν οὐρανῷ ἴσως παράδειγμα ἀνάκειται.

after an incorporeal and Godlike pattern.' Traces of the
same notion are found in another Jewish book, with marked
Alexandrian affinities, the *Wisdom of Solomon*, e.g. ix. 8 :
' Thou gavest command to build a temple in thy holy
mountain, and in the city of thy habitation an altar, a
copy (μίμημα) of the holy tabernacle (σκηνῆς), which thou
didst prepare beforehand from the beginning.' The
closing words indicate that ' the holy tabernacle ' is not
the historical edifice (although that also may be before the
writer's mind), but the sanctuary of the invisible and truly
real world. It is noteworthy that this very language
occurs in Heb. viii. 2, where Christ, as the High Priest,
who has entered the heavenly sphere, is described as
' officiating in the sanctuary, the real tabernacle (τῆς σκηνῆς
τῆς ἀληθινῆς) which the Lord erected, not man.' And
in the same context (ver. 5) the priests of the Mosaic order
are said to ' serve a mere pattern (ὑποδείγματι)[1] and
shadow (σκιᾷ) of the heavenly, as Moses was instructed
when he was about to fashion the tabernacle : See, said
God, that thou makest everything according to the model
(τύπον) shown thee on the mountain.[2] In chap. ix. 11
there is a further reference to ' the greater and more perfect
tabernacle, not made with hands, that is, not belonging
to the present creation.'

The same type of phraseology occurs throughout. In
xi. 3, the visible world (τὸ βλεπόμενον) is said to have
come into being by means of the Divine word, 'independently
of the phenomenal ' (μὴ ἐκ φαινομένων) : [3] in xii. 27, the
' created ' world, as ' shaken,' passes away : the ' un-
shaken ' kingdom endures. Numerous additional examples
might be quoted, but enough has been said to show that
this fundamental antithesis between the visible and the
invisible, the earthly and the heavenly, the temporal and the

---

[1] Phrynichus advises the use of παράδειγμα as more correct than
ὑπόδειγμα (see Rutherford, *New Phrynichus*, p. 62).

[2] Exod. xxv. 40. The writer finds this passage in admirable harmony
with his general standpoint.

[3] Dr. Moffatt's phrase, ' out of the invisible,' scarcely brings out the
full force of the words.

eternal, the world of copies and the world of the ideal, which is the truly real, is normative for the writer of Hebrews.

But he uses the Philonic scheme as an instrument of Christian apologetic. The visible and transient order is, for religion, exemplified in the legal ritual of Judaism and the covenant which that ritual is supposed to ratify and maintain. The invisible realm is that to which those who have accepted the revelation of God in Jesus Christ, the ' better ' covenant, are already linked by a hope resting on the Divine promises, which is ' as an anchor of the soul secure and steadfast,' cast already from earth into heaven (vi. 18, 19). Although still involved in an imperfect order, they have already ' tasted of the powers of the world to come ' (vi. 5). In the great series of contrasts by which he works out his argument in favour of the finality of the Christian religion, which he pictures as ' the new covenant ' —Christ and the angels, Christ and Moses, Christ and the Aaronic priesthood in all the details of its service—his object is to prove that in each instance Christ has achieved the heavenly or spiritual realisation of those aims which the legal institutions of the Old Testament attempted to reach on earthly or physical lines. As Feine has aptly pointed out, Philo endeavoured to disclose the relation of the Old Testament revelation to the ideal world by allegorising its contents. He had no other reality to set over against it.[1] Hebrews has the revelation of Christ, who has actually entered the world of heavenly reality as the Forerunner and High Priest of His people. Of this revelation, which is a genuine *facsimile* of the unseen, those ordinances by which the people of God sought to draw near to Him in the Levitical ritual were but a dim outline (σκιά, ἀντίτυπα).

We must relate this fundamental presupposition of the contrast between the copy and the pattern, the physical symbols and the spiritual reality which they represent, to every stage of our investigation of the leading ideas of the Epistle. Meanwhile, various further traces of Alexandrian

[1] *N. T. Theologie*, p. 551.

influence ought to be noted. Our author is true to his training in his employment of the allegorical method of exegesis so characteristic of Philo. This is typically exemplified in his use of the Old Testament figure of Melchizedek, described as king of Salem in Gen. xiv. 18-20, who met Abraham as he returned from his victory over the kings of the East, gave him his blessing, and as a priest-king received tithes from him. The source from which he derives his illustration is Ps. cx. 4, a passage interpreted Messianically both in Judaism and in the early Church. For the purposes of his argument the writer emphasises the etymology of Melchizedek's name, ' king of righteousness,' [1] and of the name of his kingdom, ' peace,' to bring out their resemblance to Messianic ideals. And he dwells on the fact that no genealogy of Melchizedek is mentioned, and no history, in order to contrast him with the Aaronic priests, who succeed to office because of their pedigree and pass away in ever-changing succession, and to accentuate the parallel with Christ, who becomes priest because of His inherent worth, and remains a priest for ever. Philo, too, has used the figure of Melchizedek for purposes of allegory, but curiously enough he seems to make no reference to Ps. cx. 4. Indeed, his application of the significance of this Old Testament passage follows, as usual, another direction than that in Hebrews. Like our author, he calls attention to the etymology of ' Melchizedek ' and ' Salem,' but he identifies him not with any Messianic ideal but with the Logos, ' as the common reason of mankind, that higher principle of personality by which we are brought into contact with Divine thoughts and precepts.' [2]

Of more essential importance for the theology of our Epistle is the relation of the author's conception of Christ to Philo's Logos-doctrine. Here we must beware of

---

[1] His derivation is not scientifically accurate : the name probably means, ' my king is Sidiq ' (a Phœnician deity).

[2] Drummond, *Philo*, ii. p. 227. The meaning of the description of him in Genesis as ' a priest of the most high God ' is that ' Reason is a priest, having the Self-existent as his portion, and entertaining high and sublime and magnificent thoughts about him ' (*Leg. Alleg.*, iii. 82).

identifying too exclusively with Alexandrian ideas that
strain in New Testament thought which sets forth the
cosmic significance of Christ. And it has also to be
observed that the central element in the Christology of
Hebrews, the high-priesthood, does not correspond to
anything Philonic.[1] For when Philo speaks of God's
'first-born divine Logos' as high priest (ἀρχιερεύς), the
temple in which he ministers is the ordered universe, and
he evidently represents the Reason which gives its meaning
to the entire system of things.[2] But there can be little
doubt that our author has been influenced by Alexandrian
thought and terminology in setting forth the unique position
of Christ. Especially noteworthy is the description in the
opening paragraph of Chap. I. Strangely enough, he does
not make use of the term 'Logos': his highest conception
of the essential nature of Christ is expressed in the title,
'Son of God,' which is found repeatedly in Philo as the
equivalent of the Logos.[3] Here, as in the case of the
Melchizedek-story, Philo moves in a realm of abstractions.
For him 'Son' of God has no suggestion of personality.[4]
The writer of Hebrews, on the other hand, is above all else
impressed by the real human life of Jesus Christ. Yet he
does not hesitate to apply to Him the very language employed
by Philo. Thus, in i. 2 he speaks of Him as God's instrument
in creation : just as Philo says of the Logos that, in creating
the world, God used him as His instrument (ὀργάνῳ).[5] He
describes the pre-existent Christ (i. 3) as the 'effulgence'
(ἀπαύγασμα) of God's glory, and the 'impress' or 'stamp'
(χαρακτήρ) of His essence : as Philo calls the Logos the
impress (χαρακτήρ) of the seal of God (De Plantat. 18), and

[1] Professor MacNeill admits that the conception of Christ's high-
priesthood in Hebrews is 'essentially that of the O.T.,' but he adds that
it 'is touched with the more refined, mystical, abstract conception of
Philo' (op. cit., p. 107). Surely it is anything but abstract. It may
possibly be termed 'mystical,' but the mysticism is that of Christian
experience, not of Judaising Platonism.

[2] De Somniis, i. 215.

[3] E.g., De Confus. Ling., 63 : τοῦτον . . . πρεσβύτατον υἱὸν ὁ τῶν ὅλων
ἀνέτειλε πατήρ, ὃν ἑτέρωθι πρωτόγονον ὠνόμασε.

[4] See Drummond, op. cit., ii. pp. 185, 186.

[5] Leg. Alleg., iii. 96.

as in the Alexandrian *Wisdom of Solomon* the heavenly Wisdom is depicted as the ' effluence ' (ἀπόρροια) of God's omnipotent glory and the ' effulgence ' (ἀπαύγασμα) of everlasting light (vii. 25, 26). A comparison may also be drawn between Christ as Mediator of salvation and the Logos as representing for Philo a channel of mediation between God and man. But in the remarkable passage which describes the Logos as ' between the extremes . . . beside Him who planted as a pledge that what has come into being . . . shall not depart . . . and beside that which has grown for a firm ground of hope that the gracious God will never ignore his own work,' [1] it is plain once more that Philo is thinking of a mental force or energy and not of personalised spirit.

B. *Fundamental Conceptions of the Epistle*

(a) *The New Covenant*

1. *The New Covenant and the Old*

Over against the background of the two sharply contrasted world-orders, the visible and transient, and the invisible and eternal, our author sets his central conception of religion as a covenant between God and men. To understand his position, we must glance at the significance of this idea for the Old Testament. Throughout the religious history of Israel, the covenant-conception is normative as expressing the fact that God had graciously drawn near to them as His people, and that they recognised Him as their God. Such recognition was manifested in worship and service. The essential aim of their worship was access to God's presence, fellowship with Him as a community. But, in order to attain this relationship, the worship must be worthy of its object. The great hindrance was the defilement of sin. For the removal of this defilement the sacrificial system was instituted. It must be noted that the system only applied to those within the

[1] *Quis Rer. Div. Her.*, 206.

covenant. If unbelief in the living God became manifest, the relationship was thereby invalidated. Otherwise,
there was the possibility of atonement for transgressions
both ritual and ethical. For the covenant could only be
maintained through God's forgiveness of the sins of the
people. Atonement was of course made through sacrifice,
and in the offering of sacrifices the priest was both the
minister and the representative of the people. The climax
of the sacrificial ritual was to be found in the great vicarious
action of the high priest, once a year, on the Day of
Atonement, when, after slaying the victim, he carried its
blood into the Holy of Holies and sprinkled it on or before
the mercy-seat as an atonement for the sin of the covenant-
people, that God might continue His gracious relation of
fellowship with them.[1]

We cannot here dwell on the representation in the Old
Testament of historical covenants made at special epochs.
But attention must be called to that which inaugurates the
national history as described in Exod. xxiv. 4-8,[2] because
our author, like other New Testament writers, assigns to it
a special importance. After receiving the precepts enumer-
ated in chaps. xx.-xxiii., Moses is represented as communi-
cating them to the people, who answered with one voice :
' All the words which the Lord hath said will we do.'
Thereupon he built an altar and caused sacrifices to be
offered. Finally he ' took half of the blood, and put it in
basons : and half of the blood he sprinkled on the altar.
And he took the book of the covenant, and read in the
audience of the people : and they said, All that the Lord
hath said will we do, and be obedient. And Moses took the
blood and sprinkled it on the people, and said : Behold the
blood of the covenant, which the Lord hath made with you
upon all these words.' It seems probable that here the
ritual primarily symbolises the communion of men with
God through the blood of the sacrificial victim which is its
life. But, as Robertson Smith has shown (*Religion of the*

---

[1] See Lev. xvi. 15 ff.
[2] The section belongs to the Elohistic document.

Semites, p. 302), the idea of sacramental communion in
early Semitic religion seems always to have carried with it,
in germ at least, the notion of atonement.   Accordingly,
as in the ceremonial of the Day of Atonement, the sprinkling
of the blood also sets forth the covering or removal of the
sin of the community, so that God can accept them.   In
this inaugural act of the nation's existence as the people
of God, Moses himself is the mediator of the covenant.
Hence our author associates the most impressive aspects
of the covenant-idea as an effective force in the life of the
community—its inauguration in the distant past of the
nation's history, and its renewal or continuance in the yearly
atoning sacrifice offered for the sins of the people—with
Moses and the Aaronic order of priests.   But we may
here note that for the writer's mind the sacrificial ritual so
completely embodied the religion of Israel that it stood for
the entire earlier revelation of God.   Now according to an
influential Jewish theologumenon, which finds expression
in Acts vii. 53, Gal. iii. 19, and the LXX of Deut. xxxiii. 2,
that earlier revelation of the Divine will, codified in the Law,
was administered by angels as bridging the gulf between
God and the world.   They also stand behind the 'first
covenant' (Heb. ix. 15), and are in a sense responsible
for it (ii. 2).

But before we touch upon the 'better covenant' (vii. 22)
of which Jesus is the pledge, we must observe the remarkable fact that the author himself finds in the Old Testament a far-reaching forecast of the new order.   He quotes
Jeremiah's memorable words : ' This is the covenant which
I will make with the house of Israel after those days, saith
the Lord : I will put my laws into their mind, and upon
their hearts will I write them, and I will be to them a God,
and they shall be to me a people.   And they shall not teach
each his fellow-citizen and each his brother, saying, Know
the Lord, for all of them shall know me from the least unto
the greatest.   For I will be gracious to their iniquities,
and their sins I will remember no more.' [1]   This prophetic

[1] Jer. xxxi. 33-34 (quoted in Heb. viii. 10-12).

utterance is rich in meaning. The complex sacrificial ritual is ignored. No minute distinction is drawn between various classes of sins, those which admit of forgiveness and those which do not. Although the covenant is still described with reference to the community, the method of its realisation brings into the foreground the religious individual. That implies a deepening of the conception of sin. And the inwardness of its nature clearly shows that the centre of gravity has been shifted from a code of precepts to a renewed and inspired heart. The presupposition of all is a great act of Divine grace : God's free and complete pardon of His people's sins. The quotation is in no sense incidental. For in x. 16, 17 the author comes back to the passage and singles out those elements in it which have left the profoundest impression upon him : ' I will put my laws upon [1] their hearts, and upon their mind will I write them, and their sins and their iniquities I will remember no more.' The inwardness of the new relationship to God and its basis in the forgiveness of sins—these appeal to him as the crucial factors in the prophet's splendid vision.

Now already Jeremiah's forecast had been interpreted for the Christian consciousness. For there can be little doubt that Jesus had it in view when, at the Last Supper, so closely associated with the passover festival, He speaks of ' the new covenant in my blood.' [2] The addition found in Matthew xxvi. 28, ' shed for many to obtain the forgiveness of sins,' is at any rate true to the circle of ideas in which His mind was moving. For those to whom the Old Testament conception of the covenant was familiar, Jesus' words could have only one meaning. His death signified the inauguration of a new covenant, a new relation between God and men. That relation was initiated by the Divine

---

[1] Probably he uses 'upon' ($\epsilon\pi\iota$) in analogy to the inscribing of the older laws upon tables of stone. Cf. the contrast in 2 Cor. iii. 3.

[2] We deliberately take St. Paul's account in 1 Cor. xi. 23 ff. as the most authoritative. The arguments which have been used to discredit it are wholly arbitrary. We also recognise that, in all likelihood, such passages as Isa. xlix. 8, where the ' Servant of the Lord ' is described as ' a covenant of the people,' and (possibly) Zech. ix. 11, where the deliverance of captives is associated with ' the blood of the covenant,' were before our Lord's mind.

grace, and it depended essentially on the forgiveness of
sins, of which Jesus Himself, in His self-sacrificing love,
was the eternal pledge.

It is important to note that Paul makes scarcely any use
of the covenant-idea as a reciprocal relationship between
God and man, even although he was aware of its prominence
in the mind of Jesus. His view of the redeeming grace of
God in Christ was, as we have seen, indissolubly linked to
his personal experience. Release from the bondage of
legalism as a code of precepts on whose observance salvation depended—this was the moral problem which had
confronted the unsatisfied Pharisee. It was not, primarily
at least, the question of efficacious approach to God through
the sacrificial ritual, although in 2 Cor. iii. 6, entirely in the
spirit of Jeremiah, he speaks of himself as a minister of the
'new covenant, not of the letter but of the spirit.' For
Paul, the thought of the Divine initiative, already prominent
in the Old Testament idea of the covenant, is expressed by
a term belonging to the circle of covenant-ideas, namely,
the Promise. That occupies a large place in his Epistles.
In an illustration of the Promise, resting on the fact that
God had entered into gracious relationship with Abraham
before any legal code had been thought of, and assuring him
of a great future for his descendants apart from any burdensome restrictions, Paul uses the ordinary term for 'covenant'
($\delta\iota\alpha\theta\eta\kappa\eta$) in its allied sense of 'testament' or 'will'
(Gal. iii. 15), but entirely for illustrative purposes. Our
author, on the other hand, introduces this meaning into
one significant passage (ix. 15-18), taking the pleasure which
all Alexandrian exegetes found in a word with a two-fold
sense.[1] 'For this reason,' he says, 'Jesus is mediator of
a new covenant ($\delta\iota\alpha\theta\eta\kappa\eta$), that those who have been called

---

[1] Nothing could be more futile than the attempt to force the meaning
of 'will' or 'testamentary disposition' on $\delta\iota\alpha\theta\eta\kappa\eta$ throughout the Greek
Bible, whether O. T. or N. T., as, e.g., Deissmann does (Licht vom Osten,
p. 243). The evidence of piles of Hellenistic papyri is of no value whatever against the covenant-conception of the O. T., which was a religious
axiom for a Jew. The misunderstanding lies in interpreting the conception of covenant primarily as a bargain. In the O. T. it rests upon and
represents the Divine grace.

may obtain the eternal inheritance which has been promised
them, now that a death has occurred which redeems them
from the transgressions belonging to the first covenant.
For in the case of a will ($\delta\iota\alpha\theta\acute{\eta}\kappa\eta$), the death of the testator
must be announced. For a will only holds in cases of
death : it is never valid while the testator is alive. Hence
even the first *covenant of God's will* was not inaugurated
apart from blood.' [1] The phrase in italics (from Dr.
Moffatt's translation) brings out the connection of the two
ideas. The author's purpose here seems obvious. In the
great paragraph which precedes (vv. 11-14), he has
emphasised Christ's sacrifice of Himself ' through eternal
spirit ' as once for all realising the true purpose of sacrifice,
the purifying of sin-burdened consciences from a sense of
guilt so that they could serve the living God and thus
maintain the covenant-relation unbroken. Hence the
entire ritual of atonement has been antiquated. But he
desires also, following in the Master's own footsteps, to
associate Christ's sacrifice with the inauguration of the New
Covenant (ver. 18). This, as in the case of the Old, involves
the slaying of a victim whose blood is held to atone for
sin.[2] Instead of saying this directly, he uses what seems
to us a somewhat irrelevant argument, by passing from the
meaning of ' covenant ' to that of ' will,' and pointing out
that the testator *must die* before his will can have any
significance. This mode of demonstration, while suiting
his immediate purpose, is really no more than an illustration.[3] He passes from it immediately, returns to the
description of the ancient ceremonial in Exodus, and
contrasts that with the ' better sacrifice ' of Christ
(vv. 18-26).

[1] Chiefly M.

[2] There can be little doubt that for the later Judaism in which the
writer of Hebrews had been trained, the idea of atonement was crucial
in the inauguration-ritual.

[3] There is force in Professor Bruce's words : ' One wonders at the
introduction of so elementary and inferior a view close upon the grand
conception of verse 14. But . . . he is not at all sure that his grand
thought will strike his readers as it struck him, and so he falls back on
this cruder view as more level to childish apprehension ' (*Ep. to the Hebrews*,
p. 360).

For our author, then, Christ is both the inaugurator of the New Covenant, and the atoning sacrifice which pledges its eternal validity. But that New Covenant really belongs to the invisible realm. The great High Priest is in the heavens, a ministrant in the ' real tabernacle which the Lord erected, not man ' (viii. 2). He has not entered ' a holy place made with hands, the antitype of the genuine sanctuary, but heaven itself, now to appear in the presence of God on our behalf ' (ix. 24).

The central place of the conception of the covenant in the writer's thought is somewhat obscured by the method he has followed in constructing his apology. He first demonstrates the superiority of Christ, as the Son of God, to the angels ; secondly, to Moses ; and finally, to the Aaronic priesthood. Only in this final comparison, which is by far the most elaborate, does he introduce the idea of the covenant. But, as a matter of fact, all the terms of the contrast which he works out are selected because of their relation to the covenant-conception. It is as mediators of the earlier Divine order in which the people sought to realise their fellowship with the God who had revealed Himself that the angels, Moses, and the Aaronic priests are set over against Christ, the Mediator of the New Covenant. Hence the various elements which disclose the finality of the one in contrast with the temporary validity of the other will appear as we discuss the writer's comparison of Christ with the earlier mediators associated with the religion of Israel. It may be noted that he lays supreme emphasis on priestly mediation, because he connects with atoning sacrifices both the inauguration and the maintenance of a covenant between God and men. And thus the priesthood of Christ constitutes the main theme of the Epistle.

2. *Superiority of Christ, the Mediator of the New Covenant,
as Son of God, to :*

α. *Angels*

All that the author says about Christ has as its presupposition His Divine Sonship.   Whatever He has done or
is doing He does as the Son of God.   Attention has been
already called to the close parallel between various descriptions of the Logos in Philo and the statements regarding
Christ as Son of God in the opening verses of our Epistle.
Although a similar train of thought appears in such
utterances of Paul as 1 Cor. viii. 6 and Col. i. 16, 17, with
which the writer was probably acquainted, there can be
little doubt that his mode of expression in i. 1-4 has been
directly influenced by Philo and Alexandrian Judaism.
The use of such terms as ' effulgence ' and ' impress ' can
scarcely be accidental.   It is also noteworthy that Philo
repeatedly calls the Logos the ' first-born Son ' (πρωτόγονος)
of God.   But it would be altogether precarious, as we
have seen, to equate Philo's conception of the Logos with
our author's designation of Christ as Son of God.   The
title is one which he must have found in early Christian
usage, for he feels it unnecessary to offer any explanation
of it.   It is possible, from the frequent reference in the
New Testament to Ps. ii. 7, that it was originally used in
an adoptive sense.   But our investigation of its significance
for Paul has already shown that its history presents a somewhat complex problem.   In any case, the writer of Hebrews
does not require to establish the Divine Sonship of Christ
by argument.   He takes for granted that his readers agree
with his position.   And that position is, to all intents and
purposes, identical with Paul's, only that this writer, for
his special purpose, has to elaborate it.   It is not enough
to say, with some authorities, that our author's association
of the Christian order with the invisible heavenly world
necessarily presupposes the pre-existence of Christ.   He
starts, like Paul, from the historical Person, and works

back to what he regards as the inevitable implications of that overpowering Reality. His Alexandrian training may have helped him in the formulation of the convictions at which he has arrived. But his statements about Christ as the ' first-born ' (πρωτότοκος, i. 6), as God's instrument in creation (i. 2), as ' Son ' *par excellence* (i. 2, i. 8, etc.), are not the consequences of a metaphysical theory. They are the inferences forced upon him by the total result of Jesus' historical mission as embodied in the Christian community, and still more as apprehended in his personal experience.

It has been noted that the Christology of the Epistle is indissolubly linked to the idea of the Christian revelation as the New Covenant. Hence the supremacy of this covenant is involved in the supremacy of its Mediator. The author, however, is not content with a general exhibition of Christ's sovereignty as Revealer of God. For his concern is to show how the later revelation overshadows and antiquates the earlier. Therefore he draws a contrast in detail between the new and final Mediator between God and men, and those temporary mediators to whom his readers were inclined to attach undue importance.

He begins with angels, because it was a current Jewish doctrine, taken over into the Christian Church, that they were concerned with the giving of the Law at Sinai.[1] It might however be objected that they were spiritual beings, and that it is illegitimate to take them as representatives of that visible and material order which is here contrasted with the invisible realm of the spirit. But, as Prof. Peake points out, ' Jewish theology connected them closely with the material universe, so that each thing had its angel.' [2] There is scarcely a tone of disparagement in his reference. The angels have a valuable function to perform in the history of redemption (i. 14, ii. 2). But they are thrown into the shade by the essential dignity of Christ. He is Son. They are ' ministering spirits,' barely

---

[1] Cf. Acts vii. 53 ; Gal. iii. 19 ; Deut. xxxiii. 2 (LXX).
[2] *Hebrews* (Century Bible), p. 18. Cf. Paul's use of στοιχεῖα in Gal. iv. 3, 9.

conceivable as personalities. As such they may be transformed into natural forces to carry out in this medium
the behests of God (i. 7). Christ's exaltation is eternal.
He shares God's throne for ever, raised above all mutation
of being (i. 8, 10-12). No angel has ever been invited into
this lofty partnership with God (i. 13). Rather are they
bidden to bow down in worship before the First-born of
the eternal world (i. 6). Finally, their sphere of administration is the present, with all its imperfection. Christ is
Lord of the coming order, and His lordship is the pledge
that frail men shall have that glorious invisible world as
their heritage (ii. 5-9).[1] Two moments in the career of
Jesus are skilfully worked into this contrast : His con-
descension in sharing flesh and blood with His brethren,
and His exaltation to God's right hand (ii. 9, 14, i. 3, 4).
We call attention to these, because again and again in the
course of his argument the writer pauses to dwell upon
them (e.g. iv. 14, 15, v. 7-10, xii. 2). No doubt in this he
is above all else carrying out the chief object of his letter,
the bracing up of his readers in loyalty to Christ. He can
assure them of their Master's sympathy because He has
entered into their experiences, and can urge home the great
spiritual principle that suffering is the path to victory.
Probably also he has the apologetic aim of setting the
humiliation of Christ, which may have been to some a
stumbling-block, in its true perspective as a necessary
stage in the accomplishment of salvation. Nor can we
overlook his eagerness to prepare his readers' minds, as
he does by so many similarly subtle hints, for his great
central exposition of Christ's all-sufficient priesthood.

β. Moses

One of the supreme glories of Jewish tradition was the
mediatorship of Moses. On him had been conferred the

---

[1] The details of the contrast between Christ and the angels are based
on O. T. passages which the author, no doubt in common with the whole
early Christian community, interprets Messianically. These would have
the force of proof-texts for his readers, although to us his method is altogether foreign.

unique privilege of acting as the channel of the Divine will
to Israel in the formative period of its history. No name
stood higher on the national roll of honour. The writer's
estimate of his heroic figure is plain from chap. xi. 23-28.
No other personage in the catalogue of worthies is marked
out for such distinction. The special characteristic of
Moses selected for emphasis in the present comparison is
taken from the statement of Numb. xii. 7 (LXX) that he
was 'faithful in all God's house.' Obviously in that
passage, 'house' stands for 'community' or 'common-
wealth.' [1] His fidelity is manifested in his administration
of Israel as the community of God. Now for a mind steeped
in the Pentateuch, the foundation of the community would
be directly associated with the inauguration of the covenant
at Horeb. So that, in accord with his general scheme of
thought, this moment probably lies in the background of
the writer's mind. We know that Moses stands out as the
medium between God and the people in the great act of
dedication which, in Exod. xxiv. 8, is called a 'covenant,'
an act which is the response to the gracious entrance of
God into their history. For our author, a new epoch of
history, the final epoch, has begun with Christ. He
stands between God and man as Moses did. His fidelity
is evident to all who are acquainted with the story of His
mission. In no respect does He come behind Moses in this,
the most important quality demanded of any one who is
entrusted with the fulfilling of a high vocation. Now, as a
matter of fact, Moses' aim was only partially attained.
Although the whole community entered through him into
the covenant, the loyalty of many broke down, and the
promise embodied in the covenant was in their case
thwarted. Even Joshua, the successor of Moses, was not
able to lead them to the desired end (iii. 16-19, iv. 6-8).
Here, although the contrast is not made explicit, there is a
suggestion that it remained for Christ to make possible in
the New Covenant that satisfying relation to God for which
they had craved. This, however, is not the central point

[1] See Dillmann, *ad loc.*

of the comparison. Moses, the writer shows, was after all
only a servant in the consecrated community. Christ, as
the Son of God, who of His grace founded the community,
has authority over it as the vicegerent of God, the Founder.
That is to say, on its new basis, the consecrated community is not at one remove from God, as reaching the
knowledge of God through one of its own number. In
Christ it is brought directly into the Divine fellowship,
for as the Son He knows and represents the Father
perfectly.

γ. Aaronic High Priests

It is at first sight almost startling to find the remarkable
passage which describes the human experience of Jesus
as perfect sympathy with the needs and trials of His
brethren (ii. 9-17) culminating in the statement : ' in order
to become a compassionate and faithful high priest (for
them) in relation to God.' We are not prepared for this
abrupt introduction of the idea of priesthood. With equal
abruptness this conception is made the pivot of the exhortation which closes the elaborate warning against
unbelief in iii. 7—iv. 13, only that now an important note
of explanation is added : ' As we have, therefore, a great
high priest who has passed through the heavens, Jesus the
Son of God, let us hold fast our confession ' (iv. 14). The
words really form the climax of the writer's thought up to
this point, and they reveal the lines along which his mind
has been silently moving. He began the Epistle by dwelling
upon the glory of Jesus as Son of God, through whom the
Father has given His final revelation to men. But this
Jesus humbled Himself to enter the lot of tempted
humanity. His aim was to understand men through and
through. Now He is exalted to God's right hand. There
He still bears the burdens of His brethren, and represents
their needs in God's presence, and thus in an altogether
new and glorified fashion performs the function of high
priest, keeping them in fellowship with the Divine mercy
and grace. From this point up to x. 32 the main theme

of the Epistle is the high-priesthood of Christ, viewed in various aspects as the great ministry through which men are able to draw near to the living God.

From the elaboration of the writer's leading thesis we can gather the steps by which he has reached his position. The *order* of subjects in the Epistle presupposes rather than indicates these steps.[1] We have already collected and examined the data which determine the writer's general outlook. Let us recall its main features. Fundamental is the antithesis between the realm of the visible and transient, embodied for religion in the legal ritual of Judaism, and that of the invisible and eternal which has projected itself into human experience in the Christian revelation. Now the end of religion is to bring men near to God. This relation of access to God found expression in the Old Testament conception of the covenant. The writer retains the idea, which makes so powerful an appeal to all Jewish minds, and through the medium of Jeremiah's great picture of the New Covenant finds it marvellously exemplified in Christianity. But the function of a covenant being to maintain the community in fellowship with God, and that maintenance, according to the Law, depending on appropriate sacrifices, everything will turn on the existence of an adequate priesthood, that can represent the community in making offerings to atone for their sins. In the Christian dispensation Christ is the all-sufficient Priest. His one sacrifice of Himself both inaugurates the New Covenant, a ceremony which in the ritual of the Pentateuch involved a sprinkling of blood, and constitutes an eternal atonement for the sins of His people, which would otherwise interrupt their fellowship with God.

(1) *Christ's Priesthood included all the valuable qualities of a worthy High Priest of the Aaronic Order*

We are now in a position to discuss the writer's comparison of Christ's high-priesthood with that of the Aaronic

[1] See p. 201, *supra*.

order. First, he sets himself to show that it included all the valuable qualities of a worthy high priest of the Aaronic order. Now the primary function of the high priest was to take direction of the worship of the community. As the worship of Israel, like that of all ancient peoples, was chiefly sacrificial, his main business was to see that the offerings of the people were presented to God in the manner prescribed by religious authority. These offerings, the writer assumes, are usually intended to make atonement for sin, to remove whatever defilement may hinder the people from finding access to their God. His language, however, suggests that the high priest who is true to his sacred calling will not be a mere official ministrant of sacrifice. He will take a larger view of his vocation than that. He will feel the obligation to deal with burdened consciences, to offer spiritual counsel, and all in a spirit of sincere sympathy, for we know that confession of sin for the post-exilic community formed the very core of the sacrificial ritual.[1] Hence the high priest, a frail man himself, must be able ' to deal gently with the ignorant and the erring ' (v. 2). The remarkable term here used to describe his attitude ($\mu\epsilon\tau\rho\iota o\pi a\theta\epsilon\hat{\iota}\nu$) implies the mean between censorious severity and mere good-natured leniency. He will not terrify the penitent by unqualified condemnation, and yet he dare not make light of any moral lapse. In virtue of his office he can declare the will of God, but at the same time he will be fully alive to the frailty which besets even those whose purposes are good. Further, no man of himself would choose a vocation of such tremendous responsibility (v. 4). He simply enters upon it according to Divine appointment, and the sense of a Divine purpose encourages him when otherwise he would shrink from his task. Here, of course, the author has in view the Jewish tradition of a priesthood hereditary by Divine prescription in the tribe of Levi.

Christ possesses both of the specific qualifications laid down. On the one hand, He is able to sympathise with

---

[1] See Wheeler Robinson, *Religious Ideas of the O. T.*, p. 167.

the infirmities of His brethren, because He was ' tempted
in all points' like them ' yet without yielding to sin' (iv. 15).
No writer outside the Synoptic Gospels gives so prominent
a place as this to Jesus' discipline of suffering [1] as the
condition of His final fitness to be Saviour. The subject
seems to fascinate him. No doubt, as has been already
hinted, he finds in it a strong ground of consolation to
offer to his readers who are undergoing severe trials. It
reminds them not merely that their living Lord understands their situation, and can therefore give them the
succour they require, but also that the way of suffering is
that which leads to ultimate perfection. But at the same
time it directly answers the author's central purpose of
exhibiting Jesus Christ as the completely adequate High
Priest who can accomplish what has never been accomplished before : who is able to remove all the barriers
which separate God from His children whom He desires
to ' bring to glory ' (ii. 10). On the other hand, this
function of Christ is assigned to Him by the Father. That
is taken for granted again and again in the Epistle. When
the writer wishes to demonstrate it, he quotes two passages
from the Book of Psalms, which were always interpreted
Messianically (v. 5, 6). His method, which to us appears
so external, would appeal forcibly to his readers. The
second of his quotations, ' Thou art a priest for ever
according to the order of Melchizedek ' (Ps. cx. 4), strikes
the keynote of the elaborate discussion of Christ's high
superiority to the older priesthood which occupies the
body of the Epistle.

(2) *Christ's Priesthood possessed in addition those qualities
for lack of which the Aaronic Order of Priests failed in
its religious Office*

It is important to observe that in seeking to establish
this superiority, the author is not simply at the mercy of
an imposing theory. The basis of all his elaborate argu-

[1] *E.g.* ii. 9, 10, 14, 17, 18 ; iv. 15, 16 ; v. 7-9 ; xii. 2.

ment lies in his personal experience of Jesus Christ. This
man, who from his earliest days has been familiar with the
sacrificial system of his nation, who is aware of the firm
hold it has taken even of spiritual minds, has discovered
for himself that in Christ he has actually come into that
fellowship with God which the traditional ceremonial had
promised, but which it had never achieved. Here is the
New Covenant which Jeremiah had foretold in real operation. Its existence is intrinsically involved in that of the
exalted Christ, ' who ever lives to make intercession for '
His people. Hence it is thoroughly relevant to his own
religious history as well as to the pressing needs of his
readers to set forth with reverent care those qualities by
which Christ, in contrast to the Aaronic line of officials,
has realised for His people the true function of High Priest.

(a) *Christ belongs to a new order of priesthood.* The
elaborate discussion of this theme in vii. 1-25 has been skilfully prepared for by a three-fold introduction of the
phrase, ' a high priest (or, priest) according to the order
($\tau\acute{a}\xi\iota\nu$) of Melchizedek,' [1] and the discussion itself starts
from a characteristically Alexandrian treatment of the
primitive story in Genesis, of which the priest-king
Melchizedek forms the centre. Two considerations have
prompted the introduction of this strange figure. On the
one hand, there is the psalmist's phrase which, in the judgment of Jews and early Christians, describes the priesthood
of Messiah and therefore directly refers to Christ (Ps. cx. 4).
On the other, the author, entirely in the Philonic manner,
finds the most impressive feature of the ancient narrative to
be the *timelessness* of Melchidezek as a historical personage.
He sees the psalmist's description, ' a priest for ever,'
exemplified in this man, who appears without any setting
of lineage or family : who is not represented, like the
Aaronic priests, as belonging to any succession : who, on
the sacred page, ' has neither beginning of days nor end of

---

[1] v. 6, 10 ; vi. 20. Holtzmann's attempt to find in the author's
emphasis on Christ's priesthood the influence of Philo's description of the
Logos as high priest in one or two places is far-fetched (*op. cit.*, ii. p. 334).
But it may have been one of the factors in the formation of his thought.

life,' and thus, so far as Scripture is concerned, 'abides a priest for ever.'[1] Here is a priest-king who occupies his station, not on account of legal arrangement, but in virtue of his own personality. His is the order to which Christ belongs. He has become priest 'not according to the law of a fleshly commandment, but according to the power of an indissoluble life' (vii. 16). Christ's priesthood invalidates the old Aaronic order. That depended on heredity. His depends on personality, a fulness of life which cannot be quenched. He who has come to impart to men 'overflowing life,' in the Johannine phrase (John x. 10), is the true priest for men, the true medium between God and them. His priesthood, from the nature of the case, is eternal and inviolable (vii. 23, 24). The full significance of the eternal priesthood emerges at a later stage of his argument. But the new order of priesthood implies essentially the establishment of the New Covenant.

(b) The all-important function of the priest is to offer sacrifice, as representing the people before God. *The New Covenant established by Christ involves a new type of sacrifice.* The contrast between the old and the new is drawn in detail. The Aaronic priests offered their sacrifices in an earthly sanctuary. But its inner chamber, the special place of the Divine Presence, was closed except for a single day in the year, on which the high priest entered, carrying the blood of the sacrificial victim, which he sprinkled on and in front of the mercy-seat, the first time as an atonement for his own sin, the second, for the sins of the people. On this great day, by a similar ceremony, the holy place itself, with its furniture, was 'atoned for,' or purged from sin.[2] These actions, as we have seen, were intended to 'purify' ($\kappa\alpha\theta\alpha\rho\iota\zeta\epsilon\iota\nu$) or 'sanctify' ($\dot{\alpha}\gamma\iota\dot{\alpha}\zeta\epsilon\iota\nu$) the people, that is, to preserve them in covenant-relation with their

---

[1] vii. 3. It is unnecessary for our purpose to ask whether the phrase 'for ever' in Ps. cx. 4 is associated for the psalmist, as for our author, with the Melchizedek-figure as described in Genesis. Obviously the latter so regards it, and justifies the association by his exegesis. For a suggestive explanation of the phrase, see Peake on Heb. i. 13. Kittel (*Die Psalmen*, pp. 400, 401) contests the ascription of Ps. cx. to the Maccabean period.
[2] See Lev. xvi. 11-19.

God.[1] The writer brings into close connection with the
ritual of the Day of Atonement that belonging to the
inauguration of the covenant as described in Exod. xxiv.
(ix. 18-20). Indeed his reference to the sprinkling of holy
places and vessels is introduced as if related to the latter.
But throughout he draws no clear distinction between the
inauguration of the covenant and its maintenance, as is
plain from ix. 15, where, in describing the death of Christ
as the initiation of the New Covenant, he goes on to
declare that that death had as its aim the forgiveness of the
sins committed under the earlier covenant. That is to
say, the same event is regarded both as an inaugural and
an atoning sacrifice. As a matter of fact, the basal idea
in his mind is expressed in ix. 22 : ' Apart from shedding
of blood, there is no remission of sins.' Both these types of
sacrifice have as their purpose the forgiveness of sins,
which are the violation of the covenant. Probably the
dictum laid down is an axiom for the writer, as it was for
the Hebrew mind in general. He does not theorise on its
significance. Blood, regarded as the seat of life, atones.
But his description of the Levitical ritual, as it culminated
in that of the Day of Atonement, emphasises its *inadequacy*.
The same ceremonial was repeated year after year. The
Holy of Holies where God was to be met remained closed
save for one day annually. The sacrifices themselves were
bound up with a system of ' meats and drinks and various
purifications.' They consisted of the blood of bulls and
goats.[2] As regards these, the writer bluntly declares that
' it is impossible that they should remove sin ' : that
' they have no power to perfect (τελειῶσαι) the worshipper
in his conscience,' *i.e.* to remove his sense of guilt so that
he may have the assurance of real fellowship with God.
The very fact of this repetition pointed to the abiding
consciousness of guilt.[3] And he boldly appeals to Ps. xl.
6-8 as scriptural evidence that God had no pleasure in

[1] In ix. 9 τελειῶσαι, 'to perfect,' is used in the same sense. See Feine,
op. cit., p. 559.
[2] ix. 25, ix. 7-9, ix. 10, ix. 12.   [3] x. 4, ix. 9, x. 2.

sacrifices, but that His delight was in the obedient will (x. 5-9). Hence we may take as his general principle the statement made with reference to the priesthood : ' The earlier commandment is cancelled on account of its feebleness and futility, for the law brought nothing to its goal ' (vii. 18 f.).

The question naturally arises : Did the writer hold that the older ritual had been simply labour lost ? That would be a most precarious inference. It was an integral part of the religious system of Israel, and although ' the law brought nothing to its goal,' it contained nevertheless ' a shadow of the blessings to come,' and its ministrants served ' a copy of the heavenly realities ' (x. 1, viii. 5). But while the ' shadow ' is very different from ' the fac-simile ' which is presented in the Christian faith, it is better than nothing. It provided a ritual cleansing for the community (ix. 13), a cleansing which, for devout minds that could penetrate beneath the letter to the spirit, must have often meant a sense of restoration to the Divine communion. But at best the machinery was cumbrous : at best the pathway into God's presence was dimly lighted. No wonder that a man who had in his own experience grasped the significance of Christ could affirm that the old sacrifices ' were of a kind which could never remove sin ' (x. 11) : no wonder that he exulted in ' the new and living (i.e. effective) way ' into the sanctuary of God's presence, inaugurated by the sacrifice of Christ.[1] Christ, in contrast to the Aaronic priests, is ' a minister of the genuine taber-nacle,' which is the heavenly world, the real abode of God's presence. As exalted above all that is material and imperfect, He represents His people in the Holy of Holies ' not made with hands.' He too has made an offering, but not on His own behalf, an atoning sacrifice in virtue of which He could enter the Divine presence, to give His worshipping people the assurance that their sins were purged away. This He did once, and once for all. The offering was Himself, in His spotless purity. It was made

---

[1] x. 19, 20.

'through eternal spirit.'[1] This differentiates it from the animal sacrifices. It had the whole power of His deathless personality in it : it was an embodiment of all that He was. So its worth can never fade. Its moral significance is that it realises the Divine will. It is an act of perfect obedience. Its effect corresponds to its character. It does completely what the earlier ritual had never achieved : it cleanses the conscience from dead works to serve the living God.[2] The description is very remarkable. The living God is God manifested as He truly is, in Jesus Christ, 'all active in putting Himself forth to men, and all responsive to their putting of themselves forth to Him.'[3] As soon as the conscience is unburdened of its sin, it passes out of the sphere of death into that of life, which is the sphere of God. For the first time the human spirit finds its real home. This new condition the writer describes by the old ritual term, 'sanctify' (ἁγιάζειν). The word retains its association with the covenant-idea. But it implies a covenant 'which has been enacted on the basis of better promises.'[4]

This, then, is the assurance brought to the believing heart by the sacrifice of Christ. The writer sets forth, as usual, in the language of *cultus*, the transformation which had been wrought in his own life and that of his fellow-Christians by coming into relation with Christ and His redeeming activity. It is for him concentrated in His death and (as we shall see) His exalted life of intercession. 'Having been perfected,[5] he became the cause of eternal salvation to all who obey him' (v. 9). But what He has done carries with it the total impression of His career as Saviour. To each element alike we may apply what Prof. Bruce has said of Christ's sacrifice, that it 'acts on the conscience through the mind interpreting its significance, and in proportion as it is thought on.'[6] Such interpretation and reflection would necessarily be coloured by

---

[1] viii. 2, vii. 26, ix. 11, vii. 27, ix. 12, x. 12, ix. 14.
[2] x. 9, 10 ; ix. 14.　　　　　　　　　[3] Davidson on Heb. iii. 12.
[4] x. 10, 14, 29 ; viii. 6.
[5] His τελείωσις was effected by suffering and death ; it was realised in His exaltation.　　　　　　　　[6] *Epistle to the Hebrews*, p. 350.

the author's presuppositions.   When these presuppositions
are modified in the course of a long development of religious experience the interpretation inevitably receives an
enlargement of range and an enriching of content.

(b) Consummation of the New Covenant in the World to Come

1. Christ's High Priesthood a Link between the Present and the World to come

The ultimate issue of our author's conception of the
high-priesthood of Christ finds expression in viii. 1 :
' We have a high priest of such a character that he sat
down at the right hand of the throne of majesty in the
heavens.' Christ's exaltation completely overshadows His
resurrection in this Epistle, while of course presupposing
it. And it is invariably linked to the atoning sacrifice of
Himself which He offered as High Priest for His people :
' Having offered one sacrifice for sin of eternal value, he
sat down at the right hand of God ' (x. 12). The latter
phrase which he uses so often has come from his favourite
Psalm, the 110th. But he always interprets it from the
point of view of Christ's high-priesthood. By the pathway
of His sacrificial death, which, as we have seen, was at
once the inauguration of a new relationship to God and the
pledge that such a relationship should never be broken,
He passed into the Divine presence and abides there for
ever. There can therefore be no interruption to the approach of those ' who come unto God by him, seeing he
ever lives to make intercession for them ' (vii. 25). A
barren controversy has been waged around the question :
When did Christ become high priest ? Was it at His
death or when He entered heaven ? The author draws
no such distinction. According to the symbolism used, He
must have been high priest when He offered the sacrifice,
but the sacrifice is not complete until it is presented before
God. But Christ never leaves the heavenly sanctuary,
therefore He is an eternal high priest. His people can

always count on His interest in their needs. They may always be sure that He ' can bring to bear all the resources of the Almighty for the complete and final salvation of his brethren.' [1]

A remarkable turn is given to the idea of Christ's high-priesthood, which reveals a further range of the writer's thought. It is introduced almost as if incidentally, but it belongs to a fundamental element in his scheme of conceptions. In describing the hope of the Christian as an anchor cast within the heavenly world, that world which is at present veiled from his eyes as the Holy of Holies was curtained off from the gaze of the worshippers in the ancient tabernacle, he reminds his readers that Jesus has penetrated behind the veil as their High Priest, but also as their Forerunner ($\pi\rho\delta\delta\rho\omega\mu\omega\varsigma$).[2] Here is a vital transformation of the picture. The Aaronic high priest was permitted once a year to pass within the Holy of Holies, but no worshipper could ever expect to follow him. At best their fellowship with God was mediated. Christ has entered the true sanctuary in the heavenly world, not to spend a brief moment there but to abide for ever. But in so doing He has prepared the way by which His people are destined to follow Him. The veil has been withdrawn. Their perfecting will be on the same lines as His (v. 9). It will mean entrance into the real sanctuary, complete and immediate communion with God. That will be the consummation of the New Covenant.

Now a most important feature in our author's outlook is the conviction that already Christians have entered upon this consummation, have begun to live in the world to come, the invisible heavenly order. At an early stage in our discussion we found how central for the Epistle was the contrast between the present, as the world of shadows, embodied for religion in the ritual of Judaism, and the world to come as the realm of realities, which have their true copy in the Christian dispensation. The author ventures to go further than this, and to declare that, in a

---

[1] Bruce, *op. cit.*, p. 280.   [2] vi. 20.

sense, the world to come, the Messianic age of ardent Jews, has already broken in, has already projected itself into the closing epoch of this present age. That is the real meaning of the New Covenant. It is not merely a hope : it is already fruition. Here he touches the thought of Paul. Paul too has the belief that Christians are even now 'delivered from this age which is evil.' Their common-wealth is already in heaven. Their lot has been cast in 'the closing hours of the world.'[1] This phrase has a marked resemblance to that of Heb. i. 2 : 'the close of these days,' an epoch signalised by the manifestation of Jesus Christ.[2] His appearance, or at least His high-priestly service on behalf of His people, has virtually inaugurated the coming era. Their present access to God through Him is a genuine anticipation of the future. They know that they possess a better than any earthly heritage, one that endures. They have already 'tasted the heavenly gift . . . and the powers of the world to come' ($\mu\epsilon\lambda\lambda o\nu\tau os$ $a i\hat{\omega}\nu os$).[3] In Jesus Christ their representative High Priest and Forerunner, who has carried with Him into the heavenly order the life and experience in which He became one with His brethren, they are now 'partakers of a heavenly calling.' They have come 'to Mount Sion, the city of the living God, the heavenly Jerusalem, to myriads of angels in festal gathering, to the assembly of the first-born enrolled in heaven.'[4] The Christian is thus living a two-fold life. 'Actually he still lives within the lower order. But ideally he has already transcended it, and he confidently looks forward to the time when the actual shall be one with the ideal.'[5] Even now, in wondrous fashion, the ideal is translated into the real through faith.

---

[1] Gal. i. 4 ; Phil. iii. 20 ; 1 Cor. x. 11 (M.).
[2] Cf. ix. 26 : $\epsilon\pi\grave{\iota}$ $\sigma u\nu\tau\epsilon\lambda\epsilon\acute{\iota}a$ $\tau\hat{\omega}\nu$ $a i\acute{\omega}\nu\omega\nu$ . . . $\pi\epsilon\phi a\nu\acute{\epsilon}\rho\omega\tau a\iota$, 'at the end of the ages . . . he has been manifested.'
[3] x. 34 ; vi. 4, 5.   [4] iii. 1 ; xii. 22, 23 (M.).
[5] Peake, *Hebrews*, p. 21.

2. *Faith, the indispensable Attitude of Members of the New Covenant*

In our examination of Paulinism it became clear that faith, for Paul, primarily means a surrender of the whole being to the once crucified and now living Christ, with the close intimacy of spirit which that involves. This was a re-shaping, on the ground of personal experience, of a conception which held a place both in the Old Testament and Judaism. There can be little doubt that in the school of Gamaliel Paul would hear and take part in discussions of the ' faith ' of Abraham, the classical believer of Hebrew tradition (Gen. xv. 6). In the Book of Psalms, with which he was familiar, trust is emphasised as the fundamental attitude of the devout soul to God. Now through his three-fold reference to Abraham's faith in Rom. iv.[1] there shines the regular Old Testament idea of faith as confidence in the fidelity of God, and the same idea belongs to Isa. xxviii. 16, which Paul deliberately adjusts to his own Christian conception.[2] Meanwhile Philo had given faith a central place in religion. It is true that here and there it assumes a highly intellectual cast. But when discussing, as he delights to do, the faith of Abraham (Gen. xv. 6), he clearly brings out its religious value : *e.g. De Migrat. Abr.* 132, ' It was after Abraham believed that he is said to have drawn near to God ' ; *De Abrah.* 268, ' So the only genuine and sure blessing is faith towards God, the consolation of life, the fulness of gracious hopes.' [3]

It is possible, but perhaps scarcely necessary, to suppose that the prominence which our author gives to faith is partly due to Philonic influence.[4] In any case, his statement regarding Moses in xi. 27, ' for as seeing the invisible

---

[1] Gen. xv. 6, quoted in Rom. iv. 3, 9, 22.

[2] It is interesting to note that while Hab. ii. 4, ' the righteous man shall live by his faithfulness,' is quoted by Paul (Rom. i. 17, Gal. iii. 11) as an O. T. argument for the typical faith of the Christian as the apostle himself has formulated it, it appears in Heb. x. 38 in its original sense of ' fidelity,' although, of course, this fidelity is the product of trust in God.

[3] Cf. *Quis Rer. Div. Her.*, 90-95.

[4] So Holtzmann, *op. cit.*, ii. p. 346 f.

he endured,' is a genuine reflection of the Old Testament standpoint which Philo also discerned.   True to the bias of his mind, he assigns to faith the crucial function in the life of the Christian under the New Covenant.   The famous muster-roll of Old Testament heroes of faith is another demonstration that the new order is the consummation of the old.   They ' died in faith, not having attained the promises, but only seeing them afar off and hailing them ' (xi. 13).   For Christians the Divine promises have been put on a totally different footing by Christ, who, Son of God as He was, became one with His brethren, shared their discipline of trial, made that final sacrifice for their sins which gave Him free entrance into the very presence of God, where He abides as a pledge that they may follow in His steps.   Hence, faith for the Christian receives a far richer content than it ever could have had under the Old Covenant. It has become a new attitude, of which Christ is the founder and perfecter.[1]   With altogether fresh cogency they may be convinced of the reality of the invisible world, because now they are able to draw near to God without restriction.

It ought to be noted that this emphasis on faith has a directly apologetic bearing.   The readers were in danger of losing touch with that good news of Christ which had once illumined them, and had enabled them to endure a hard conflict of sufferings.[2]   Confidence, therefore, is what above all else they require, and the steadfast endurance which confidence brings.   They had begun most hopefully.   They must hold fast their glad courage and the hope in which they had exulted firmly to the end (iii. 6).

We do not need to dwell upon the celebrated definition of faith given in xi. 1, nor upon its familiar expansion in xi. 6.   In these passages, which have a distinctly Philonic flavour, the writer wishes to lay a broad basis for the attitude of faith, one which will hold good of all stages in the history of religion, even the most rudimentary.   And he at once relates his definition to the experience of Old Testament worthies, who, as he observes later, could not

---

[1] xi. 39, 40 ; xii. 2.   [2] ii. 3, 4 ; vi. 4 ; x. 32.

reach their goal apart from the higher order inaugurated
and maintained by Christ (xi. 40). Thus there is an
element of truth in Bruce's statement that in this Epistle
'faith derives its virtue from its psychological character as
a faculty of the human mind, whereby it can make the
future present and the unseen visible.'[1] In this aspect of
it we can trace Philonic affinities. But if the author may
be allowed to reveal a certain psychological interest in the
conception, as Philo unquestionably does,[2] that is completely overshadowed by its religious application, which is
always in the forefront.

Some scholars have emphasised the notion that in
Hebrews faith is not associated, as in Paul, with the
beginning of the Christian career, but rather with its
development. Certainly, in addressing this particular community, the writer is not concerned with beginnings, as he
deliberately asserts,[3] and so he does not require to deal
with an initial faith. But it is noteworthy that among
the elementary Christian doctrines he mentions faith in
God; and when he reminds his readers that they, like the
ancient Israelities, have received a Divine message (iv. 2),
he warns them against the fate of their forefathers, who
gained no benefit from that which they heard, because
'it was not mixed with faith for the hearers.'[4] The
words surely imply that faith, in the author's sense of
confiding in the revelation of God, belongs not merely to
the progress but also to the starting-point of a Christian
course. That is corroborated by his conception of Christ
as the founder as well as the perfecter of the Christian
faith. It is obviously difficult in such a connection to draw
a sharp distinction between faith and obedience. So we
are not surprised to find the writer setting forth obedience
as the condition of salvation.[5] For if a Gospel is really

---

[1] *Op. cit.*, p. 448.
[2] See Bousset, *Die Religion d. Judentums*,[2] pp. 514, 515.
[3] vi. 1.
[4] Reading συνκεκερασμένος instead of -νους, which, although better
attested, does not give nearly such good sense.
[5] v. 9 : cf. ii. 1.

accepted as the appeal of the living God, it is bound to be
obeyed.

Now, if such a Gospel lays hold of the mind in the form
of a promise of eternal blessedness to be consummated in
the heavenly world, faith will operate largely as the immov-
able basis of a splendid hope. That is the position of
Hebrews. The two ideas are virtually interchangeable.
' We desire each of you,' he says, ' to give the same proof
(as they had done in Christian service) of your eagerness to
maintain your hope in full vigour to the end, so that instead
of being slack you may imitate those who by their faith
and patience are in possession of the promises ' (vi. 11, 12).
Thus from first to last the Epistle rings with the note of a
steadfast hope, a hope which is not the mere dream of
heated imaginations, but rather the anchor of the soul,
cast within the invisible world of realities through the
power of faith in a God who cannot deceive.[1] A faith so
daring and yet so closely linked to actual experience already
spans the gulf between earth and heaven. The believer
may well give thanks that even now he receives from the
God to whom he has drawn near through Christ, the great
High Priest, a realm which, unlike this terrestrial order,
can never be shaken.[2]

[1] vi. 18 f.   [2] xii. 28.

PART III

THE THEOLOGY OF THE DEVELOPING CHURCH

(a) Shaping Forces

As already noted in the introductory chapter, we regard the Epistles to Timothy and Titus, those which bear the names of James and Jude, and the Second assigned to Peter as monuments of the Theology of the Developing Church. Before we examine the dominating features of this phase of early Christian thought, we must take a brief glance at the forces which gave it shape.

When we pass from the Letters of Paul to such documents as the First Epistle of Clement to the Corinthians, the so-called Epistle of Barnabas, the Teaching of the Twelve Apostles, and the Shepherd of Hermas—all of them probably belonging to the period between 95 and 150 A.D.— we are conscious of a changed atmosphere. Even the familiar Pauline terms, which frequently occur, seem to be infected with a curious dryness. It is not that the writers lack religious earnestness. But their religion is more or less prosaic in its type. Indeed Hermas himself seems alive to the situation, when he represents the young man who appears to him in one of his Visions (iii. 11) as saying : ' Your spirit has grown old and is now withered, and it has lost power.' The splendid enthusiasm of Paul's spirituality has vanished, and in its stead there has emerged a correct, commonplace piety which claims from its adherents self-control, patience, obedience, and brotherly love, and furnishes them with an elaborate series of maxims, intended to regulate their conduct from day to day. We sorely miss the freshness and spontaneity of Paul's experience. There are no surprises of heroic faith, no outbursts of self-forgetting devotion to Christ, no bold ideals of service and consecration. ' A common greyness silvers everything.' At this lower level of thought and feeling larger room is left for a somewhat mechanical repetition of Jewish ideas, which have come to form part of the Church's religious equipment, and for an emphasising of ecclesiastical ordinances and arrangements, which brings into relief the external rather than the inner requirements of the Christian society.

Now it would be an exaggeration hastily to group with these documents the later New Testament Epistles which we are investigating. Yet the unprejudiced reader who chooses to make the comparison will be struck with many remarkable parallels between them, and a careful study will show that in these later books we have at least the beginnings of the tone and temper which are clearly manifest in the writings of the Apostolic Fathers.

The question, therefore, arises : What is the explanation of this divergence of spirit, how shall we account for the diminution of religious vision and intensity which undoubtedly confronts us ? We must, it is true, beware of over-straining the contrast. For passages may be quoted from these post-Pauline Epistles which recall the fervour of the great apostle, and move among the same fundamental ideas. But we have specially to attend to that which is typical rather than to isolated expressions which reveal the earlier vigour. And when we speak of this ' earlier vigour ' we would include First Peter and the Epistle to the Hebrews, although the latter has various interesting points of contact with the documents under review. First of all, we miss the accent of eager religious individuality. Paul was the very embodiment of extraordinary creative energy. Peter reveals the freshness of impression which characterises a mind and heart in direct touch with the beginnings of the Christian movement. The writer to the Hebrews, while reflecting something of the later Church-consciousness, is a man who has wrestled in a highly original fashion with the problem of the relation of Christianity to Judaism, and his solution bears the stamp of independent thinking. The authors of our Epistles, sincere as they are in their efforts to preserve ' the faith once for all delivered to God's people ' (Jude 3), and zealous for the Church as ' the pillar and bulwark of the truth ' (1 Tim. iii. 15), are primarily inheritors of a tradition. ' The truth ' is a phrase which constantly recurs, and it of course implies a settled body of doctrine which is the criterion for the Christian profession. Its correlative is the Church, regarded not so much from the Pauline standpoint as the Body of Christ, but rather as a carefully organised institution, administered by special functionaries. Spiritual gifts have fallen into the background. The important offices are assigned to men who possess a well-marked range of qualifications.

All this presupposes a fresh stage in the development of the Christian society. A generation was growing up which had been born within the community, and its conception of the faith was not so vivid or immediate as that of the preceding epoch. There had also been an influx of members in the mass, carrying with them into the Church survivals of pagan ideas and pagan habits. Moreover, many of the converts had been won by missionaries whose grasp of the faith was far less sure and comprehensive than that of Paul. In any case, as the diffusion of the new religion became wider, more numerous points of contact would be established with heathen society, and the tendency to compromise would find freer scope. The fact that many adherents of Christianity had already formed close associations with the synagogue meant the inevitable intrusion of central elements from Judaism. A monotheism implying a uniquely transcendent God, a strict doctrine of retribution, a legal conception of the Divine will as manifested in a code of detailed injunctions—these became factors of regulative importance in the Theology of the Developing Church, and that, not merely because they had already been influential in the experience of pagan seekers after

God, but also because they corresponded to certain pressing needs of the time.

The foundations of Christianity had been laid by the great missionaries of the earlier era. In the period which here concerns us the clamant necessity was the actual practice of those Christian virtues which were the outgrowth of its fundamental experiences. Hence a duty which lay close to the heart of every Christian teacher was that of pressing home the obligation of consistent Christian living. In many circles there would still be much confusion regarding the profounder doctrines of the faith. Side by side with this immaturity of conviction there arose men of subtle intellect who seized on special aspects of the apostolic tradition, blended these with ideas from Judaism or Hellenism, and by asserting high claims of an esoteric nature formed sects either within or outside the Church. As so frequently in esoteric coteries, laxity of morals accompanied arrogant spiritual pretensions. For these various reasons the demand for an ethical standard high above the average recognised by pagan sentiment gradually came to overshadow the sources of inspiration from which alone such a standard could be supplied.

(b) Moralistic Tendency in Religion

Here we are confronted by what may be called the moralistic tendency inherent in the documents of our period. Let us avoid any misconception of what is meant. No Christian teacher has ever laid more drastic emphasis than the apostle Paul upon the unity of religion and morals. As uncompromisingly as his Master, he proclaims the crucial test for Christians : ' By their fruits ye shall know them.' But this ethical activity is, for the apostle, in the strict sense, fruit. It is the product of a definite principle of life, that principle which he calls the Spirit.[1] If that Spirit, which is the very life of Christ Himself, operates in

---

[1] See especially Gal. v. 22.

the individual, only one kind of result can ensue. So that for Paul the all-important matter is to secure the free play of this Divine energy in the soul of the Christian. It is bound to express itself in all kinds of worthy action. And that action will be spontaneous. From the point of view of the individual it will be inspired by a sense of obligation to Christ. Adoring love and gratitude require no compulsion.

We have already suggested various reasons for the accentuation of the demand for a good life in the Epistles which we are studying. Of special interest is the manner in which this demand is formulated. Its burden is the necessity for ' good works.' Thus, in 2 Tim. iii. 17 the purpose of Old Testament Scripture is described as that of thoroughly equipping the man of God ' for every kind of good work.' In ii. 21 consecration to God means ' being prepared for every kind of good work.' Widows who desire a place on the Church's roll must be ' attested by good works ' and have shown a zealous interest in them (1 Tim. v. 10). The rich are charged ' to be wealthy in good works,' for these lay the foundations of eternal life in the world to come (vi. 18, 19). Those who are accused of pollution and disobedience have as their supreme condemnation their ' uselessness for every kind of good work ' (Tit. i. 16). Titus, as chief overseer of a Christian community, is urged to show himself to his younger brethren as a pattern of good works (ii. 7). Even the object of Christ's redemption itself is described as that of purifying a people for Himself who should be eager for good works (ii. 14). The author delights to enlarge upon the theme with solemn emphasis : ' True is the saying (and I wish you to insist upon this) that those who have come to believe in God must give diligent attention to good works : [1] this is good and useful for men ' (iii. 8). It is impossible in examining these passages in the light of their context to avoid the impression that good works constitute the special badge of

[1] Not ' profess honest occupations,' as R.V. *mg.* and Moffatt. The whole tone of the Epistle demands the translation in the text.

the Christian, and have to be urged upon him, very much as the observance of the Law was urged in Judaism.

Specially instructive is the well-known definition of religion in James i. 27 as ' visiting orphans and widows in their distress, and keeping one's self unspotted from the world.' This as pure religion is contrasted with the futile religion of the man who cannot bridle his tongue. And its significance for the author is more fully brought out by the famous discussion of Faith and [good] Works (James ii. 14-26). It is needless for our purpose to inquire whether the passage contains a polemic against Paul's doctrine of justification by faith alone. What is important to note is that the writer sharply controverts a faith which is little more than the assent to a creed (ii. 19), a faith which need not have any relation to conduct at all. Well may he describe such a faith as ' inherently lifeless ' (ii. 17). The whole section illuminates the religious atmosphere of the post-Pauline epoch. It would, of course, be rash to generalise from particular instances like this. But the same tendency is attested somewhat later in such a statement as Hermas, *Mandat.* x. i. 4, which speaks of ' those who have never searched into the truth, nor investigated the Divine nature, but have only believed ($\pi\iota\sigma\tau\epsilon\acute{u}$-$\sigma\alpha\nu\tau\epsilon\varsigma$ $\delta\grave{\epsilon}$ $\mu\acute{o}\nu o\nu$), and have got mixed up with business and wealth and heathen friendships.' These examples are sufficient to show the necessity of injunctions bearing directly upon Christian practice.[1] It is true that Divine grace still forms the presupposition of the Christian life (*e.g.* James i. 18). But it has to be reinforced by good works, and these supply material for the final verdict of God.[2] Obviously, when the original inspiration of the Spirit is lacking, increasing importance will be attached to the keeping of the commandments of God, the rendering of adequate service, an idea common to Judaism with the reformed Stoicism of the period. Hence the cleft becomes

---

[1] Moffatt (*op. cit.*, p. 464) instructively points out that in the 108 verses of the Epistle of James there are fifty-four imperatives.

[2] *E.g.* 2 Pet. i. 10, 11.

gradually wider between the Pauline conception of ' faith
working through love,' an energy which covers the whole
area of moral action, and that more painful and anxious
attention to detailed precepts which is called forth by a
sense of spiritual insecurity. The subsequent sections will
illustrate the more definite forms in which this moralistic
tendency is manifested.

(c) *Thinning of Redemptive Ideas*

When we turn from the earlier Epistles, and especially
those of Paul, to the Theology of the Developing Church,
perhaps the most powerful impression made upon us is
a sense of what may be called the thinning of redemptive ideas, of the great conceptions formulated to express
the experience of salvation. Certain central features in
Paul's religious thought are either conspicuously lacking,
or are handled without confidence. Reconciliation with
God, death to sin and resurrection to newness of life in
Christ crucified and risen, union with Christ by faith,
possession of the Spirit of sonship as the pledge of eternal
life and the source of unhampered spiritual energy—these
splendid convictions of the earlier time are barely recognised. There is an evident loss of inwardness and freedom.
The need for authoritative guidance is paramount. A
lower level of Christian experience has to be reckoned
with. It would be going too far to say that Paul is no
longer clearly understood. The recognition of the grace of
God, for example, as fundamental in salvation still holds
good.[1] The forgiveness of sin is still felt to be an integral
element in the spiritual history of the Christian.[2] But
changed conditions and circumstances have shifted the
points of emphasis. The tremendous controversy between
legalism and spiritual freedom, which set Paul's soul on
fire and struck out his wonderful conceptions glowing with

[1] Cf. 1 Tim. i. 14 ; 2 Tim. i. 9 ; Tit. ii. 11 ; Jude 4 ; and see Titius,
Die vulgäre Anschauung von der Seligkeit, pp. 161, 191.
[2] *E.g.* 2 Pet. i. 9 ; 1 Tim. i. 15 ; Tit. ii. 14.

the white heat of inspiration, has long since become a spent force. The creative energy of the first missionary period has yielded to the careful organising efforts of the second and third generations. Jewish and Hellenistic influences have asserted their power, not merely through natural environment, but by the medium of multitudes of converts who have carried former presuppositions and tendencies into their new spiritual home. Above all, the necessity has arisen of resisting that indifference to moral obligations which besets those who have shaken themselves loose from traditional standards of law and custom and have entered a realm in which the love and grace of God are supremely exalted.

Let us examine some typically Pauline and early Christian ideas in their new setting. For Paul, as we know, faith meant complete surrender of the whole being to Jesus Christ, who had loved men and given Himself for them. As such, it brought into play every energy of the soul, and established a contact of all with the Divine life in Christ. Thus, on the human side, it constitutes the fundamental attitude in salvation. And all God's saving gifts are received by faith. But as soon as the experience of Christ becomes less rich and profound, as soon as a traditional element begins to be influential in Christianity, faith is apt to pass over into the sense of an acceptance of the truth of the Gospel, an assent to the testimony borne by the apostles to Christ, and even more generally the belief that God will do as He has said. The deeper significance is occasionally found in our Epistles.[1] But the other is much more common, especially in that development of it which virtually identifies faith with the recognised Christian doctrine of the Church as the criterion for all its members.[2] So it becomes a synonym for orthodox belief.[3]

[1] *E.g.* 1 Tim. i. 16 ; 2 Tim. i. 12, iii. 15.
[2] *E.g.* 1 Tim. i. 19, iii. 9, iv. 6, v. 8 ; 2 Tim. iii. 8, iv. 7 ; Tit. i. 13, ii. 2 ; Jude 3.
[3] See the preceding examples. Very instructive is the fact that in the documents under review the verb ' to believe ' ($\pi\iota\sigma\tau\epsilon\acute{\upsilon}\epsilon\iota\nu$), denoting the personal relation to Christ, and central in Paul, the Synoptics, and the Johannine literature, is scarcely found at all.

But such belief may become a mere empty profession.
Hence the possibility of the arresting statement in the
Epistle of James that ' faith without works is dead '
(ii. 20). Such a statement would be inconceivable in Paul.
The later writer makes it the theme of an earnest discussion,
thus indicating the process through which the conception
has passed. Just because faith is no longer regarded as
the vital energy of the entire Christian life, good works
have to be demanded as an additional obligation which
makes up what may hitherto have been lacking.[1] That
explains the position of James in the celebrated passage
referred to, and illuminates the prominence assigned to
good works throughout the literature of this period.

In the Epistles of Paul the first great result of faith is
justification. In the case of those who are willing to
identify themselves with Christ crucified and risen in His
attitude both to God and to sin, God, of His pure grace,
is ready to see the end in the beginning, and, although they
are still frail and defiled, to accept them as sons in Christ
Jesus, to justify or declare them righteous, and so give
them the assurance of eternal life. Their new relation to
God Paul calls righteousness, and that is also the designation
of God's way of acting towards them. It may be said that
this profound group of ideas, which attempts to describe
the apostle's personal experience, has completely receded
in the Theology of the Developing Church. Almost invariably righteousness now means right conduct, an ethical quality rather than a religious relationship.[2] Highly
suggestive in this connection is 2 Pet. i. 1, ' those who
have received a faith of like value with ours by the
righteousness of God,' where righteousness plainly means
impartiality.[3] There is one instance of the conception of
justification which recalls the Pauline usage, in Tit. iii. 5 ff.:
' Not as the result of works done by righteousness, which

---

[1] W. Bauer (*Die katholischen Briefe*, p. 18 f.) compares Ignatius' idea
of faith and love as the two separate pivots of the Christian life, pointing
out that the exercise of love does not grow out of faith, but comes in
when one obediently submits to the ' royal law.'

[2] *E.g.* 1 Tim. vi. 11 ; 2 Tim. iii. 16 ; Jas. iii. 18 ; 2 Pet. ii. 5.

[3] See Bigg, *ad loc.*

we did ourselves, but according to his mercy he saved us, through the bath of regeneration and the renewing of the Holy Spirit, which he poured out upon us through . . . Jesus Christ . . . that having been justified (δικαιωθέντες) by His [God's] grace we might become heirs according to the hope of eternal life.' This fine passage, which almost stands alone, echoes Paul's phraseology.[1] Yet there is no mention here of faith, which is the very nerve of Paul's position. And the prominence given to the bath of regeneration points to the development of Catholic doctrine. The use of ' justify ' in the Epistle of James (ii. 21, 24, 25) is typical of the period. Paul's daring religious paradox as to the justification of the ungodly is no longer appreciated. The man is now said to be justified who commends himself as a Christian by obeying the revealed will of God in a life of worthy activity.

It is impossible in Paul's teaching to distinguish sharply between justification and forgiveness. The latter is implied in the former, and both are intimately associated with the death of Christ. There is no reference to this normative idea even in the unique passage quoted above. Hence we are not surprised to find that when forgiveness is mentioned (James v. 15, 20), its affinity is closer to Jewish than to distinctive Christian conceptions. Indeed the whole view of salvation which meets us in this epoch lacks the freshness of profound experience. Terms are used which remind us that Paul's teaching and that of the early apostolic Church are still influential. But the significance of such a passage as Tit. ii. 14, ' Who gave himself for us that he might redeem (λυτρώσηται) us from all iniquity (ἀνομίας) and purify for himself a people to be his possession (λαὸν περιούσιον),' must be estimated in the light of the fact that its most important phrases are derived from the Old Testament.[2] The ideas, when examined in their context, have a somewhat stereotyped

---

[1] Moffatt places these verses in inverted commas, regarding them, probably with justice. as a doctrinal statement current in the Church.
[2] Ps. cxxx. 8 (LXX) ; Exod. xix. 5 (LXX).

character.[1] They are accepted as authoritative doctrines, but their full force is scarcely appreciated. Even as they stand they suggest that redemption is viewed not primarily as deliverance from that guilt which is attested by a bad conscience, but rather as the spring of moral renewal. This aspect is clearly visible in Tit. ii. 14. Hence no special emphasis is laid upon the inner meaning of Christ's death and resurrection. We have nothing here corresponding, e.g., to Rom. iv. 25. The purification achieved by Christ is regarded as bringing into activity certain Christian virtues.[2] These qualities, in their turn, form the basis of security for the eternal future.[3] Even the Divine calling requires them, if it is to be stable and sure.

Nothing, however, more plainly indicates the change of atmosphere revealed by these documents than the important place assigned to Knowledge. In a large number of passages it is synonymous with salvation. It would be hazardous to lay the chief emphasis on the intellectual element involved. For the more recent investigation of Hellenistic religion has shown that knowledge means constantly spiritual experience of God and the unseen. But the material with which we are occupied again and again suggests that here a mental apprehension of truth belongs to its very essence. Thus, in 1 Tim. ii. 4, God is spoken of as desiring ' that all men should be saved and should reach a knowledge of the truth.' In 2 Tim. ii. 25 the object of repentance is described as ' knowledge of the truth.' In the address of the Epistle to Titus, Paul's apostleship is defined as being ' in accord with ($\kappa\alpha\tau\acute{\alpha}$) [4] the faith of God's elect and the knowledge of the truth that belongs to piety.' Such passages of course presuppose the existence of a body of doctrine which has come to be recognised as authoritative. We have noted the genesis of this conception. They also indicate the impact of a

---

[1] Cf. 1 Tim. ii. 5, 6.

[2] This is made plain by the sequence of thought in 2 Pet. i. 2-9, a state-ment very typical of our period.

[3] See especially 2 Pet. i. 10, 11.

[4] It is possible to take $\kappa\alpha\tau\acute{\alpha}$ here as expressing destination (so Moffatt, N. J. D. White, Winer).

mode of thought characteristically Greek upon early
Christian ideas. Numerous parallels may be found in the
sub-apostolic literature, as, *e.g.*, *Didache* x. 2 : ' We thank
thee . . . for the knowledge and faith and immortality
which thou hast made known to us through thy servant
Jesus.' The sequence of terms in this quotation is highly
significant. And we may compare 2 Clement xx. 5 : ' The
Saviour and author of immortality through whom he revealed
to us truth and the heavenly life.' Here the redemptive
work of Jesus is viewed primarily as a revelation to the
mind. That conception definitely appears in 2 Tim. i. 10,
where Jesus is said to have ' brought the knowledge
($\phi\omega\tau\iota\sigma\alpha\nu\tau\sigma$) of life and immortality through the gospel.'
Of course there are some statements closely akin to this
in the earlier period, as, *e.g.*, 2 Cor. iv. 6, but these have to
be interpreted in the light of Paul's central conceptions of
the significance of Christ's redemption, in relation to which
they occupy a quite subordinate position. The importance of the function assigned to the truth or knowledge
which has come to the world in Jesus may be illustrated
from our period by such statements as James i. 18 : ' Of
his own will he begat us by the word of truth,' in which
the instrument of regeneration is the revelation contained
in the Gospel rather than the Spirit,[1] as in Paul ; and
2 Pet. ii. 20, where ' the knowledge of the Lord and Saviour
Jesus Christ ' is that which saves men from the contamina-
tion of an evil world. Obviously the way is being rapidly
prepared for that slightly later phase of Christian thought
in regard to which Harnack can say, ' All that Jesus
Christ brought may be summed up as $\gamma\nu\hat{\omega}\sigma\iota\varsigma$ and $\zeta\omega\acute{\eta}$ or
even as the knowledge of immortal life : to possess complete
knowledge was in wide circles an expression for the sum
and substance of the Gospel.' [2]

[1] Cf. i. 21. A glance at the Concordance will show how extraordinarily
the conception of the Spirit has fallen into the background in our period.
One obscure use of the term occurs in James, one, referring to prophetic
inspiration, in 2 Peter. In the Pastorals, apart from a prophetic allusion
in 1 Tim. iv. 1, the only relevant passages are 2 Tim. i. 14 and Tit. iii. 5.
Contrast this with the richness of usage in Paul and 1 Peter.

[2] *Dogmengeschichte*, i. p. 123.

(d) Prominence of the Church-Consciousness and the resulting conception of Piety

At this point and in the light of the preceding paragraphs we must elaborate one or two general statements made in the opening section of the chapter. The phenomena of our Epistles are unintelligible apart from a recognition of the extraordinary growth of the Church-consciousness among Christians of this period. It lies outside our purpose to attempt even the briefest sketch of that ecclesiastical organisation which is presupposed in the documents before us. But certain features stand out clearly. The strictly apostolic era is past. The communities no longer depend directly on the unique spiritual endowment of prophets and teachers who journey from place to place sharing their gifts with their brethren. This practice still, indeed, holds good,[1] and such persons continue to enjoy esteem. But the wide diffusion of the faith and the passing away of the great leaders of the earlier time have made it essential that a careful structure should be built up throughout the Christian society. Already in Paul's day the process has begun. He knows of bishops and deacons in the Church of Philippi (Phil. i. 1). Even in 1 Thessalonians, the earliest of his letters, he speaks of ' those who preside over you in the Lord ' (v. 12). And the very important list of functions in the Church which he gives in 1 Cor. xii. 28 reveals the variety of capacities which were at the disposal of the Christian brotherhood. His own attitude, moreover, in dealing with the practical needs of his converts as disclosed in that letter, indicates his sincere interest in questions of organisation. But at that stage everything still appears fluid. Now, the Church, which had been for Paul the Body of Christ, a mystical fellowship, has become an institution managed by carefully chosen officials.[2] Strict rules are laid down for the appointment of bishops and deacons. We hear of ordination at the hands of the

---

[1] See *Didache*, chaps. xi.-xiii.
[2] *E.g.* 1 Tim. iii. 1-5 ; v. 3, 9, 16.

presbytery. Regulations are provided for the support of
needy persons from the Church funds.[1]

But above all else the Church is ' the pillar and bulwark
of the truth.' She is the guardian of ' the faith once for
all delivered to God's people.' We have already observed
that the objective aspect of faith has begun to overshadow
the subjective, so that it has become practically equivalent
to ' sound doctrine.' [2] This conception is one of the chief
watchwords of our documents. Typical is the warning
of 1 Tim. vi. 3 against ' any one who teaches novelties
and refuses to adhere to the sound ($\dot{v}\gamma\iota\alpha\acute{\iota}\nu o\nu\sigma\iota\nu$) words of
our Lord Jesus Christ, and the doctrine that accords with
piety.' [3] Such doctrine largely constitutes Christianity.
Slaves are exhorted to prove their trustworthiness, ' that
they may adorn the doctrine ($\delta\iota\delta\alpha\sigma\kappa\alpha\lambda\acute{\iota}\alpha\nu$) of God our
Saviour in all things ' (Tit. ii. 10).[4] It is plain that the
development has taken this direction owing to the emergence of false teaching. The nature of the latter must
be discussed immediately. Meanwhile, let us note the
criterion of truth and falsehood. The true doctrine is that
which has been handed down in the Christian community
from the apostles. ' Model yourself,' we read in 2 Tim.
i. 13, 14, ' on the sound instruction you have received from
me . . . guard the good deposit ($\pi\alpha\rho\alpha\theta\acute{\eta}\kappa\eta\nu$) through the
Holy Spirit that dwells in us.' This term, ' deposit,' is
specially characteristic of our period. It occurs also in
2 Tim. i. 12 and 1 Tim. vi. 20, and suggests the idea of
a fixed body of teaching which must be normative for the
individual Christian. But even apart from so technical a
phrase, the notion of an authoritative tradition is central.
' Be strong in the grace which is in Christ Jesus, and what
you heard from me in presence of many witnesses, hand on
to trustworthy men, who shall be fit to teach others also.' [5]

[1] *E.g.* 1 Tim. iii. 2-7, 8-13 ; Tit. i. 7-10 ; 1 Tim. iv. 14 ; 1 Tim. v. 3, 16.
[2] Cf. 1 Tim. iv. 6 : ' trained in the truths of the faith and the right
doctrine of which you have become an adherent ' ; cf. Jude 20.
[3] Cf. 2 Tim. iv. 3 ; Tit. i. 13, ii. 1.
[4] Cf. 1 Tim. vi. 1, where the ' name of God ' and ' the doctrine ' are
grouped together as representing the content of Christianity.
[5] 2 Tim. ii. 1, 2. Cf. iii. 14 ; 2 Pet. ii. 21, iii. 2 ; Jude 17.

Here the accredited doctrine has been further attested by
the Christian community, so that its sanctions are inviolable.[1]
It is hardly necessary to connect this conception of a
doctrinal tradition with Jewish usage.[2] The tendency is
inevitable as soon as any religion throws out a frame-work
of organisation.

Among the most interesting phenomena of our Epistles
are the traces of formulated confessions of faith, which in
any case might be assumed to be an accompaniment of
the movement sketched above. The most obvious is
that of 1 Tim. iii. 16 :

> ' Who was manifested by means of flesh,
>   justified by means of Spirit,
> seen by the angels,
>   preached among the nations,
> believed on in the world,
>   received up into glory.'

It throws light on such noteworthy hints as 1 Tim. vi. 12 :
' Fight the good fight of the faith, take firm hold of that
life eternal to which you were called, when you made the
great confession in the presence of many witnesses.'
Probably the reference here is to the time of baptism.
Some phrases in the very next verses, ' God the giver of
life to all,' and ' Christ Jesus who bore witness to the great
confession in the presence of Pontius Pilate,' sound like
fragments of liturgical formulæ. And these have perhaps
left their mark on such passages as 1 Tim. ii. 5, 6, and
2 Tim. ii. 8.

The famous confessional statement of 1 Tim. iii. 16 is
prefaced by a sentence highly significant for the religious
thought of the developing Church : ' without denial,
great is the mystery revealed to our piety (εὐσεβείας).'
The words seem primarily intended to enhance the reverence due to ' the Church of the living God ' (ver. 15), which
has had so precious a trust committed to its charge. Incidentally they bring out the special aspect under which,

---

[1] Cf. the constant use of the phrase, ' trustworthy is the saying,' in the
Pastoral Epistles.
[2] So Titius, *op. cit.*, p. 205 f.

in our period, religion is regularly viewed, the aspect of piety (εὐσέβεια). The term has a peculiarly Greek flavour, and it is worth noting that noun, verb, and adjective are rare in the LXX, except in Sirach, which has many non-Jewish affinities, and that they occur above all in 4 Maccabees, which is the most typically Hellenistic work in the Pseudepigrapha preserved by the LXX. Out of fifteen instances of the noun in the New Testament, only one falls outside our documents, and it occurs in Acts, which has many points of connection with these. It perhaps retains something of that external tone which belongs to the public religion of Greece. Its content very markedly exemplifies the tendencies of the period. On the one hand, piety has the most intimate association with sound doctrine, the truth which has been attested by the apostles. Thus the Epistle to Titus speaks of ' the knowledge of the truth that accords with piety ' (i. 1), and in 1 Tim. iv. 6 ff., Timothy, after being reminded of his careful instruction in the right doctrine, is urged to train himself for piety. In vi. 3, the ' doctrine that accords with piety ' is contrasted with the teaching which departs from the wholesome standard of the Church. On the other hand, piety must express itself in good works (1 Tim. ii. 10).[1] Hence those members of the Christian community whose conduct is a scandal have merely the form of piety, and have renounced its power (2 Tim. iii. 5). Piety is the regulating force for action. To live righteously and piously in the present age is the result of the discipline brought to men by the saving grace of God (Tit. ii. 12). It is the express aim of that spiritual endowment which has been bestowed on men by the Divine power through the knowledge of Jesus Christ (2 Pet. i. 3). But piety looks beyond the present. It also receives the pledge of that eternal life which will be fully realised in the future (1 Tim. iv. 8). Hence it may be said to sum up Christianity as an actual force in human experience, having its genesis in that unadulterated teaching

---

[1] See the previous section. The term used here is θεοσέβεια, which is equivalent to εὐσέβεια.

which goes back to Christ and has been handed down by
His Apostles, and authenticating itself in a course of
ethical activity.

(e) Conception of God

Its conception of God must be normative for every
phase of religious thought, and some valuable light from
this direction is thrown upon the period with which we
are dealing. Here, as in many other sections of our
inquiry, we need not expect to find the outlines of the idea
so clearly marked as to reveal at a glance the features in
which they differ, say, from the Pauline conception. We
must be content rather with hints and impressions. It is
true that in our documents there are one or two important
descriptions of the nature of God,[1] but the value of these
for our purpose is slightly discounted by the fact that they
evidently belong to liturgical formulæ which had taken
shape in the Church. Still, they express beliefs widely
current, and it may be possible at times to recognise the
forces which have produced them.

To begin with, the view of God exhibited in this post-
Pauline literature is to a real extent determined by the
missionary aim of the Church. In contrast with the
religious ideas of its heathen environment, it sets in bold
relief, as Paul has also done, and as was customary with the
propaganda of Hellenistic Judaism, the thought of God as
the One, the Living, and the Creator of all things.[2] In
His supreme majesty He is immortal, dwelling in light
unapproachable, the Father of the heavenly lights who
knows no change of rising and setting, invisible to mortal
eyes, the King of Kings and Lord of Lords.[3] Affinities
may be found for certain of these predicates in the Old
Testament,[4] and perhaps they are derived from Judaism.

[1] 1 Tim. i. 17, vi. 15, 16, possibly Tit. iii. 4, 5.
[2] 1 Tim. i. 17, ii. 5, vi. 15 ; Jas. iv. 12 ; Jude 25 ; 1 Tim. iii. 15, iv. 10,
vi. 16 ; 1 Tim. vi. 13, iv. 3, 4 ; Jas. i. 17, 18 ; 2 Pet. iii. 5.
[3] 1 Tim. i. 17, vi. 16a ; 1 Tim. vi. 16b ; Jas. i. 17 (M.) ; 1 Tim. i. 17,
vi. 16 ; 1 Tim. vi. 15.
[4] Feine (op. cit., p. 541) compares Deut. x. 17 (LXX), Ps. cxxxvi. 3
(LXX) with 1 Tim. vi. 15, and Ps. civ. 2 (LXX) with vi. 16.

But there is some ground for supposing that they are
emphasised in view of those Gnostic tendencies which had
now begun to disturb the Church. The prominence assigned to Christ as sole Mediator between God and men
(1 Tim. ii. 5) gives colour to the significance of this background.

It is quite possible that the interesting reference
to the light which encircles God has regard to Gnostic
speculations on dark and malevolent powers. God casts
no shadow, and is the source of those heavenly bodies
(Jas. i. 17) to whose influence so high a place was ascribed
in the religious syncretism of the time. To a similar
reason may be due the importance attached to the creative
activity of God. We know that in Gnostic theories a
distinction was drawn between the supreme God, the
Father of Jesus Christ, and the Creator, who is an inferior
deity as responsible for the evil world of matter. ' Everything created by God is good,' says 1 Tim. iv. 4. Only
good gifts come down from above (Jas. i. 17). Hence the
remarkable description of God in the Pastorals and Jude
as Saviour (σωτήρ).[1] The God of creation is also the God
of redemption. With the exception of Luke i. 47, which
echoes Old Testament hymns of praise, and the documents
before us, the title ' Saviour ' is invariably given in the
New Testament to Christ. But the LXX frequently
employs this term to translate two Hebrew words for
salvation, when used (especially in the Psalms) as descriptions of God. We must not therefore ignore this Old
Testament usage, while, at the same time, recognising that
' Saviour ' had become a prominent term in Hellenistic
religion, more particularly in those phases of it which strove
to meet the prevalent yearning for redemption. The
important point in the present connection is that God,
who is Himself the blessed (1 Tim. vi. 15),[2] is the source of
all blessedness, the ultimate author of salvation. Not

---

[1] 1 Tim. i. 1, ii. 3, iv. 10 ; Tit. i. 3, ii. 10, iii. 4 ; Jude 25.
[2] Holtzmann (*op. cit.*, ii. p. 299) calls this the Christian application of
the Greek phrase, μάκαρες θεοί, ' the blessed gods.'

only is this highest of all the Divine functions expressed
by the title Saviour, but mention is made of ' the grace of
God fraught with salvation,' of ' the graciousness and kindness of God,' of His ' pity,' of His desire for the salvation
of all men.[1] In this crucial matter the theology of the
developing Church maintains inviolate the position of the
earlier days.

All the more noteworthy is the somewhat colourless use
made of the profound conception of the Fatherhood of God.
At no point has Paul more completely grasped the thought
of Jesus than at this, and from beginning to end his
Epistles thrill with wonder and adoration as he sets
forth the glory of Christian sonship. Very rarely is God
designated ' Father ' in our documents,[2] and the name
is more or less formal, as in the stereotyped epistolary
address (1 Tim. i. 2 ; 2 Tim. i. 2 ; Tit. i. 4). As constantly
in the Apostolic Fathers, it is found in 2 Pet. i. 17 in correspondence with a statement regarding the Son. The usage
of James is also instructive as revealing the intimate connection of thought between this stratum of Christian
literature and the contemporary non-canonical books.
In i. 27 and iii. 9, the title ' Father ' appended to the Divine
name seems little more than an element in the traditional
designation current in the Church. But when (i. 17) he
calls God ' the Father of the heavenly lights,' he shows
that already the idea of Fatherhood was being identified
with that of Creation. This identification appears continually in Philo, and notably in 1 Clement, who speaks of
' the Creator and Father of the ages ' (xxxv. 3), and of
the ' Father and framer of the entire universe ' (xix. 2).
These phenomena indicate that the intimacy of that view
of God which Paul had learned from Jesus was, in spite of
the recognition of the Divine grace in salvation, giving
place to a more detached conception, which, in the sub-
apostolic epoch, finds characteristic expression in the

[1] Tit. ii. 11, iii. 4 ; 1 Tim. i. 2 ; 2 Tim. i. 2 ; Tit. iii. 5 ; Jude 2 ; 1 Tim.
ii. 4, iv. 10 ; 2 Pet. iii. 9.
[2] Once in each of the Pastorals, 2 Peter, and Jude, and thrice in James.

term ' ruler ' (δεσπότης),[1] Clement's favourite designation of God.

(f) The Law of Liberty

We have observed that in the period under review ' good works ' may almost be called the badge of a Christian career.   But the interesting question emerges :   How is a Christian convert to know what will satisfy the requirements ?   What precisely is to constitute the standard of his new activity ?   It has already become clear that a certain body of teaching, authenticated by the leaders of the Church, was recognised as the test of an adequate Christianity, of that piety which embraced both doctrine and conduct.   But it was easier, probably, to agree upon a general confession of faith than to give authoritative directions for the complex situation which must confront immature members of the Christian society in their daily duties.   In the earlier days, the enthusiasm of the new life in Christ would overcome many difficulties by means of its inherent vigour.   As the Church settled down into the forms of an organised institution, a more stereotyped condition of things must inevitably arise.   The originality of a decisive Christian experience would frequently be lacking.   The sense of a need of definite training in morality would be enhanced.   But those who had entered the Church from Judaism, in the Diaspora as well as in Palestine, brought with them the tradition of such a training, and so did the many proselytes from heathenism who came to Christianity by way of the synagogue.   They were all imbued with the idea of a rule of life embodied in that moral Law which was the revelation of the will of God. On the other hand, the ethical revival which was operating in the Hellenistic-Roman world had as its chief watchword, ' conformity to law, whether the law of nature or the law of God.' [2]   Now, in proportion as the profound ideas of the Gospel shaped by the rich and unique experience of

---

- In these post-Pauline writings it is not applied to God, but, what is more remarkable, in two passages (Jude 4, 2 Pet. ii. 1) to Christ.

[2] M'Giffert, Christianity in the Apostolic Age, p. 450.

Paul were less securely grasped in the Christian community, and the founding of faith in living fellowship with Christ and the outworking of its energies as the product of an inner Divine life in the soul became obscured to the average mind, the conception of a definite code of precepts was bound to assert its influence.

The claims of the ritual side of the Law were no longer dominant. Its moral injunctions alone were in question, but forces had been operative even in the earliest phase of the Christian society which might easily raise these injunctions to a controlling place in its later development. To minds disciplined by a legal system, the fresh and, in many aspects, revolutionary interpretation of it given by Jesus in the Sermon on the Mount might well appear the promulgation of a new Law for the Messianic community. There can be little doubt that this was the actual position taken in the Mother-Church at Jerusalem. Ordinances which Jesus had not dealt with retained their validity, even although these were in real conflict with the principles He had enunciated. It required Paul's marvellous spiritual intuition to discern the perilous issues which such an attitude involved. He it was who rescued the Christian mission from the bondage of Jewish legalism. But he himself recognised the necessity of a moral standard. And we have an instructive example of his teaching on the subject in Gal. v. 14 : ' The whole law is fulfilled in one saying, namely this : Thou shalt love thy neighbour as thyself.' Here, as always, he identifies himself with the teaching of Jesus in Mark xii. 28-31. It may therefore be taken for granted that Jesus' restatement of the earlier ethical code continued to have absolute authority in the expanding Church. Now as the memory of Paul's burning controversy with his Jewish-Christian brethren faded, the prejudice roused against the Jewish Law in many heathen-Christian communities would disappear. In typically Jewish sections it had never existed. Hence, not only the tradition of Jesus' ethical principles but the moral code of Judaism must soon have asserted its claims.

Appeal could be made to Paul himself in such statements
as Rom. vii. 12 : ' The law is holy, and the commandment
holy and righteous and good.' Yet a very interesting
instance of the position adopted in our period, which occurs
in 1 Tim. i. 5 ff., shows that the acknowledgment of the
Law meant something different from that of the earlier
time. ' The aim of the Christian discipline is the love
that springs from a pure heart, from a good conscience,
and from a sincere faith. Certain individuals have failed
here by turning to empty argument : doctors of the Law
is what they want to be. . . . Now I am quite aware that
" the Law is admirable " provided that one makes a lawful
use of it : he must keep in view that no law is ever made
for honest people, but for the lawless and the insubordinate,
for the impious and the sinful.' [1] This is essentially Paul's
view, and can in no real sense be called legalism.

Perhaps the standpoint of the Epistle of James indicates
a somewhat closer approximation to the Judaistic position.
James virtually describes the content of the Christian
message as ' the perfect law, the law of freedom ' (i. 25),
and the context shows that the claim of compassion is
chiefly before his thoughts. The injunction, ' Thou shalt
love thy neighbour as thyself,' he describes as the ' royal
(*i.e.* supreme) law.' [2] After emphasising the danger of an
inadequate standard of conduct, he reminds his readers
that they are to be judged by ' the law of freedom ' (ii. 12),
and as an example of what he means, he refers to the
obligation of kindness : ' The judgment will have no mercy
on the man who showed none, whereas the merciful spirit
will triumph in the face of judgment ' (ii. 13, partly M.).
And then he proceeds to challenge a conception of faith
which fails in deeds of loving service. Primarily these
passages show that his mind is saturated with Jesus'
teaching on love.[3] While he describes the obligation of

[1] So Dr. Moffatt admirably translates the passage.
[2] ii. 8 : plainly, like Paul in Gal. v. 14, he has in view the teaching of
Jesus in Mark xii. 31, Matt. xxii. 40.
[3] Cf. iv. 11, 12, where the Law is associated with the very same circle
of ideas.

love as a ' law,' he deliberately sets in the forefront the
spirit of freedom and spontaneity with which it is fulfilled,
taking for granted that the Christian has inwardly identified himself with its principles, so that, as the Epistle
of Barnabas strikingly expresses it, ' the new law of our
Lord Jesus Christ is freed from the yoke of compulsion'
(ii. 6).   Nevertheless in such an atmosphere as that of the
close of the apostolic and the beginning of the sub-apostolic
age, when the Church was confronted by a definitely
antinomian movement, larger conceptions of the Law
like that of James and Barnabas were bound to give place
to something more formal and restricted.   It is interesting,
indeed, to notice that the writers with whom we are concerned prefer, as a rule, to speak of ' commandment,' [1]
perhaps to avoid confusion with the Mosaic Law.   But as
soon as the idea of keeping commandments begins to
overshadow the spontaneity of a spiritual life which receives
its ethical impulses from its relation to Christ, the way is
prepared for that new legalism of which we have so
significant an example in the first ten chapters of the
Didache.

(g) *Eschatological Outlook*

It would be an exaggeration to say that in the religious
thought of the developing Church salvation is regarded as
the reward of obedience to the Divine commandments.
We have seen that it continues to be viewed under its
Pauline aspect as a gift of God's loving-kindness.   Yet the
tendency to such a position appears here and there, *e.g.*
2 Pet. i. 10, 11 : [2] ' If you exercise these qualities, you
cannot stumble : rather will you be richly furnished with
the right of entrance into the eternal kingdom of our Lord
and Saviour Jesus Christ.'   The words remind us that the
gaze of these Christians was eagerly turned towards the
future, in which eternal life and blessedness awaited them.
No wonder that their leaders urged them to make sure
of the high vocation to which they had been called.

[1] *E.g.* 1 Tim. vi. 14 ; 2 Pet. ii. 21.   [2] Cf. 1 Tim. vi. 14.

Their predominant conception of salvation may be described as Eternal Life. The idea is familiar from the letters of Paul. There it appears with a rich variety of content, always closely associated with the possession of the Spirit or the indwelling of Christ in the soul. For Paul too the conception has a strongly eschatological character, which accords with the entire trend of his religious thought. But his personal history has re-shaped the idea, which was already current in Jewish eschatology, in the direction of laying marked emphasis upon it as a present experience known and enjoyed, whose consummation belongs to the final establishment of the Kingdom of God. An examination of the usage in our documents shows that for them the eschatological aspect of Eternal Life is paramount. Sometimes it is described as a hope and a promise. Sometimes the picture is that of a prize awarded to the victor in a hard contest. Again, it is the goal of faith and patience. And once, as synonymous with immortality, it is declared to be the content of that good news which has been brought by Christ, the conqueror of death.[1] The more closely these Epistles are investigated, the more deeply embedded in their substance does this conviction appear to be. Here we have the embodiment of the central faith of the universal Church. Perhaps its most prominent element is now that of immortality. This feature is emphasised, even where there is no specific mention of eternal life, as, *e.g.*, when 2 Peter speaks of God's ' exceeding great and precious promises ' by which men ' may become partakers of the Divine nature, escaping the destruction created in the world by lust ' (i. 4). And its atmosphere is ' eternal glory ' (2 Tim. ii. 10). The kinship with Paul's thought is evident. Only, the conception is presented in a more superficial form, and lacks that profound sense of contrast with the old, sin-burdened nature which has been vanquished in the power of the living and life-giving Lord.

[1] Tit. i. 2, iii. 7 ; 2 Tim. i. 1, 1 Tim. iv. 8 ; Jas. i. 12, 1 Tim. vi. 12 ; 1 Tim. i. 16, Jude 21 ; 2 Tim. i. 10.

In discussing the theology of Paul, we found that the
expectation of the return of Christ formed a permanent
part of his eschatological picture. It was based, as was
then pointed out, partly on the tradition of the Master's
teaching, partly on the prophetic and apocalyptic forecasts
of the coming of Messiah. In the earlier Pauline Epistles
it stands in the forefront. Later, while always recognised,
it remains side by side with convictions as to the experience
of the Christian soul after death which are really independent
of it. That is to say, the Parousia, the resurrection, and
the judgment continue to be grouped together as the great
crisis of the end, but the deeper currents of Paul's spiritual
life seem to demand a more immediate relation of the soul
to Christ, to be realised as soon as the hampering conditions
of the body are removed.[1] A similar variation of emphasis
appears in the thought of the developing Church. Everywhere the Messianic eschatology survives. An incidental
evidence is, perhaps, the constant use of the term ' arrival '
($\pi a \rho o v \sigma i a$) to denote the return of Christ.[2] Here attention
is called, not so much to the *second* advent of the historical
Jesus, as to the advent in glory and power of the Messiah,[3]
an expectation which is, of course, pledged by the redemptive career of Jesus. Hence no forecast of the End can
dispense with the conception of the Parousia. Further,
the conviction is general that Christians are living in ' the
last days.' [4] But the relation of the close of the age to
the return of Christ is variously conceived. There can
be little question that the pressure of trial and temptation
intensifies expectancy. Thus James can urge his brethren
to be patient and to strengthen their hearts, ' for the
arrival of the Lord is near ' (v. 8). In the Pastorals the
outlook is less definite. First Timothy speaks of ' the
appearance of our Lord Jesus Christ which that blessed

---

[1] See especially Phil. i. 23 ; 2 Cor. v. 8.

[2] Jas. v. 7, 8 ; 2 Pet. i. 16, iii. 4, 12. The Pastoral Epistles prefer the
typically Hellenistic term, $\epsilon \pi \iota \phi \acute{a} \nu \epsilon \iota a$, ' manifestation,' ' appearance,'
which is really identical in meaning.

[3] James speaks of ' our Lord Jesus Christ, who is the Glory ' (ii. 1).
See on this whole question, Titius, *op. cit.*, p. 31.

[4] 2 Tim. iii. 1 ; Jas. v. 3 ; 2 Pet. iii. 3 ; Jude 18.

and only Sovereign will disclose at his own time ' (vi. 14, 15).
Here, without any speculation or feverish eagerness, the
future is left in God's hands, while the Church is encouraged
to go on with its work of consolidation. A similar impression of unhasting quietness of mind is made by the description
of Christians as living ' a life of self-control, righteousness,
and piety in this present world, awaiting the blessed hope
and the appearing of the glory of the great God and of our
Saviour Jesus Christ ' (Tit. ii. 12, 13).

But a problem inevitably presented itself. As the days
went on, devout souls, troubled by the apparent triumph
of evil, must have been perplexed by the delay in the fulfilment of their expectation. No doubt the delay was used
by vigorous natures as an incentive to watchfulness. But
the question, which in 2 Pet. iii. 4 is put into the mouth of
scoffers, ' Where is the promise of his advent ? ' must have
found an echo in many a believing heart. And the answer
given by the writer indicates how such hearts were com-
forted. He never falters as to the certainty of the crisis,
which rests on the evidence of apostles (i. 16, 17, iii. 2)
and has long since been predicted by the prophets (i. 19 ff.),
yet he refrains from specific chronological forecasts. The
day of the Lord will come suddenly, and it will bring
destruction by fire upon the existing universe, even as of
old the world of that day was destroyed by the deluge
(iii. 6, 7). Here the author follows a tradition of the two-
fold destruction of the world current in Judaism.[1] But
the explanation of the delay is to be found in the nature of
God. Men measure His processes by their limited ideas of
time. ' With the Lord a thousand years are as one day '
(Ps. xc. 4, used, as in Jubilees iv. 30, by 2 Pet. iii. 8).
It is nothing but His long-suffering, His desire that all

---

[1] Windisch quotes interesting passages from the *Vita Adae et Evae*, 49,
and Joseph. *Ant.* i. 2, 3, and refers to *Sibylline Oracles*, iv. 172-182, v. 155-
161, 274 f., 512-531. Perhaps Isa. lxvi. 15 ff. should be added. The
notion of a world-conflagration is widely diffused, being found not only
in Jewish sources, but in Persian eschatology, and in the Stoic doctrine
of ἐκπύρωσις. Many scholars trace its origin to Babylon. See excursus
on 2 Pet. iii. 10 in Windisch, *op. cit.*, p. 100.

should repent before it is too late, which prompts Him to
suspend the final crisis.

(h) Influence of Heretical Movements

It has been suggested in the course of the previous
discussion that various phenomena in the theology of the
developing Church were due to reaction against the influence of heretical teachers. Reference was made to the
emphasis on morality and the claims of a definite ethical
standard as a protest against tendencies to moral laxity
involved in their doctrines. These doctrines themselves
must have helped to crystallise the idea of a body of sound
teaching, representing the authoritative Christian tradition
handed down by the followers of Jesus and incorporated
in confessions of faith which were required of candidates
for admission to the Church. Piety, we saw, consisted in
adherence to the well-attested apostolic deposit of truth,
and the living of a life of worthy activity in accordance
with the Gospel. Further, in our investigation of the
current conception of God, it seemed possible to explain
certain aspects of that conception as at least thrown into
prominence by way of antithesis to positions which were
being adopted by disloyal members of the Christian community. Perhaps we may add that the departure from
some of Paul's bolder and more original religious standpoints and the acceptance of a more commonplace outlook may have had a real connection with dangerous
exaggerations of such ideas as spiritual freedom and the
boundless generosity of the Divine grace. And if, as there
is reason for supposing, Gnostic influences are to be included among the perils of the Church of our period, it
cannot be accidental that so large a place is assigned to the
value of a true knowledge of Christ and the revelation of
God which He has made.

When we come, however, to examine the material
presented by our Epistles for estimating the precise
features of these heretical movements, we pass into a

region of obscure hints and shadowy outlines. The chief reason is that the authors are concerned not with describing but with denouncing the false teachers. Their vague allusions would be quite clear to their readers. The terminology which is so opaque to us shone for them against a background which we cannot fully reconstruct. Still, a provisional attempt may be of value, and in making it let us start with the data whose interpretation cannot be doubted.

First of all, it may be observed that the more important of the perils confronted appear throughout our literature. It is far more likely that this bears witness to a widespread group of tendencies than that it merely represents literary dependence. Indeed we find traces of a similar movement in Paul's letter to the Church at Colossae. And we should probably be justified in supposing that the entire area of Hellenistic Christianity was exposed to its inroads.

The most prominent phase of this aberration from the Gospel may be called Libertinism. Its adherents are ' impious persons who distort the grace of our God into immorality.' They are people ' seared in conscience,' who ' fall in with the polluting appetites of the flesh,' who ' profess to know God, but by their deeds deny him.' [1] Here is a distortion of the meaning of salvation. Paul had taught that through the boundless grace of God men were raised above all the hampering restrictions of a religion of mere routine and endowed with a spiritual freedom responsible to God alone. But the apostle himself had to warn against a degeneration of that splendid liberty into licence. His warnings were being disregarded with fatal results. These false teachers promised freedom to their disciples, while they themselves were the slaves of corruption (2 Pet. ii. 19). Now Irenæus, in describing those who claimed to have perfect knowledge, and were therefore called Gnostics ($\gamma\nu\omega\sigma\tau\iota\kappa\omicron\iota$), tells how they, as ' spiritual ' ($\pi\nu\epsilon\upsilon\mu\alpha\tau\iota\kappa\omicron\iota$) men, ' affirm that good conduct is necessary for us (i.e. Christians belonging to the Church, whom they

[1] Jude 4 ; 1 Tim. iv. 2 ; 2 Pet. ii. 10 (M.) ; Tit. i. 16.

called 'psychical,' or unspiritual) : otherwise it is impossible to be saved.   But they hold the doctrine that they
themselves will be saved in any case, not because of their
conduct, but because they are by nature spiritual. . . .
And so, without fear, the most " perfect " among them
perform all the forbidden things, regarding which Scripture
declares that " those who do such things shall not inherit
the Kingdom of God." ' [1]   Surely this is precisely the
standpoint which Jude has in view when he speaks (ver. 19)
of ' the people who draw sharp distinctions (*i.e.* between
themselves and others), unspiritual ($\psi v \chi \iota \kappa o i$), not possessing the Spirit.'   Just because they deliberately indulge
their lusts,[2] they give the lie to the title of ' spirit-possessed '
which they arrogantly claim, and earn the name of ' unspiritual ' which, in contempt, they assign to others.

The Pastoral Epistles contain hints of this exclusive
standpoint.   Thus 1 Timothy speaks of ' the God who
desires *all* men to be saved,' and of ' the living God, the
Saviour of *all* men.' [3]   The emphasis is noteworthy.
Moreover, Timothy is warned against ' the profane
jargon . . . of what is falsely called knowledge ' (vi. 20, M.).
Throughout our documents vague allusions are found to
the contents of this profane jargon.   It is connected with
the study of ' myths and interminable genealogies.' [4]
No more apt description could be given of the material
used in Gnostic speculation.   It has constructed a genuine
mythology of cosmological principles, many of them
literally derived from earlier mythological systems.[5]   It
might be rash to explain the genealogies as referring to the
Gnostic doctrine of emanations.   But apart from that,
there is evidence of their eagerness in tracing the descent
of those half-personified principles which are central in
their scheme of the universe.

Confusion has been brought into the discussion of this

---

[1] *Contra Omn. Haer.* I. vi. 2, 3 (ed. Stieren).
[2] ' With their immoral practice a definite theory went hand in hand '
(Hollmann, *Die Schriften d. N. T.*,[2] ii. p. 571).   [3] ii. 4, iv. 10.
[4] 1 Tim. i. 4 (M.) ; 2 Tim. iv. 4 ; Tit. i. 14, iii. 9 ; 2 Pet. i. 16.
[5] See, *e.g.*, Bousset, *Hauptprobleme d. Gnosis*, pp. 9-21, 83 ff., 160-175,
223-237, 320-322.

subject by the attempt to explain it completely from a
Jewish point of view.[1] Recent research has shown how
Gnostic movements assimilated elements from every type
of Oriental religion, and not least from the Jewish.[2] Strange
hybrid sects were the characteristic phenomenon of this
age of religious syncretism.   Some of these had their
roots in Judaism.[3]   Now the obverse side of the Libertinism
mentioned above appears from our Epistles to have been a
rigid asceticism.   This of course accords with one of the
fundamental tenets of Gnosticism, the dualistic theory
that matter is incurably evil.   On that assumption the
body and its passions may be ignored as matters of indifference : hence the indulgence of fleshly lusts as lying wholly
apart from the realm of spirit.   Or on the other hand, all
that is material may be subjected to the severest discipline.
Thus the seared in conscience of 1 Tim. iv. 2 are also men
' who prohibit marriage and insist on abstinence from foods
which God created for believing men ' (iv. 3, M.).   ' For
the pure all things are pure, but nothing is pure for the
polluted and unbelieving ' (Tit. i. 15).   It is plain that a
theory of asceticism could be powerfully buttressed by
the Jewish Law.   And our documents supply evidence
that the false teachers aimed at interpreting the Law, that it
entered into the controversies which they had stirred up.[4]
Furthermore, we hear of ' insubordinate creatures who
impose on people with their empty arguments, particularly
those who have come over from Judaism ' (Tit. i. 10, M.).
So that there is reason for regarding the heretical movement
assailed in these Epistles as being a widely diffused phase
of incipient Jewish-Christian Gnosticism, revealing, on its
ascetic side, traces of kinship with the similar movement
attacked by Paul in his letter to the Colossians.[5]

---

[1] So, e.g., Hort, *Judaistic Christianity*, pp. 132-146.
[2] See, e.g., Bousset, *op. cit.*, pp. 194-202, 324-328.
[3] See Cumont, *Les Religions Orientales*,[2] pp. xx, 94, 182, 367 (n. 59).
[4] 1 Tim. i. 7 ; Tit. iii. 9.
[5] The curious medley of elements in these speculations is brought out
by the fact that, while in the Colossian heresy angel-worship is prominent
(Col. ii. 18), one of the features of this later phase is a contempt for angelic
powers (Jude 8-10 ; 2 Pet. ii. 10-12).

(i) *Hellenistic Colouring*

Attention has been called at isolated points to the impact
of Hellenistic thought and feeling on the theology of the
developing Church. It lies beyond our scope to deal
with the large and complex problem of the range and
ultimate issues of such impact. To attempt any estimate
we should require to cover a wide area of early Christian
literature. But the material which directly concerns
us brings into view the atmosphere in which nascent
Christianity was obliged to construct its religious thought.
That it does so by unconscious hints makes it all the more
valuable for our purpose.

A peculiarity of the *vocabulary* of our Epistles is the
occurrence of various typically Hellenistic terms which
either do not appear at all, or with extreme rarity, in
the rest of the New Testament. The regular word used in
the Pastorals for the ' appearing ' of the exalted Christ in
glory ($\epsilon\pi\iota\phi\acute{a}\nu\epsilon\iota a$) is only found once elsewhere in New
Testament literature. But it is constantly applied to
actual ' manifestations ' of God in human history by 2 and
3 Maccabees, both of them in all likelihood products of
Alexandrian Judaism. Its real background is disclosed
by various Greek inscriptions in which it is the technical
term for the ' appearing ' of a god.[1] It came to be applied
to deified rulers in the Græco-Roman world, and thus we
have as an extraordinary parallel to the words of Tit. ii. 13:
' awaiting the blessed hope and the appearing ($\epsilon\pi\iota\phi\acute{a}\nu\epsilon\iota a\nu$)
of the great God and of our Saviour ($\sigma\omega\tau\hat{\eta}\rho o\varsigma$) Christ
Jesus,' an inscription of Ephesus [2] which celebrates Julius
Cæsar while still alive as ' the god . . . who has appeared
($\epsilon\pi\iota\phi a\nu\acute{\eta}$), the universal saviour ($\sigma\omega\tau\hat{\eta}\rho a$) of the life of
men.' The combination with ' Saviour ' is noteworthy,
and reminds us of the significant fact that this word, so
prominent in Hellenistic religious usage, occurs no less
than sixteen times within the short compass of our docu-

[1] See Dittenberger, *Orientis Graecae Inscriptiones Selectae*, i. 90, *n.* 19.
[3] Dittenberger, *Sylloge*,³ 347, 6.

ments, while Paul has only two instances of it. In this connection we may mention another typical term of the Hellenistic *milieu*, which in Tit. iii. 4 is associated with the ' appearing ' of the Saviour, namely, the Divine ' kindness ' (φιλανθρωπία).[1]

The opening paragraph of 2 Peter reflects the Hellenistic atmosphere of the author's thoughts in every sentence. In setting forth the ethical requirements of the Christian's religious life, he heaps up characteristic qualities of the highest contemporary ideal, ' virtue ' (ἀρετή), ' knowledge ' (γνῶσις), ' self-control ' (ἐγκράτεια), ' piety ' (εὐσέβεια). It has already been pointed out that piety may almost be called the watchword of the Pastoral Epistles.

No less remarkable is the Hellenistic strain in the Epistle of James. This appears not merely in arresting expressions like ' the wheel of existence ' (iii. 6), which is common to our author with late Greek philosophical commentators such as Simplicius and Proclus, and the metaphors used in iii. 3, 4, but in a large number of striking parallels to Philo and the Alexandrian Wisdom of Solomon, in cases where these are indebted to the Hellenistic culture of their time.[2] And here it may be observed that Alexandrian Judaism has evidently been an important medium of Greek influence for our group of documents.[3]

Even more suggestive than the use of special Hellenistic terms is the appearance of typical ideas. Thus in 2 Pet. i. 4 the bestowal of the priceless promises of God has for its aim the participation of those who receive them in the Divine nature (θείας κοινωνοὶ φύσεως) and their escape from that destruction which is produced in the world by lust. The conception of sharing the Divine nature is not found elsewhere in the New Testament, although, of course, there are approximations to it in Paul. But Paul never has the notion of a metaphysical deification, which is

---

[1] This word occurs so often in the Greek inscriptions of the East that in the index to his selection from these Dittenberger considers it needless to give the references.

[2] For details, see an article by the present writer on ' The Hellenistic Atmosphere of the Epistle of James,' in *Expositor*, 1912, pp. 37-52.

[3] See the examples in the succeeding paragraphs.

characteristically Hellenistic. It means primarily that
the goal of the religious life is the attainment of an incorruptible essence, as is plain from the second clause of our
passage. The idea was fraught with momentous consequences for the development of early Christian theology,
for it carried with it the tendency to shift the emphasis from
the ethical to the metaphysical. The subsequent history
of Christian doctrine bears eloquent testimony to the
perilous issues involved. This conception occurs repeatedly
in Philo, *e.g. De Decal.* 104, where he speaks of the heavenly
bodies as ' possessing a share in the divine and blessed and
beatific nature.' [1]

The negative clause of 2 Pet. i. 4 is equally significant.
Plato, in a famous passage of the *Theœtetus* (176 A, B),
which shows how evils hover around the earthly nature and
the material sphere, declares through the lips of Socrates that
' we must try to fly from hence yonder as quickly as possible, for flight means likeness to God (φυγὴ δὲ ὁμοίωσις Θεῷ)
as far as this can be, and likeness means becoming righteous
and holy along with understanding' (φρονήσεως). Philo,
who quotes these words verbatim (*De Fuga et Invent.* 63),
is engrossed with the idea, and follows his master in such a
passage as *De Migrat. Abrah.* 9 : ' Depart then from the
earthly element that encompasses you, and flee with all your
might and main from that accursed prison, the body, and
its pleasures and desires which may be called your jailors.'
He speaks also of souls ' rooted to the earthly body which,
when purified, are able to soar on high, exchanging earth
for heaven and destruction (φθοράν) for immortality.' [2]
Here is the atmosphere of our passage, apart from its
Christian adaptation, and the emphasis which our author
lays on knowledge [3] as the pathway to blessedness finds
a direct parallel in Philo's doctrine that immortality is
attained by knowledge of the Divine essence.[4]

---

[1] Windisch gives this and other instances in his admirable note on
2 Pet. i. 4.
[2] *Quis Rer. Div. Her.*, 239.
[3] *E.g.* i. 2, 3, 8, ii. 20, iii. 18.
[4] See Windisch, *Die Frömmigkeit Philos*, pp. 4-6.

Finally, the ethical ideal of high-minded natures in contemporary Hellenism is mirrored in the description given by Tit. ii. 12 of the aim which God's redeeming love sets before men, ' to renounce impiety and worldly lusts and to live in self-control (σωφρόνως), and righteousness (δικαίως), and piety (εὐσεβῶς) in this present world.' Righteousness is that attitude towards one's fellow-men which recognises their just claims. Piety describes the proper relation to supernatural powers. Self-control is the most characteristic of Hellenic virtues, that principle of order and balance, which preserves the real unity of a life by maintaining its elements in their due proportions.

BIBLIOGRAPHY

(SELECTED WORKS)

I. ENVIRONMENT OF EPISTLES

(a) Jewish

BOUSSET.   *Die Religion des Judentums*, ed. 2, 1906.
CHARLES.   *The Apocrypha and Pseudepigrapha of the Old Testament*, 1913.
HORT.   *Judaistic Christianity*, 1894.
MATHEWS.   *The Messianic Hope in the New Testament*, 1905.
SCHECHTER.   *Some Aspects of Rabbinic Theology*, 1909.
SCHÜRER.   *The Jewish People in the Time of Jesus Christ* (E. T.), 1890-96.   (4th German ed., 1901-11.)
VOLZ.   *Jüdische Eschatologie*, 1903.

(b) Hellenistic

ANGUS.   *The Environment of Early Christianity*, 1914.
BONHÖFFER.   *Epiktet und das Neue Testament*, 1911.
BRÉHIER.   *Les Idées Philosophiques et Religieuses de Philon*, 1908.
CUMONT.   *Les Religions Orientales dans le Paganisme Romain*, ed. 2, 1909.
DILL.   *Roman Society from Nero to Marcus Aurelius*, 1904.
GLOVER.   *The Conflict of Religions in the Early Roman Empire*, 1907.
HARNACK.   *The Mission and Expansion of Christianity* (E. T.), 1908.
KENNEDY.   *St. Paul and the Mystery-Religions*, 1913.
NORDEN.   *Agnostos Theos*, 1913.
RAMSAY.   *The Church in the Roman Empire*, 1893 ;   *St. Paul the Traveller*, 1895.
REITZENSTEIN.   *Die hellenistischen Mysterienreligionen*, 1910.
WENDLAND.   *Die hellenistisch-römische Kultur*, ed. 2-3, 1912.

II. THE THEOLOGY OF THE EPISTLES AS A WHOLE

FEINE.   *Theologie des Neuen Testaments*, 1910.
HOLTZMANN.   *Neutestamentliche Theologie*, ed. 2, 1911.
M'GIFFERT.   *History of Christianity in the Apostolic Age*, 1897.
STEVENS.   *The Theology of the New Testament*, 1899.
WEINEL.   *Biblische Theologie des Neuen Testaments*, 1911.

WEISS, J.   *Christus*, 1909 ; *Das Urchristentum*, 1 Teil, 1914 ; 2 Teil, 1917.

WEIZSÄCKER.   *The Apostolic Age* (E. T.), 1894-95.

WERNLE.   *The Beginnings of Christianity* (E. T.), 1903.

III. PAULINISM

(1) *Commentaries of special value for Pauline Theology*

Romans, DENNEY (Exp. Greek Test.), 1900 ; KÜHL, 1913. 1 *Corinthians*, FINDLAY (E. G. T.), 1900 ; J. WEISS (9th ed. of Meyer), 1910. 2 *Corinthians*, DENNEY (Expos. Bible), 1894 ; HEINRICI, 1887. *Galatians*, LIGHTFOOT (ed. 9), 1887 ; FINDLAY (Expos. B.), 1889. 1 *and* 2 *Thessalonians*, MOFFATT (E. G. T.), 1910 ; VON DOBSCHÜTZ (7th ed. of Meyer), 1909. *Ephesians*, ARMITAGE ROBINSON, 1903 ; HAUPT (7th ed. of Meyer), 1897. *Colossians*, LIGHTFOOT (ed. 8), 1886 ; PEAKE (E. G. T.), 1903 ; HAUPT (6th ed. of Meyer), 1897. *Philippians*, LIGHTFOOT (ed. 8), 1888 ; HAUPT (6th ed. of Meyer), 1897.

(2) *General Studies*

BACON.   *The Story of St. Paul*, 1904.

DEISSMANN.   *St. Paul* (E. T.), 1912.

FINDLAY.   Art. *Paul* (H. D. B.).

MOFFATT.   *Paul and Paulinism*, 1910.

MORGAN, W.   *The Religion and Theology of Paul*, 1917.

PFLEIDERER.   *Paulinism* (E. T.), 1877.

SABATIER.   *The Apostle Paul* (E. T.), 1891.

STRACHAN, R. H.   *The Individuality of St. Paul*, 1917.

WEINEL.   *St. Paul* (E. T.), 1906.

WEISS, J.   *Das Urchristentum*, 1 Teil, 1914, pp. 103-416.

WERNLE, P.   *Jesus u. Paulus*, 1915.

WREDE.   *Paulus*, 1904.

(3) *Special Subjects*

DENNEY.   *The Theology of the Epistle to the Romans* (*Expositor*, vi., vols. 3, 4), 1901.

DIBELIUS.   *Die Geisterwelt im Glauben des Paulus*, 1909.

DICKSON.   *St. Paul's Use of the terms Flesh and Spirit*, 1883.

FEINE.   *Jesus Christus und Paulus*, 1902.

GRAFE.   *Die paulinische Lehre vom Gesetz*, ed. 2, 1893.

GUNKEL.   *Die Wirkungen des Heiligen Geistes*, ed. 2, 1899.

KAFTAN.   *Jesus und Paulus*, 1906.

KENNEDY.   *St. Paul's Conceptions of the Last Things*, 1904.

MÉNÉGOZ.   *Le Péché et la Rédemption d'après St. Paul*, 1882.

OLSCHEWSKI.   *Die Wurzeln der paulinischen Christologie*, 1909.

ROBINSON.   *The Christian Doctrine of Man*, 1911, pp. 104-136.

R

SOKOLOWSKI. *Geist und Leben bei Paulus*, 1903.
SOMERVILLE. *St. Paul's Conception of Christ*, 1897.
TITIUS. *Der Paulinismus unter dem Gesichtspunkt der Seligkeit*, 1900.
WARNECK. *Paulus im Lichte der heutigen Heidenmission*, 1913.

IV. EARLY CHRISTIAN THOUGHT INDEPENDENT OF PAUL

(1) *First Peter*

(a) *Commentaries valuable for Theology*: BIGG, 1901; HORT
(incomplete), 1898; WINDISCH (in Lietzmann's *Handbuch zum N. T.*),
1911.

(b) *Studies*: CHASE, Art. *First Epistle of Peter* (H. D. B.);
MOFFATT, *Introduction to the Literature of the N. T.*, 1911, pp. 319-344;
B. WEISS, *Der petrinische Lehrbegriff*, 1855.

(2) *Hebrews*

(a) *Commentaries*: DAVIDSON (Bible Handbooks), 1882; DODS
(E. G. T.), 1910; A. NAIRNE, *The Epistle to the Hebrews* (C. G. T.),
1917; PEAKE (Cent. Bible), n.d.; B. WEISS (6th ed. of Meyer), 1897.

(b) *Studies*: BRUCE, *The Epistle to the Hebrews*, 1899;
H. MACNEILL, *The Christology of the Epistle to the Hebrews*, 1914;
MÉNÉGOZ, *La Théologie de l'Épître aux Hébreux*, 1894; G. MILLIGAN,
The Theology of the Epistle to the Hebrews, 1899.

V. THE THEOLOGY OF THE DEVELOPING CHURCH

(1) *Commentaries*

Pastoral Epistles, BERNARD (Camb. Greek Test.), 1899; VON
SODEN, ed. 2 (Handcommentar), 1893. *James*, KNOWLING, 1903;
Mayor, ed. 3, 1910; WINDISCH (in Lietzmann), 1911. *Jude and
2 Peter*, BIGG, 1901; MAYOR, 1907; WINDISCH, 1911.

(2) *Studies*

W. BAUER, *Die katholischen Briefe*, 1910; CHASE, Artt. *Epistle of
Jude* and *Second Epistle of Peter* (H. D. B.); GRAFE, *Die Stellung
und Bedeutung des Jacobusbriefes*, 1904; HOENNICKE, *Das Juden-
christentum*, 1908; TITIUS, *Die vulgäre Anschauung von der Seligkeit
im Urchristentum*, 1900; VON DOBSCHÜTZ, *Die urchristlichen
Gemeinden*, 1902, pp. 176-205.

INDEX

I.—SUBJECTS

theism of, 19, 86; conscience in, 26, 38; flesh in, 33 f., 36; soul in, 36; spirit in, 37, 88 ff.; mind in, 37 f.; relation of, to Stephen, 47 f.; relation of, to historical Jesus, 49, 53, 98 ff., 158; grace in, 51, 61, 74, 91 f., 95, 133, 137; conversion of, 51 ff.; apostolic consciousness of, 58-60; meaning of election for, 58-62; eschatology of, 64, 77 ff., 95, 108 f., 140; ethics of, 65 f., 107, 142 ff., 225; missionary preaching of, 63-67; influence of conversion of, on thought, 66, 68, 74, 86, 91 f., 97, 119, 143; and the original apostles, 98; and the Gospel of Matthew, 99; knowledge of Jesus' life in, 103 f.; on transformation of Christians,139 f.; on slavery, 146; on woman, 146; on the state, 147; creative energy of, 223.

Pax Romana, 147.

Perfecting (of Christians), 189, 212.

Persecutions, 163-165.

Peter, First, author of, 10; composition of, 161; date of, 165; practical character of, 166; relation of, to Paul, 167 f.; divergence of, from Paul, 169 f.; use of O. T. in, 171; reminiscences of Synoptics in, 173; affinities of, with Hebrews, 173, 174 *n.*; influence of prophets on, 174 f.; descent to Hades in, 180 f.

Philo, 24, 26 *n.*, 38, 124 *n.*, 155 ff., 190, 192-195, 202, 218 ff., 240, 253 f.

Piety, 237, 255.

Plato, 34, 38, 43, 190, 254.

Powers, evil, 20, 40, 46, 65, 78, 154.

Priesthood, Aaronic, 206 ff.; of Christ, 209 ff.

Psalms of Solomon, 80.

RECONCILIATION, 130, 134 f.

Redemption, 24, 25, 65, 106, 108. 154, 189.

Retribution, 134, 135.

Righteousness, 21, 136, 230, 231. *See* Justification.

SACRAMENTS, 133 *n.*, 150-152.

Sacrifices, 130, 195 196, 214.

Saviour, 239, 252, 253.

Septuagint, 23, 83, 84, 237.

Sermon on Mount, 11 *n.*, 173 *n.*, 242.

Servant of Jehovah, 72, 116-118, 128.

Sin, and flesh, 33 f., 129; origin of, 39; relation of, to death, 126.

Sonship, 94 f., 106 f., 137, 138.

Spirit, Holy, as criterion of Christian life, 86; in O. T., 87, 113; Paul's conception of, 88-90; relation of, to Christ, 88 f., 111, 123; in Messianic age, 88, 113; transformation of doctrine of, 90 f.; promise of, in Acts, 112; teaching of Jesus on, 114 *n.*; in Christian conduct, 142; receding of idea of, 233 *n.*

Stoicism, 23, 25 f., 155, 227.

TARSUS, 14, 25.

Tradition, authority of, 224, 235, 248.

UNION with Christ, 119-124, 132.

WISDOM-LITERATURE, 21, 24, 26, 87, 156, 158, 191, 195, 253.

Works, good, 226, 227.

World-soul, 24, 155.

II.—BIBLICAL REFERENCES

(1) OLD TESTAMENT

Printed by T. and A. CONSTABLE, Printers to His Majesty
at the Edinburgh University Press